DATA PROCESSING
PROJECT
MANAGEMENT

DATA PROCESSING PROJECT MANAGEMENT

by Alfred O. Awani

PETROCELLI BOOKS
Princeton, New Jersey

Library of Congress Cataloging-in-Publication Data

Awani, Alfred O.
  Data processing project management.

  Bibliography: p.
  Includes index.
  1. Electronic data processing—Management.
2. System design.   I. Title.
QA76.9.M3A93   1986   658.4'038   86-22507
ISBN 0-89433-234-1

CONTENTS

v

PREFACE

Data processing management appears to have entered an era of identity crises in the last decade—gradually relinquishing an autonomous role in organizations to adopt one of developing bridges to link the organization to its environment through involvement in technological and societal needs. This move from a traditional hierarchical position of downward supervision to a facilitating and coordinating responsibility within complex economic, social, political, and technological systems calls for a much-needed look at its structure and process which formed it. While management theory has made great progress in the development of scientific tools and methodology for solving complex resource allocation problems, the organizational interfaces that affect the outcome of the application of these resources are not fully understood.

Organizations emerge to satisfy the need for pooling collective effort. The development of organization theory took its modern shape in response to the requirement for an interface between two isolated segments of society—one represented by society's need for products and the other by the availability of scientific management

xi

methods and discoveries. Based on this, one might hypothesize that the "business" that data processing management is in is the interaction between these two segments. Today, when a subsistence level of product demand has been largely satisfied in our society, and when people are playing a more aggressive role in controlling their organizational destinies, the data processing manager emerges in a somewhat different role.

Contemporary data processing managers play two key roles in their implementation function. First, they are responsible for a given organization—their direct supervisory duties. Second, today's data processing manager also acts in a facilitating capacity, bringing about effective organizational interfacing with technical, social, economic, and political systems. It is this new role that this book on data processing project management directly addresses.

In recent years there has been an increasing volume of books, reports, articles, papers and lectures dealing with various aspects of project management. However, to those who enter this domain either as graduate students with some background in business management or those transferring from other fields, this vast amount of literature becomes a proverbial haystack of information, often with the result of looking for a needle that isn't there. But even those who are professionally engaged in some aspect of data processing project management may experience the need for a reference text on project management in the data processing field, this book may fulfill at least some of their requirements.

This book was written with this goal in mind. On one hand the objective is to provide an understanding of the project management phenomena of the data processing field, and on the other, to furnish tools for effectively directing and controlling data processing activities and projects of all types.

To achieve this dual aim, "Data Processing Project Management" is designed to help data processing managers and potential managers visualize all the operations of a project for which one does not have previous experience; to arrange these operations in their proper sequence; to achieve confidence that one understands each operation; to acquire the know-how and means necessary to perform it; and to feel convinced that the method for performing each operation is the most economical. Such confidence is achieved only through systematic planning, scheduling and controlling techniques.

This book is dedicated to my family.

Alfred O. Awani
Mesa, Arizona

NOMENCLATURE

a   Optimistic Time

b   Pessimistic Time

BMP   Batch Message Processor

CPM   Critical Path Method

CPU   Central Processing Unit

DFS   Demand Forecasting Systems

DP   Data Processing

DPC   Direct Project Cost

EDP   Electronic Data Processing

ET   Earliest Time

FF   Free Float

ICS   Inventory Control System

I/O   Input/Output

LT   Latest Time

m   Most Probable Time

NASA   National Aeronautic and Space Administration

PAR   Program Appraisal and Review

PCAM   Planning Card Accounting Machines

PERT   Program Evaluation and Review Techniques

PPBS   Planning Programming Budget System

Chapter
1
INTRODUCTION TO DATA PROCESSING PROJECT MANAGEMENT

Data processing project management (DPPM) at many installations today is faced with the very difficult task of deciding how to efficiently allocate resources to jobs and projects. (A project is a complex of nonroutine activities that must be completed with a set amount of resources and within a set time interval.)

The backlog of work in a data processing organization can be substantial. Some of these jobs are small, of course, such as minor changes to existing programs, but others involve complete new programs. Not only is data processing management faced with choosing between these jobs, it also has the uncomfortable feeling that there are other, more important projects that ought to be considered. They hear about developments in on-line systems, in data communications, and in new methods for computer input and output. Data processing management recognizes that some attention must be paid to such developments, but with a sizeable backlog of projects already confronting them, it is hard to divert resources to investigate these new developments.

Thus, data processing industries have emphasized the term project management which is concerned with planning, scheduling,

1

and controlling the complex of nonroutine activities that must be completed to reach the predetermined objective(s) of the project.

So, DPPM need improved methods to help decide where best to allocate resources. In short, they need a better approach to choosing the direction of the company's data processing activities. Their problem is getting more complex as new technological developments occur.

The net effect of these many data processing projects is that project selection, planning, and scheduling becomes much more difficult than it has been in the past. Clerical savings, never a really good measure of project selection, becomes less and less a factor as these new areas are considered. "Experience" provides fewer guidelines for decision-making because there are few precedents to follow. Snap decisions and "quarterbacking" cannot begin to cope with the complexity of the problem. What is needed is a systematic means of project evaluation, planning, and scheduling for guiding the data processing project.

EVALUATION OF PLANNING AND SCHEDULING TECHNIQUES

Planning and scheduling have always played an important role in project-type operations. However, most previous planning systems had deficiences resulting from the use of techniques which were inadequate for dealing with complex projects. Generally, the several groups concerned with the work did their own planning and scheduling. Since much of this was independent, the results often reflected a lack of coordination. In addition, it is traditional in project operations to develop detailed schedules from gross estimates of total requirements and achievements based on past experience. Plans and schedules based on this data tend to be oversimplified because unaided human beings are simply unable to consider all the pertinent factors bearing on the problem at one time.

As a consequence, many undesirable effects may arise. Some important aspects of the operation which should be dealt with at the outset are ignored and unrecognized. In the course of the project much confusion arises. Uncoordinated interpretations and improvisations become common. Under such circumstances, data processing project management falls to the coordinators and expeditors. When it appears that a schedule change is required, corrective action has tended to be across-the-board to all jobs since the complexity of the situation has not permitted rapid, economical analysis to single out the particular jobs affected by a change. In effect, management has lost control and doesn't know whether or not its objectives are being met.

The lack of adequate tools and techniques has been primarily responsible for these conditions. Most of the traditional scheduling techniques are based on the Gantt or bar chart (see Chapter 8) which has been in common use for over 50 years. Although it is still a valuable tool, its use is limited in the scheduling of large-scale data processing operations. In particular, the bar chart fails to delineate the complex interactions and precedence relationships which exist among the data processing project activities. The milestone system used extensively by the military and industry for the management of major projects prior to the advent of Program Evaluation and Review Technique (PERT) was an important link in the evaluation from Gantt chart to the network concept. Milestones are key events of points in time which can be uniquely identified when reached as the project progresses. The milestone system provides a sequential list of the various tasks to be accomplished in the project. This innovation was important because it emphasized the functional elements of the program, reflecting what is now the project work-time breakdown or product indentured structure. This system increased awareness, if not the effective display, of the interdependencies between tasks.

The milestone system is still widely used in spite of the limitation that the relationship between milestones is not established. Milestones are merely listed chronologically and are not related in a logical sequence. Therefore, the essential interrelationships cannot be displayed. The system was an important early recognition of the need for awareness and discipline at lower management levels and forces outcome-oriented planning of all segments of the project.

The need for procedures which allow simulation of the possible future stages of a project through to completion led to the adoption of the network as a desirable means of depicting the elements of a project and the relationships among them. This network idea is the basis of all critical path analysis (CPM) schemes and is used to depict a project plan. Much of the early success of PERT/CPM was based on the explicitness being essential to the construction of a network. Being explicit about what was to take place at some much later time was a new experience for many. Improved communications among those concerned with a given project were a standard result of networking the project plan.

NETWORK TECHNIQUES

Today's data processing project managers use network techniques to assist them in their tasks—the management science techniques of PERT (program evaluation and review technique) and CPM (critical path method). With the experience gained to date in these techniques, it is logical to assume that they would be used for developing the time-and-action schedule for the data processing project.

Detailed descriptions of CPM and PERT are given in chapters 11 and 12, respectively. Suffice it to say that these network methods start with a list of jobs that have to be done ("activities") in order to accomplish the overall project, along with time and resource requirements for each such activity. These activities are then arranged into a logical sequence—a network diagram. Laying out the diagram and analysis of its implications can point out such things as the fact that the whole data processing project cannot be completed as soon as desired, that some activities have been overlooked, or that more than the available resources are being committed during some time period. The use of network technique will point out, better than previous methods, the time schedule and resource utilization of the data processing project.

The networks for the various data processing projects will provide a good basis for developing the detailed plans. Subnetworks generally will be necessary to break down the total project network; for example, the data processing project network might have an activity named "study data processing activities of the order department". For detailed plans, a network might be developed for this particular study, showing more specifically what is to be done, and when.

We shall discuss networks in terms of estimating elapsed time and resource utilization; in PERT terminology, these are called PERT/TIME network (see Chapter 12). The network concept has also been extended to the estimating and control of project costs through what is called PERT/COST (see Chapter 13). Under PERT/COST, logical groups of work activities are identified as "work packages". In general, every activity must be a member of one and only one work package, but some things do not lend themselves to a nice clean assignment. Maintenance work is an example; it is hard to predict just what will need maintenance, or when. However, the work package concept is useful. Cost estimates are prepared for the work packages, and costs are controlled by these packages. So the time networks provide a good basis for developing detailed work plans and budgets for the project.

There are two basic systems of networking currently in use—the arrow diagramming, or activities-on-arrow (A-O-A) system, and the precedence diagram, or activities-on-nodes (A-O-N) system. Both systems are used throughout this text.

In this text, we shall discuss some of the data processing technological developments that are pressing in on data processing management, and to show how the network-based procedures of PERT and CPM can be used to assist management in planning and controlling data processing projects of all types.

REFERENCES

Awani, Alfred O. *Project Management Techniques*. Princeton: Petrocelli Books, Inc., 1983.

Canning, Richard G. and Sisson, Roger L. *The Management of Data Processing*. New York: John Wiley & Sons, Inc., 1967.

Gray, Clifford F. *Essentials of Project Management*. Princeton: Petrocelli Books, Inc., 1981.

Chapter
2
COMPONENTS OF DATA PROCESSING

A terse but accurate definition of data processing is: the execution of a systematic sequence of operations performed upon data. A broad term may be "data automation" which implies many other activities such as systems analysis and equipment selection. They are all part of the total concept of making the collection, storage, and processing of data automatic. Generally, the term "data" is used to denote the representation by numbers, letters, or symbols of facts, figures, conditions, or factors which are the basic elements used to communicate information.

Processing of data has certain essential characteristics regardless of whether it is done manually, mechanically, or electronically. Processing changes the form of data so that it becomes information. In the process, the elements of data may be classified, recorded, communicated, sorted, calculated, summarized, or some combination of these steps. Classifying identifies data and distinguishes one kind from another. Recording means the writing of data either by hand or by machines. Communication takes place when data are transmitted from one place to another, or when documents are transported. Sorting arranges the data in a desired sequence. Calculating is the performance of add, subtract, multiply and/or divide. Summarizing condenses or groups the data with totals.

Three other operations may also be added to the list of processing steps. Data are *stored* when filed or held for future reference. They are *retrieved* when searched for, located, and taken or copied from storage. They are *reproduced* when duplicated for use in other processes.

Raw data have not been processed and may not be in machine-sensible form.

Master data are contained in master files and are the basic material for processing operations. They are relatively static, used frequently, and are altered or changed as infrequently as possible.

Transaction data are the record of the occurrence of a new event pertaining to an individual record in the master file (also referred to as detail data). Occurrences are random and unpredictable.

Test data are specifically developed to test computer runs or programs. They are often actual data from previous runs with artificially created data added to test the program's reactions to all possible situations under all known conditions.

Control data are coded entries to identify a record for subsequent processing; i.e., debit/credit, gain/loss, or flag with specialized meaning.

Data processing equipment came into being primarily to satisfy the need for information under increasingly complex conditions. Programs and physical equipment are combined into data processing systems to handle data at high rates of speed with self-check accuracy features. The physical data processing equipment consists of various units, such as input and output devices, storage devices, and processing devices to handle information at electronic speeds. From the above definition, it can be seen that data processing is the heart of the organization's information system.

The basic role of an information system is to provide information to decision-makers in a form most suitable for developing high-quality decisions. Data processing, as the functional part of the information system, provides the tools and techniques used to achieve this task and relates to the rest of the organization in a staff fashion. Data processing is part of the information system, but it is not the entire system and has no proper decision-making or policy-making function outside of the information system. In the performance of its duties as part of the information system, data processing makes use of several definitive techniques, such as data collection, classification, recording, data storage, sorting, calculating, summarizing, and communication.

DATA PROCESSING FILES

The framework of a data processing system is its files; it is through the proper planning and control of these that the system can function efficiently and comprehensively. The term "file" as used in data processing has a more precise meaning than in manual systems. A data processing file is a collection of data in the form of "records". Each record is discrete and is labelled by a "key" that is held as an identifier within the record. The various arrangements of files, records and keys are legion and are devised to suit the requirements of a particular system. Nevertheless, the theme of file, record and key is maintained throughout all systems.

What are the main purpose of data processing files?

1. To hold data in a form that enables it to be processed rapidly by the computer.
2. To make every record accessible to the computer, either individually or *en masse*.
3. To obtain security and compactness for the data.

These purposes are all achievable provided suitable hardware is made available for the system and its files are employed in a well-planned manner.

CONTENTS OF FILES

Virtually any data processed by a computer is held in a file at some time or other. This may be either temporary or permanent depending on the type of data and its purpose. An example of temporary data are the details pertaining to the issue of an item from factory stores; this data is valuable up to the point at which it amends a stock level or other information, thereafter becoming increasingly valueless. An example of permanent data is the stock level of an item in the stores; although this level is continually changing, it is held permanently in the file for as long as the item is handled in the factory.

In some applications the distinction between temporary and permanent data is less obvious, but in general terms, temporary data applies to momentary events, and permanent data to reasonably stable facts. Typical examples of temporary data are the details from stores transactions, job tickets, goods delivered, and cash received. In permanent files we might well find selling prices, stock levels, manufacturing operations details, and standard costs.

CLASSIFICATION OF FILES*

The development of hardware and its usage in data processing has spawned an extensive amount of jargon and terminology. Unfortunately, these are by no means standardized, so that knowledge of one manufacturer's terminology does not guarantee an immediate understanding of another's. After a data processing system has been designed and the hardware chosen, this difficulty disappears—for a time at least!

Because of the very wide application of files in data processing, it is worth considering the various ways in which they can be classified. Files are most suitably classified according to their four main facets (see below), and every file falls into one category within each of these faceted classifications at any point of time. As will be real-

---

* Selection from *Systems Analysis for Business Data Processing* by H. D. Clifton. Copyright © 1974 by Van Nostrand Co. Inc. All right reserved.

ized, a file may, during processing and to a varying degree, change its category within one or more classifications. Thus, the classification of a file is not necessarily static, but can depend upon its operational state during a computer run.

CLASSIFICATION ACCORDING TO CONTENTS

The contents of a file can be considered as falling into one of three categories—movement data, transition data, and master data.

Movement data (transaction data) files hold records that have been created from source data and which are a straight copy of the paper tape, punched cards, or other source medium. The records normally contain all the data from the source and no other data. A movement file may be sorted into a different sequence from its original, but will still remain a movement file if the contents are unchanged. There is often an unpredictable total of records in the file, and a variable number, including none, having a particular key. For instance, a file of job dockets will vary in size from week to week, and each person may have a different number of dockets.

The contents of movement files are not retained for long, but are replaced periodically by further movement data. It is always possible to reproduce the source data from a movement file by making a straightforward printed copy, after resorting if necessary.

Transition data files generally stem from movement files as a result of changes made to the contents of the latter. The insertion or deletion of fields causes a movement file to become a transition file, the insertions usually being derived from master files. A typical example of this process is the insertion of piecework rates into a job docket (movement) file from a rates (master) file.

Master data files form a permanent feature in a data processing system, and hold records pertaining to ranges of items of diverse natures. A range is usually semistatic as regards both its size and contents, and there is one record for each item covered by the file. The records may be of fixed or variable length. Typically, master files with fixed length records are payroll records, commodity prices, stock levels, personnel records; and with variable length records are sales ledgers, purchase ledgers, parts operations, product and assembly contents.

A characteristic of master files not applicable to movement and transition files is that during their life they are frequently "updated," "amended" and "referenced".

> *Updated* refers to regular attention to each record in a master file in order to maintain it in an up-to-date condition. This is normally carried out at regular intervals, and it is expected that a substantial proportion of records are updated on each occasion, such as the monthly updating of a sales ledger with invoice and payment data, or the weekly updating of the payroll record.
>
> *Amendment* refers to the addition of new records, the deletion of obsolete records, and changes made to existing records that are not expected to occur regularly. The amendment of a master file is not intended to occur at regular predetermined intervals, nor effect more than a small minority of records, although sometimes practical circumstances destroy both of these intentions. An instance of amendment is the change made to a price file when new commodities are introduced or when price adjustments are made to existing commodities.
>
> *Referencing* is simply looking up a record so as to obtain data from it without changing it in any way (input mode). An example is looking up the prices of commodities during an invoicing run.

CLASSIFICATION ACCORDING TO MODE OF PROCESSING

There are four modes in which files can be processed—input, output, reconstruction, and overlay.

> *Input mode* (read mode) is the process whereby data is read (referenced) or copied from the file into the core store but is not

written back again, the data on the file remaining unchanged. The data is read in different amounts at one time, depending on the core available to receive it, the amount actually required, and the characteristics of the file hardware.

Output mode (write mode) data is transferred (or written) from the core store to the file without having been previously read from the file. This mode is employed during the creation of a file.

In the *reconstruction mode* all records in a file are transferred from the file into core store (as in the input mode); after amendment or updating, they are written back to the file, but in other locations. The starting data is preserved in its original locations so that after the run is completed there are two versions of the file—the opening and the closing file. This process is frequently employed with magnetic tape files, data being read from one reel and written to another. It can also be employed with direct access storage devices as a means of obtaining a high degree of security.

In the *overlay mode* certain records are read from the file into core store and, after amendment or updating, are written back to the original locations in the file. The original data in the file is lost because it is overwritten by the changed records. This process cannot be used with magnetic tape, but direct access storage devices may be employed in this way.

An advantage of this mode over the reconstruction mode is that it is possible to update or amend a small portion of the file without having to process the whole file. Special arrangements have to be made for records that expand during updating and cannot then be accomodated in their original locations. A disadvantage of this mode is its lower level of security due to the original data being destroyed.

CLASSIFICATION ACCORDING TO MODE OF ACCESS AND STORAGE

Mode of access is liable to be confused with mode of storage because the same terminology is employed for both concepts. In some ways, the common terminology is acceptable since the two modes are closely connected in many cases. Mode of access refers to the way in which the file is referenced, updated, or amended; it is in effect the sequence in which a string of movements are applied to a file. Mode of storage refers to a way in which the file itself is stored, either on magnetic tape or a direct access storage device. In general, maximum efficiency is obtained when the movement and the file are in the same sequence, so that the two sets of records are kept in phase during an updating run, etc. There are, however, many situations which cause the most suitable arrangements to be other than this; a significant factor in this respect is the activity of the file.

The classifications of these two modes are:

Serial access	Serial storage
Partitioned access	Partitioned storage
Sequential access	Sequential storage
Selective-sequential access	Indexed sequential storage
Random access	Random storage

A *serial access and storage* file is one in which the records are stored in adjacent locations so that the file is tightly packed and has no semblance of sequence or other organization. Typically, a batch of stock movements read from paper tape would form a serial file when written to magnetic tape or disc.

With a serial file it is not possible to deal with isolated records or groups of records; the file must be processed by starting at its beginning and proceeding through to its end. This is to say that it can only be accessed in serial mode; and moreover, serial access can apply to any of the five modes of storage.

With *partitioned access and storage,* a file consists of several members, each of which has a unique name or number, and within which the records are stored serially. It is used mainly for the storage of programs and subroutines, or as a core dump. Partitioned access implies that the computer proceeds directly to the start of a member and then deals with the records in serial access mode. Although magnetic tape can hold a partitioned file, e.g. a library of programs, partitioned access to it is not really possible because all preceding data has to be examined to find the wanted member. Partitioned access is quite straightforward on a direct access storage device holding a partitioned file.

With *sequential access storage,* a sequential file holds its records in a logical sequence of the record keys. The most popular use of magnetic tape is to hold sequential files and, apart from serial storage, this is the only mode of storage with which magnetic tape can be used. Sequential access applies only to sequential or indexed sequential storage; and, although theoretically possible, it would be very troublesome to deal with a serial or partitioned file in this manner. A random file can be accessed sequentially by a string of sequential movements, but this is in fact tantamount to random access.

With *selective-sequential access and indexed sequential storage,* to save time when looking for a particular record in a sequential file, an index is created that gives the locations of certain records in the file, and the search continues from one of these locations. This is known as an indexed sequential file, and can exist only on a direct access storage device. Selective-sequential access is applicable only to indexed sequential storage, for although it can be employed with a random file, it is effectively random access.

Random access and storage should not be confused with direct access storage. The latter refers to a hardware device whereas the first two terms apply to logical concepts. A random file is characterized by predictable relationships between the key of a record and the location of that record in the file. The records are otherwise held in a random manner, and so there is no obvious relationship between contiguous records. Random access mode provides the user with the capability of obtaining access to any record directly without having to search through the file. In its true form, random access can apply only to the random file. An interesting point about random file is that its records cannot be printed in sequence without either sorting them or reading in a sequence of keys; this is because there is no way of ascertaining the key of the next record in the sequence, and it cannot be located without this.

CLASSIFICATION ACCORDING TO HARDWARE

Files can be stored on a variety of hardware devices; these are chosen to suit the requirements of the particular system, taking other factors as well as file storage into account. The characteristics of the various types of file storage hardware can be classified into two main categories—serial access storage and direct access storage devices.

Serial access storage devices are so-called because the data on them is accessed and stored only in serial or sequential mode. The only viable form of serial access storage device is magnetic tape; other serial files in the form of punched cards or paper tape are too slow for frequent use.

Direct access storage devices can be used in any of the modes of access and storage mentioned previously. Although there are various degrees of directness associated with the different types of direct access storage devices, their main characteristic is the ability to go directly to a stored record without searching through all the preceding records. Included in this category are devices such as magnetic drums, exchangeable (or removable) disk stores, fixed disk stores, magnetic card files, and data cell drives.

REFERENCES

Brightman, Richard W. *Information Systems for Modern Management*. New York: The Macmillan Company, 1971.

Clifton, H. D. *Systems Analysis for Business Data Processing*. New York: Van Nostrand Reinhold Co. Inc. 1974.

Lord, Jr. Kenniston W. and Steiner, James B. *CPM Review Manual Data Processing Handbook* (Second Edition). New York: Van Nostrand Reinhold Co. Inc. 1978.

Chapter
3
PROCESSING MODE

The mode of operation of a computer system is not under the control of the data processing professional (e.g. programmer or operator), but is something that they must understand and be able to work with when dealing with a particular computer system.

BATCH PROCESSING

The very first uses of computers were in the batch mode. The batch mode of computerization refers to the practice of collecting and holding work to be run on the computer and executing that work later, yielding the results after all work has been collected and executed. The batch user typically submits a "worksheet" or transaction that is keypunched (or submitted through data entry). The data is then run and the results are available later.

The batch processing makes effective use of time in the sense that without it the same work would have to be done manually. In a larger sense, batch processing does not make optimal use of an individual's time. This is so because users must wait a significant amount of time to see the result of their activities. If those activities are critical to their projects (financially, strategically, etc.), the delay caused by processing from the time the information is known (i.e., entered on the worksheet) until the time the information is useable can be quite expensive. The expense comes primarily in the form of users not being able to perform the next logical sequence of their project work until the information is transacted by the computer. Other expenses occur by having personnel sitting idly waiting for the computer to complete the transacting of the activity. In addition, error correction may mean that a transaction will have to be resubmitted on the next processing cycle, delaying the completion of the project function even further. These expenses can be reduced greatly or even eliminated with an on-line system discussed in a later section.

REAL-TIME*

In real-time operation, a data processing system is synchronized with a physical process so that the results of the data processing are useful to the physical operation. Real-time processing is usually identified with great speed, but speed is relative. The essence of real-time is not speed but concurrency, or simultaneity.

Real-time computing for high-speed situations has been possible only in the last few years. Before that, computers were too slow. A few years ago, for example, if a telegraph company had wanted to use a computer to control the routing of all telegrams in a particular area, no computer was available that could handle the job. The computers of that day simply couldn't keep up with the flood of telegrams pouring in every second, each requiring a different routing.

One characteristic of most on-line time systems is that one or more human operators are often an integral part of the system. This means that problems of communication and human response

---

* From *Computer Usage Fundamentals* by Eric A. Weiss. Copyright 1969 by McGraw-Hill Book Co.

time are among the significant factors in the design of the system. Another characteristic is the availability of a wide variety of input/output equipment. This includes not only keyboards and displays for communication with the operators, but also special-purpose input equipment such as digitized radar, analog-to-digital converters, and outputs to many types of control devices and actuators for positioning valves, rotating shafts, or simply controlling off-on switches.

For a computer to operate in real-time, it must be able to perform on the same time scale as the operation with which it is involved. That is, the computer must be able to keep up with the events that occur in the environment which the computer is controlling, simulating, or working in. Actually, the computer must be somewhat faster than that; it must respond to its environment faster than the environment is itself able to react so as to be in control of the situation. However, there are still many areas where events occur too rapidly for a computer to be used in real-time. One of these is nuclear research, where atomic particles react in much less than a billionth of a second—a speed that no computer of today can match.

There are at least six different types of real-time computing:

simulation

parallel operation with a process

hybrid operation with an analog computer

performing an operational function

performing a remote communications function

controlling the operation of one or more computers.

The above real-time type of computing is examined in greater detail below.

Simulation

In a real-time simulation, a computer executes a program with the time scale corresponding to that of the process being studied.

Flight trainers are one example of real-time simulation. Using a real jet for all of a pilot's training is too expensive, so flight simulators are used. These large systems combine a precise mock-up of the pilot's cabin to process the sights and sounds that a pilot would experience in flight, and a computer with a real-time program to guide the trainer through all possible normal and emergency maneuvers. The computer must operate in real-time so that the "aircraft" will respond in real-time, and so that events are presented to the pilot just as they would occur under real conditions.

Parallel Operation With a Process

In real-time parallel operation with a process, a computer executes a program with a time scale that corresponds closely to a real process. In other words, the computer's time scale is just 60 seconds to the minute.

For example, the display of a missile's position is an important application of a real-time parallel-operation program. The range safety officer at a missile launching must know exactly where the missile is so that if it begins to veer off course it can be destroyed before doing any damage. Obviously, the computer that prepares the real-time missile-position display must be able to provide the latest up-to-the-split-second data on the missile's position to protect lives and property in case of its failure.

Hybrid Operation with an Analog Computer

Just like a digital computer, an analog computer can in many cases be programmed to operate in fast time or in slow time. If the analog computer is operating in real-time, and is connected to a digital computer for hybrid operation so as to take advantage of the digital machine's large memory and logical capabilities, then the digital computer must also operate in real-time in order to be compatible.

Let's take the example of a project utilizing a hybrid computer in studying the effect of supersonic speeds on wing designs for a jetliner. In fast time operation, several hours of flight can be compressed into minutes for a quick comprehensive look at what will happen with each design. In slow time operation, a detailed examination can be made of the events occurring during a critical moment in a particular design. In real-time operation, the action of the wing can be observed as the pilot would experience it—to see if, for instance, there is too much flutter of the wing for the pilot to be able to control the craft properly. This could not be observed under conditions of slow time or of fast time.

Performing an Operational Function

When performing an operational function in real-time, a computer is mainly an element in an external environment. That is, when a computer is involved in controlling an operation, the computer, although important, is usually a minor part of the overall picture.

In recent years, a breed of special-purpose computers known as process control computers has evolved. These computers control an actual industrial or scientific process, using feedback mechanisms to sense the status of the operations being controlled. In a petroleum distillation process, a typical project such as the precise control of the "crude tower" is important in separating the various components that constitute the crude petroleum in order to get maximum yield. A process control computer can supervise the entire operation, relying on various temperature and pressure sensors throughout the tower to provide indications as to just how the process is proceeding. These feedback devices monitor the operation and allow the computer to take corrective action if any part of the process begins to go wrong. This is especially important with unstable processes, as in the chemical industry, or with dangerous ones, such as nuclear reactors.

Performing a Remote Communications Function

A computer connected to and servicing a number of remote terminals must perform this remote communications function in real-time. The computer has to perform "on demand". The demands may come at any time, and they must be taken care of immediately.

In recent years, computers have become fast enough to be used for message switching, either for a telegraph company, as mentioned earlier, or to handle the vast number and variety of messages generated within a large corporation. In addition to the problem of the simultaneous arrival of two or more messages, the message-switching computer must also give priority to certain very important messages, must store some messages and retrieve them when required, and must convert from the code of one type of message to the code of another. In a few cases delays are tolerable, but during peak hours real-time operation is vital.

Controlling the Operation of One or More Computers

Because computer speeds are reaching their maximum, manufacturers have to turn to other ways of increasing the computing power of their machines. One answer has been to design computer systems that can run more than one program at a time. This is called multiprogramming (described later in this chapter).

To perform multiprogramming, the computer must operate with a real-time control program to handle the many simultaneous demands.

ON-LINE

On-line refers to the use of input/output equipment that may be called upon at any time to transmit to or from a computer to which it is directly connected. Thus, the on-line systems enable users to enter, retrieve, and change data in a timely fashion so that the time lag associated with batch systems is reduced to such a short period. It also enables users to access and manipulate data without waiting for a prescribed time slot for activity. This timeliness of processing maximizes two things:

the user's time, and

the speed of information flow with a project.

To illustrate the importance of speed of information flow in a company or industry, consider two institutions that depend heavily on on-line systems: airlines and banks. Airlines reservations would be much less efficient and streamlined, both to the airlines and to the traveler, without on-line systems. In banks, automatic tellers rely on on-line systems, such as with the proper maintenance of balances.

The first technical step to achieving the on-line environment is usually "going data base" because:

the data base centralizes the control of data facilities to a degree of integrity that is otherwise difficult to attain;

it eliminates the need to do all processing sequentially;

it is a natural step toward achieving control of data at the data administration level.

After the data base environment is established, the next logical step is the on-line environment. There are several standard on-line modes of operation:

24-hour on-line operation,

on-line operation with "batch windows," and

batch processing runs in conjunction with and under control of the on-line environment.

In a 24-hour on-line operation, there is no batch window; that is, there is no time when the on-line system is regularly brought down so that batch jobs may be run. The 24-hour on-line environment is typical of companies running systems worldwide or for operations or projects where the need for services can occur around the clock.

The more typical on-line environment is the one where there is a batch window. In this environment, the on-line system is brought up at some prescribed time (usually early in the morning), stays up to service the workload of on-line activity during the day, and is brought down in the afternoon or evening after the need for an on-line processing diminishes. At that time batch runs (sequential-type processing) can be made against the data base. This regularly scheduled break in on-line processing is called the batch window.

The third way of processing on-line data occurs through use of a hybrid mode of processing in which batch processing shares data concurrently with the on-line system. An example of this mode of processing is the IMS BMP (Batch Message processor). Care must be taken in the mixing of these two fundamentally different modes of processing, because there are essential differences in the two environments (e.g., sequential versus random access of data, large processing runs versus discrete processing units, etc.).

There are variations in the way in which data is processed within the on-line and batch processing modes. Some projects may do all updates in batch and use on-line facilities only for retrieval of data. This simplifies backup and recovering procedures but restricts the user in updating data. Other projects may run nothing but batch processes under the on-line controller, thus achieving a degree of data-sharing not attainable in the pure batch environment. Still other projects may run systems with a great deal of duplicating of processing and data between the on-line and batch environments.

MULTIPROGRAMING

Multiprograming pertains to the interleaved execution of multiple programs at one time. The term "concurrent operation" is used to describe the system wherein multiple programs share the time of a CPU on a one-at-a-time basis. The only simultaneous processing is that between the CPU and the various channels. Multiprogramming is basically a software system with control of the operation placed in the executive routine or control program part of the software operating system.

The rather simple hardware requirements for multiprogramming are:

a very large memory,

both main memory and fast access members of the lower hierarchy of memory, and

many channels and devices,

all of which are fundamental to the concept of multiprogramming and allow for the proper mixture of computer-bound and input/output bound types of programs, such as:

a hardware interrupt feature allowing break-in for computer attention to the channels;

a hardware memory protect feature that prevents unauthorized access to memory not assigned to the running program;

a real-time clock used solely by the executive program for time-slicing, control, and accounting purposes.

The efficiency with which a program is executed by a computer system is dependent not only on the efficiency and coordination of the hardware, but also on the nature of the program itself. Some programs require little calculation and great qualities of output, for example. Others might require considerable internal processing time but a minimal amount of time to record the results of the processing.

The first of these examples is a program typically called "I/O-bound". This means that the total throughput time required to process the program is limited by the speed of the input-output devices being used to record the output and to provide the input data to the processing unit. Other programs that require considerable processing time are known as "process-bound" because their throughput time depends on the internal speed of the processing unit. When an I/O-bound program is being executed, the processing unit spends a good deal of time waiting while the input-output devices perform their function. Similarly, when a process-bound program is being executed, input-output devices are standing idle much of the time. Multiprogramming is a feature of advanced operating systems which attempts to increase the general throughput of the computer sytem by executing more than one program at once. Ideally, the set of programs being executed together would contain a combination of process-bound and I/O-bound programs in such a way that both the processing unit and the input-output devices are operating at maximum speed. Thus, while the output device, say, is recording the results of the minimal calculations involved in the I/O-bound programs, the processor is executing a portion of the process-bound programs which does not require input or output functions. If two such programs are being executed together, it is clear that separate input-output devices are needed for each program. Computer systems so complex as to justify an operating system sophisticated enough to permit multiprogramming will be equipped with multiple input-output devices and the related hardware devices needed to control them.

Basically, multiprogramming operates as follows. An object program to be executed is loaded into memory. Let us assume that this is an I/O-bound program. Soon after execution starts, this program calls for an elaborate input-output operation. When this happens, the input-output devices involved are set to the required tasks and another program is loaded into memory, say a process-bound program. The processing unit is then turned to the operations called for in this program; these will continue until the input-output devices have completed their functions for the I/O-bound program. When this happens, the I/O-bound program is reloaded into memory after the temporary results of the other program are stored away, and execution of the I/O-bound program continues until it again calls for input-output functions, at which time the transfer of programs in memory takes place again.

This process may take place every two or three seconds or perhaps over longer intervals of time. The advantage gained is more effective use of the central processor because it can continue executing a program while waiting for the input-output devices to complete their operations. If the computer system's memory is large enough or the programs to be executed are small enough, or both, then the object programs can be stored in memory and control transferred from one to the other, thus precluding the necessity of loading and reloading each program in its turn. This, of course, would result in even more efficient throughput.

Multiprogramming works most ideally in a situation in which programs to be executed over a period of time, say a few hours or a day, are indicated to the operating system and made available to it, together with their respective data, by on-line input-output devices. The operating system, provided with information as to the frequency and duration of input-output operations of each of the programs, is then in a position to schedule which programs are to be executed when and in combination with which other programs so as to maximize the system's throughput. Elaborate operating systems capable of coping with this type of operation are generally available for use with large computer systems.

MULTIPROCESSING

In some instances, the real-time systems discussed earlier may involve the execution of a wide variety of programs and call for data from a wide variety of sources. To satisfy these diverse requirements, a system can be developed which involves more than one computer and in which a transaction presented to the system will be processed by the computer best suited to handle that particular operation. Other computers on-line to the system can be used to process other transactions and would therefore be standing idle. In this way, the system is in fact executing more than one program at once and is using more than one computer to do it. A computer employing two or more processing units under integrated control is referred to as a multiprocessor.

A more complete definition is based on both the hardware and system software characteristics of the system. There are two or more central processing units; some qualify further the definition that these must be of approximately equal capability (i.e., symmetric CPUs), and others allow asymmetric systems to be included as long as they meet all other conditions. Main processor memory must be shared and accessible by all processors; some require that all memory be common, and total sharing may complicate some of the system software problems (most definitions do allow some private memory for each processor). I/O access must be shareable to include channels, control units, and devices as appropriate. There must be a single integrated operating system in overall control of all hardware and software. There must be intimate interaction possible at both hardware and software operating levels:

At the system software level in the execution of system tasks.

At the program level for the execution of portions of the same program by several processors in turn, and the execution of an independent task of a program on a processor other than the one executing the main task (the ability to move a job).

At the data set level.

At the hardware interrupt level.

A multiprocessor then is a system with

two or more processing units,

shared memory,

shared I/O,

a single integrated operating system, and

hardware and software interaction at all levels. (Figure 3.1 illustrates the basic hardware interconnection relationships. However, it should be noted that the hardware and software interactions depend on the systems software and operating procedures as well as the interaction configuration.)

The external differences in the basic characteristics and capabilities between an operating system for a multiprocessor and that for

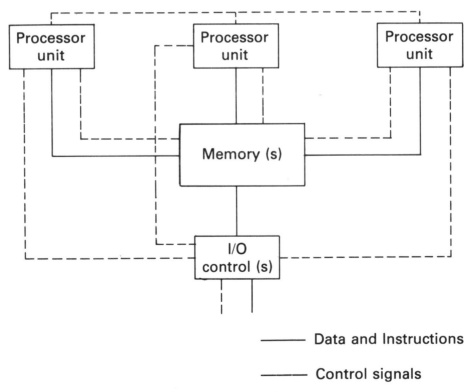

FIGURE 3.1. Basic multiprocessor configuration.

a third generation uniprocessor are not readily apparent. Internally, there is a great amount of difference. In fact, it has been operating system development that has often set the pace for the development and performance of the multiprocessor configuration. One aspect of the system software that sets multiprocessors apart from uniprocessors is the essential need for an extensive operating system to make effective use of the multiprocessor. It is possible for an experienced programmer to operate a uniprocessor without any system software, although the effective utilization of a third-generation machine operated in this manner is quite low. Such is not the case with even the simplest multiprocessor system; an operating system is usually necessary to even start it.

Although many minor variations are possible, there are three basic organizations and modes of operation for the operating system executive of a multiprocessor:

1. master/slave,
2. separate executive for each processor, and
3. symmetric or anonymous treatment of all processors.

The primary characteristics of these organizations are summarized in Table 3.1.

Although both multiprogramming-uniprocessor and multiprocessor operating systems have very similar functional capabilities, there are several important differences. One of the most important of these is software reliability. Software crashes (failures that cannot be recovered from automatically by the software recovery routines) on a uniprocessor usually do not leave the system down too long. However, in a multiprocessor, several of the CPUs may all be executing the same or different portion of the executive code, and a software error or transient hardware failure in a single CPU can quickly propagate throughout the entire system, immediately creating many conditions that are difficult, or at least time-consuming, to recover from.

The multiprocessor operating system has to do everything the uniprocessor OS (operating system) does, and also has the ability to perform several other important tasks such as resource allocation

TABLE 3.1. Characteristics of three organizations of multiprocessor operating systems.*

MASTER/SLAVE	SEPARATE EXECUTIVE FOR EACH PROCESSOR	SYMMETRIC OR ANONYMOUS TREATMENT OF ALL PROCESSORS
• Executive always runs in one (the same) processor.	• Each processor services its own needs.	• Master floats from one processor to another.
• Executive routines do not need to be reentrant.	• Supervisory code must be reentrant or replicated.	• Better load balancing.
• No problem of table conflict or lockout for the Executive. (Applications programs will still conflict over table accesses.)	• Each processor has own set of private tables.	• Conflicts in service requests resolved by priorities.
• Subject to catastrophic failure.	• Not subject to catastrophic failure from single failure; however, restart of a failed processor will probably be very difficult.	• Code must be reentrant since several processors can be executing same service routine.
• Comparatively inflexible.		• Since several processors can be in supervisory state simultaneously, access conflicts can occur.
• Idle time on slave can build up if master is not fast enough.	• In effect, each processor has own set of I/O equipment, files, etc.	• Advantages:
• Most effective for special applications and asymmetric systems.	• Reconfiguration of I/O usually requires manual switching.	Provides graceful degradation. Better availability potential. Real redundancy. Most efficient use of resources.
• Comparatively simpler software and hardware.		

*From *Multiprocessors and Parallel Processing* by Comtre Corporation (Phillip H. Enslow), copyright 1974 by John Wiley and Sons, Inc.

and management (i.e. scheduling, memory management and dispatching, etc.) that result from the nature of the hardware configuration.

REFERENCES

Brightman, Richard W. *Information Systems for Modern Management*. New York: The Macmillan Company, 1971.

Enslow, Phillip H.: Comtre Corporation. *Multiprocessors and Parallel Processing*. New York: John Wiley & Sons, Inc., 1974.

Inmon, W. H. *Management Control of Data Processing*. Englewood Cliffs: Prentice-Hall, Inc., 1983.

Lord, Jr. Kenniston W. and Steiner, James B. *CPM Review Manual Data Processing Handbook* (Second Edition). New York: Van Nostrand Reinhold Co. Inc. 1978.

Weiss, Eric A. *Computer Usage Fundamentals*. New York: McGraw Hill, Inc., 1969.

Chapter
4
SYSTEM DEVELOPMENT LIFE CYCLE

The dynamic life cycle of systems places demands on an organization different from those traditionally felt by managers. These demands have resulted in the creation of "projects" as organizational devices for coping with these new phenomena.

The natural life cycles of systems induce similar life cycles in data processing project organizations. This is particularly apparent at the level of considering the "state variables" which may be used to characterize a project as it evolves.

Such measures vary widely. For instance, in developing a new product, one might characterize the various phases of the project life cycle in terms of the proportional composition of the work force assigned to the activity. In the beginning, research personnel predominate; subsequently, their role diminishes and engineers come to the forefront; finally, marketing and sales personnel become most important. Alternatively, the level of expenditure on the development of the product may well be an appropriate way to characterize various phases of development.

Basic life cycle concepts hold for all projects. Thus, a project develops and matures according to a cycle which is much like that of a product. The measures used to define various phases of a project's life cycle might focus on its product orientation, e.g., defense versus nondefense, its personnel composition, scientists versus nonscientists, its per share earning, and so on.*

SOFTWARE LIFE CYCLE

Software management is primarily concerned with computer programs, data files and documentation rather than the computer equipment configuration that executes the programs. Even so, software designers must have a say in hardware decisions if they are to meet the goals for a computer service. The term "system" will be used here for the combination of hardware and software that provides a computer service. Since software has little purpose without hardware, the terms "system" and "software" may be used interchangeably without causing confusion.

The basic activities and decisions are best introduced in relation to the commonly recognized phases of a system's life cycle, shown in Figure 4.1. The INITIATION phase involves the assessment of an existing, inadequate system to determine the feasibility of replacing it with an improved system. The four phases, DEFINITION through TESTING, are the development period, where a new and improved software product is being designed and implemented. The OPERATION phase starts with the operation of a new system by its intended users, and includes the subsequent maintenance and minor redesigns that user experience may dictate. Eventually, maintenance no longer suffices for needed improvements, and another development cycle is begun.

Specific guidelines for each phase will be given after the following summary of the tasks included. Table 4.1 helps to understand each phase by summarizing the documents produced that are needed for quality control.

---

* Reprinted by permission from *Systems Analysis and Project Management* by David I. Cleland and William R. King. Copyright 1975 by McGraw-Hill, Inc.

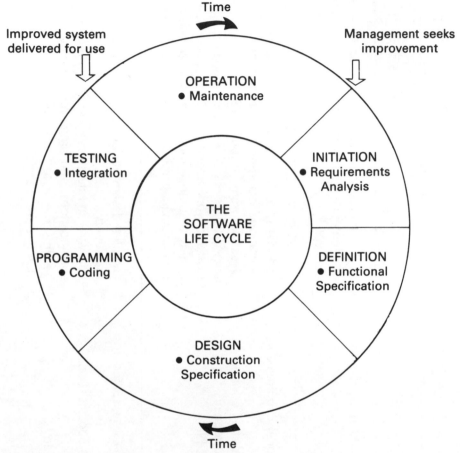

FIGURE 4.1. The life cycle of a software product.

Initiation

In the INITIATION phase, the data processing project manager assures that the technical designers understand the purpose and scope of the envisioned system, and adequately perceive its required functions.

The INITIATION phase begins when management recognizes

TABLE 4.1. Chart of basic quality control documents.

LIFE CYCLE PHASE	DOCUMENTS	GENERAL CONTENT
Initiation	Feasibility Study Report	Requirements analysis, definition and evaluation of alternative solutions, recommended software concept.
Definition	Functional Requirements	External specification of software functions and operation, including design constraints.
	Quality and Performance Requirements	Desired design attributes and quantitative performance parameters for key processing operations.
	Project Plan	Cost and work breakdown, detailed schedule including quality assurance milestones, and definition of primary management and quality control methods.
Design	Design/Coding Standards	Detailed design attributes and coding conventions for quality.
	Design Specifications	Software architecture, module definitions, interface specifications, and programming requirements.
	Test Plan	Testing criteria, testing schedule and work breakdown, standard test case specifications.

Programming	Review Reports	Identified discrepancies and recommendations from team reviews.
	Unit Test Reports	Results of unit test for each module.
	Inspection Reports	Results of inspection sessions for each subsystem.
	Software Manuals	Usage, operation and maintenance descriptions.
	Program Listings	Source Language statements for each tested module.
Testing	Test/Fault Report	Results of scheduled tests.
Operation	Fault Report	Symptoms, circumstances of detected or suspected failure.
	Specification	Functional and design specifications for maintenance and improvement work.
	Maintenance Plan	Work breakdown, cost estimate, and schedule for proposed rework.

that a need exists for new or improved computer services, and that a study should be made to formulate a software solution. During this phase, software planners or system analysts identify the intended users and investigate their work processes. The planner describes the services needed from the envisioned software, and then conceives an outline of alternative software solutions. A close working relationship with the intended users is essential. The alternative approaches should be described in basic terms that users can understand. User concurrence with the stated requirements and the recommended software approach is mandatory.

The INITIATION phase assures that the recommended software approach is technically and economically feasible. An estimate must be made of the costs and benefits for each of the potential software solutions. This will lead to a recommended solution and provide data regarding feasibility (see Chapter 5). Comparable existing systems are investigated to derive cost data and to confirm that proposed solutions are technically realizable. Any pitfalls, failures, or questionable design areas in comparable projects should be covered thoroughly. Comparisons of the proposed project to past failures or problem areas would assure that they can be avoided or resolved. General specifications must be written to show clearly the scope and character of the recommended solution. The INITIATION phase concludes with a report delineating the recommended software and supporting analysis. Management may then approve the concept and budget the recommended funds and personnel for acquisition and operation of the planned system.

Definition

The DEFINITION phase defines the functional and performance requirements in order to confirm that the software, when built, will meet its objectives.

This phase begins when management commits resources to the design or purchase of the proposed software. In this phase, detailed specifications are created for those externally apparent functions and design characteristics that are crucial to the purpose and operation of the software in the intended environment. Input and output data, processing operations, and performance goals are defined. The DEFINITION phase concludes with a specification that is sufficiently precise for outside contracting, if desired. Equally important, the specification allows the intended users to confirm that the proposed system will meet the need and will have acceptable qualities of useability, generality, etc.

The DEFINITION phase provides a project plan for managing the acquisition and installation of the system. A thorough plan for producing or purchasing the software is prepared as part of the DEFINITION phase. Projections are made of the detailed costs. A delivery schedule is laid out, including intermediate milestones and technical reviews for evaluating progress and insuring that the project will meet its goals. Working methods are defined for quality control of intermediate and final products. The plan should extend to the installation and initial operation of the system, and should include user training, document preparation and review, acceptance testing, and the continuing obligations of any contractors, vendors, or support organizations. The project plan is extremely important because it specifies how the effort will be managed, how problems will be resolved, and how the quality of the final system will be assured.

Design

The DESIGN phase produces a thorough design specification for guiding a timely and problem-free implementation of the proposed software.

The DESIGN phase begins when the functional requirements have been validated by intended users, and implementation of the system is approved. This phase results in detailed specifications of the internal construction of the software for use by programmers who will implement the design. It involves definition of the internal architecture of the software, performance trade-off analyses of algorithms, specification of individual programs or modules, specification of interactions between components of software, etc. The design specifications are important as a means for resource management and quality control during PROGRAMMING.

Programming

In the PROGRAMMING phase, software management assures that appropriate technical choices are made, and that high-quality workmanship is applied in producing codes meeting the design specifications.

The PROGRAMMING phase often is merged with DESIGN and so may have no distinguishable starting point. PROGRAMMING involves final technical choices for internal program design and the creation of programming language statements or "code" that is executable on the computer and that implements the design. Data processing management here is the day-to-day supervision of programmers, and guiding and reviewing their technical results. PROGRAMMING effort includes the testing by each programmer of his/her individual programs and the preparation of pertinent management reports and software documents. Test reports, inspection reports, and program documentation act as tangible quality controls over PROGRAMMING accomplishments.

Testing

In the TESTING phase, data processing management assures that no significant errors or design discrepancies will impede usage of the system in the intended operational environment.

The TESTING phase is concerned with verifying that the software product meets the functional specifications and contains no significant discrepancies or logical errors to impede its use. TESTING proceeds according to a test plan prepared in the DESIGN phase, and focuses on the integration of individual programmer results in an overall working system. Noted discrepancies and errors are documented for corrective action by the programming team. Gross shortcomings in the original design or functional specifications may be exposed; this should lead to a major project review in order to plan and organize additional definition and design work.

Operation

In OPERATION of a delivered system, data processing or software management assures that maintenance is as well managed and controlled as the original development.

The OPERATION phase follows the delivery and installation of the software, and involves periodic redesign and improvement. Data processing management procedures that are recommended during development can be streamlined to provide similar close control of the reduced effort committed to corrective design work. Thorough specifications, quality workmanship, effective testing, and management reviews remain highly important in directing technical efforts to meet cost and schedule targets.

During the development period, the earlier activities may be continued or repeated to remedy design defects and improve quality of the final system.

Although the successive phases defined here should be followed whenever practical, some flexibility is advisable, especially when a project involves unusual complexity or innovation. For example, it may be important to carry only a part of the system through to DESIGN and PROGRAMMING to confirm feasibility before beginning DEFINITION for the entire system. Or, with limited effort available, development of some supporting capabilities or auxiliary programs may be deferred until the mainstream processing is successfully completed. So, all parts of the software need not be at the same stage of development, and the life cycle orientation may be viewed with some flexibility.

REFERENCES

Cleland, David I. and King, William R. *Systems Analysis and Project Management.* New York: McGraw-Hill, 1975.

Fife, Dennis W. "Computer Software Management: A Primer for Project Management and Quality Control." NBS Special Publication 500-11, U. S. Department of Commerce, July 1977.

Chapter
5
DATA PROCESSING PROJECT

Most data processing projects consist of three distinct phases—initiation, execution and conclusion.

The initiation phase defines the objectives of the project being undertaken and obtains management approval to begin work on the execution phase. The execution phase utilizes the output from the first phase to assign project personnel to activities, generates detailed schedules for reporting progress, manages the work process, and summarizes the project progress into management reports. The conclusion phase terminates the project. It includes a review of the system, preparation of the project evaluation document, and acceptance by user management.

The evaluation document is filed in the project control manual and referred to in the future for similar projects. Its contents include:

A detailed description of how the final time and cost figures compare with the original budget.

The mistakes made in the project.

The things about the project that were particularly outstanding, including new design or control techniques.

Recommendations for future projects of this nature.

The user acceptance of the system—usually a special letter from the data processing project manager to the user management.

Thus, data processing project management (DPPM) should be designed to provide sustained, intensified, and integrated management of complex ventures. It should involve: (a) the focus of a substantial portion of total organizational resources on specific objectives; (b) highly interdependent specialized activities; and (c) relatively severe constraints with respect to cost, delivery, and performance of the end product. Unqualified success of the data processing project often requires a breakthrough in the technological state-of-the-art and pervasive trade-off decisions which seek whole-system optimization rather than suboptimization at the level of a single paramenter or function.

To achieve maximum intensification of managerial attention, DPPM may be assigned full responsibility for the achievement of project objectives, subject only to an overall project plan approved by top management. At the other extreme, DPPM may be assigned coordinative (or simply monitoring) responsibility for the integration of project-related activities while existing patterns of functional responsibility and directive authority remain largely intact. In most instances, DPPM are required to subcontract with either the functional organization or an outside concern for the specialized efforts required to accomplish project tasks; e.g., design, development, production, test, support, and other services.

Therefore, the usual position of the data processing activity within an organization greatly heightens the importance of the liaison functions at the management level. The data processing project manager is faced with difficult decisions; he/she often shares in making decisions that do not relate directly to his/her own project and acts as an intermediary with other departments. The problem of translating technical information into management terms is always with him/her. Finally, in day-to-day operations, he/she must act to assure a smooth, timely flow of data.

The basic data processing functions of planning, operation and management are discussed below.

DATA PROCESSING PLANNING FUNCTION

Planning is the major activity that encompasses those functions concerned with establishing a data processing installation, and with selecting, designing and preparing programs for new data processing applications. This type of planning involves the organization and scheduling of human and mechanical resources into an effective plan for establishing or changing a data processing activity. This includes the following operations:

schedule development for all tasks involved in installing the organization, applications and equipment;

budget development;

staffing plans including assignment of tasks, recruitment, selection, and training plans;

development of detailed standard for performance; and

site and facilities planning.

In addition, the functions include activities that are relative to the selection and definition of data processing applications that fulfill the objectives of the organization, such as:

review with management and other departments of information needs, and their translation into stated objectives;

economy analyses to determine the justification of the costs;

a thorough analysis of proposed applications to ascertain whether they fit into the overall plan of the data processing system; and

continuing liaison with other sections and management to review the need for new applications and the degree to which present applications are satisfying management goals.

OPERATION AND MANAGEMENT

The operating functions include the day-to-day operation of established procedures. The actual loading, unloading, setup and control of equipment that constitutes a data processing installation is included in machine operations. Data processing equipment operations require meticulous control of schedules and the maintenance of accurate records of equipment and program performance.

Data processing shares in common with other activities the many functions of administering and supervising an operating unit. Special aspects of data processing administration and supervision are good utilization of equipment (a constant concern, since meeting schedules is very important), and a combination of rigid, detailed operations and creative development work must often be simultaneously supervised.

The reporting function is an important part of any manager's job. DPPM faces two problems:

the translation of technical measures of progress and performance into commonly understood standards, and

continual reporting on planning and project performance.

CRITERIA FOR A PROJECT

*The day-to-day tasks of a data processing organization are done by assigning work to specific units. Routine work is done efficiently when done repetitively at a responsible work center. Major changes in work, new concepts, and new approaches often require a specialized unit. For instance, a major change in a data system or a conversion to an advanced generation of electornic data processing (EDP) equipment are specialized tasks that need special efforts. It may be impossible or inadvisable to charge the existing machine operations or systems division with the additional duty of planning

* Selection from CDP Review Manual Data Processing Handbook, Second Edition, by Kenniston W. Lord, Jr. and James B. Steiner. Copyright (c) 1978 by Litton Educational Publishing, Inc. Reprinted by permission of Van Nostrand Reinhold Co. Inc.

the design of a completely new system and the conversion to new equipment. It is best to assign a specialized team to the project unless the project or organization is very small; units responsible for day-to-day jobs are likely to be prejudiced in favor of doing the job in the current way and opposed to change.

A project should have certain characteristics to be separately organized and controlled. It must be unique and of vital importance with definite and measurable goals. Officially recognized and directed by top management, the project should be clearly a one-time effort, that is:

defineable in terms of a specific goal;

infrequent, unique, or unfamiliar to the present organization;

complex with respect to the interdependence of detail task accomplishment;

economically justifiable;

have sequence of specific events that leads to completion; and

have a means for measuring the results of the completed project against expectations.

TYPES OF DATA PROCESSING PROJECTS

There are a number of jobs that could qualify as separate projects in implementing a data processing system. Chronologically, they are the feasibility study, the application study, the equipment proposal, equipment selection, installation of the equipment, and the implementation/conversion.

FEASIBILITY STUDY

In the feasibility study, the data processing requirements of the organization are analyzed to determine if there is technological, operational and economic justification to change to a new system, perhaps using an advanced generation of computer equipment. The study then concerns itself with alternatives and recommendations that offer the greatest advantage to the organization. When a computer is already in use in the organization, the emphasis is on technological developments and economic factors. Can control or decision-making be improved? Will increased speed and timeliness provide a competitive advantage? What commitment of resources is involved? A major system change results in an extended period in which the organization is locked-in to the system with no opportunity to turn back or change course. The feasibility study, by identifying costs and benefits, enables DPPM to choose intelligently. Change should not be made for the sake of change. One way to lose money is to change computers as each new system is introduced. Another way is to continue an outmoded system long after it has recovered its costs and is no longer cost competitive with newer equipment. Computer replacement must be considered in much the same manner as the replacement of production machinery or capital equipment.

It may become apparent to data processors that it is time to make a major change in the data processing operation. The first step is to obtain the sanction of top management to investigate the idea. Management support is vital because time, effort, and company resources are required to do the study. Data may be required from components across organizational lines, and all components of the organization may be affected by proposed changes. Top management must make clear what it wants from the study. It should issue a letter or charter to define the study's scope and objectives and to establish the authority for the study. A data processing project manager should be appointed with the authority to select other team members.

The feasibility study develops the overall picture of some integral system of data processing requirements. It identifies the application likely to gain from using more advanced date processing techniques. It itemizes present costs and benefits for comparison to projected systems costs and benefits. Continuing or fixed costs associated with both the current and proposed system are ignored, as they do not infleunce the decision. Finally, when alternatives are presented, when advantages and disadvantages are noted, recommendations concerning new techniques and procedures should be made.

The recommendations of the project team, with supporting documentation, should be presented to the top management both as a written proposal and oral presentation. At this point, the recommendation should be a report on the feasibility of the proposed action and a record of the thinking that formed the basis for the decision.

APPLICATION STUDY

Application or system studies are detailed extensions of the feasibility study. They deal with the systems or problems to which the computer is applied. Approval to proceed with the new system may be given as a result of the feasibility study.

At this point, the proposed system must be defined in detail. The data processing project manager must first consider the output needs; that is, the information requirements of the user. From these needs he works backwards, through the processing, to the capture of the output. Block diagrams are normally used to relate the source documents, or generation of the basic data, through the processing steps to the output products.

Thus, the characteristics of an optimum system are as follows:

fast and responsive, making efficient use of equipment and having minimal time between the time data are generated and the output is produced;

accurate within prescribed limits;

reliable, consistent in operation, and virtually infallible;

adaptable, able to expand or be changed, flexible; and

economical, saving money, time, effort, supplies, and manpower.

To achieve these favorable characteristics, it is necessary to incorporate a number of concepts which lend themselves to efficient system design, such as:

1. Standardize as many terms, procedures, routines, methods and as much equipment as possible.

2. Capture data as close to the source as possible.

3. Use reporting by exception for those items that require management's attention.

4. Avoid human intervention by using machine sensible media and direct communication.

5. Provide the most useful format to the user at his/her optimum time and place.

6. Select equipment compatible to job requirements and design the system to maximize the use of this equipment.

EQUIPMENT SELECTION PROCESS

A data processing project team may be required to convert the study and design into specifications for equipment. Government agencies and many companies go to great lengths to ensure a competitive bidding situation. Hopefully, it is the means to get the best value. Qualified vendors are formally notified of a forthcoming set of data processing system specifications and are invited to express an interest in bidding. Those that do express interest are then given the specifications and the related ground rules necessary for an acceptable proposal. The vendor's proposal becomes an objective basis upon which to make a selection. This selection should provide the best equipment for the price, and all bidders would have had a fair and impartial opportunity to win the contract.

A special data processing project team may be assigned to review proposals and make recommendations on the selection. The actual selection process rests with the upper echelon of management which tends to follow recommendations but which may apply different weights to some selection factors.

It should be noted that detailed systems specifications and the proposal and bidding process are not always so formalized. Relying on previous experience with one vendor, his reputation and established competence, some companies may select a particular vendor at the outset. He may be asked to propose an equipment configuration to match the system needs. This approach can be practical if the potential user has done a thorough systems study, prescribed a detailed description of processing, and identified input and file content. Specialized computer programs that aid in selecting the right equipment can also be obtained. Benchmark applications using off-the-shelf equipment help test and validate the proposed selection.

Specialized planning may be required for the site preparation for the new equipment. Planning is also needed for the implementation/conversion to the new data system and equipment.

SELECTING AN APPROPRIATE PLANNING HORIZON

Planning is an intellectual process requiring creative thinking, conceptual ability, imagination, and the use of knowledge, experience, and wisdom in the selection of alternatives. By definition, it is the process by which a system adapts its resources to changes in environment and internal forces. It is the recognition of an intelligent cooperation with the inevitable and the anticipation of change so as to alter the course of future action. It contains controls or criteria which trigger certain actions when predetermined events occur in the future.

Time and change are implied in planning. Business, data processing activity, and the world we live in are in a constant state of change. A most important aspect of change pertaining to computer equipment is in the implementation cycle. When computers were first introduced, it was relatively easy to put them to use. Since then, there have been various generations or major technological changes that render the old models obsolete or economically impractical. Change has occurred at a rate that makes the life span of a computer about six years; one that remains in use for eight years is exceptional. A data processing activity must expect change.

The system work necessary to convert to a new generation of equipment is growing longer, however. Conversion from punched card accounting machines (PCAM) to computers was done application by application in a few weeks or at most in a few months. Conversion from PCAM to second generation equipment took a little longer for the system work and programming. Conversion from second generation to third generation equipment, particularly when immediate access storage and remote devices for updates and inquiry on a real-time basis are part of the system, often requires many months of planning before implementation. Complex management information systems and the concept of totally integrated systems may very likely require several more years of design before they are fully operational. The planning for computer conversion has become more complex and time-consuming, and a much longer lead time must, therefore, be anticipated.

Planning is the programmed decision-making process. Broad plans or goals and objectives are made at the top. These broad plans are developed into more detailed and specific plans at the next level. These more detailed plans are either standing plans, which cover routine situations, or single-use plans designed to fit a specific situation or anticipated event. Policies and certain directives are types of standing plans which guide the organization members in the conduct of their business. Usually, these policies are written in a manual or operating guide. Similarly, procedures and standards are types of plans.

Standing plans provide uniformity of operation throughout the organization. Similar situations can be handled in a similar manner, and decisions can be expedited by referring to the book. This type of plan has been referred to as programmed decision-making. It is an efficient way to handle routine and repetitive matters that fall within normal expectations. It avoids the need to go through a complex research, thinking and decision process every time a common situation arises.

Taking the concept of programmed decision-making one step further than a standing plan or policy manual is the incorporation of a planning factor into the data processing system. During the processing of data by the computer, the status of a record is compared with preplanned criteria, and if certain conditions prevail, a branch to a subroutine takes place. For instance, should processing reveal that quantity-on-hand is less than the reorder point, then the instruction is to prepare the standard procurement request.

Many decisions are not programmed. They cannot be included

in a plan when they are novel, unusual, and uninstructed. These situations must be handled by judgment, intuition, experience, and a thinking process outside of the plan. Even here, however, it is possible to use the techniques of operation research, modeling, and computer simulation to identify the best of alternate solutions, provided planning made these tools available.

DEFINITION OF SCOPE/OBJECTIVES/CONSTRAINTS

The first step in a data processing project is to determine the project objectives, although it may be necessary to modify them completely or discard them prior to the completion of the project. Since the selected objectives influence the nature of the end product, the advantages and disadvantages of each possible objective must be determined. The project team should use objectives as real, working guides for the data processing project.

A formal set of objectives forces management to give the total business environment serious thought. In the process of defining the objectives, the problems involved in attaining these objectives become more visible. Additionally, a framework or operation is evolved within which the project team knows exactly what is expected of it, the limitations under which it must work, and the time constraints under which it must function. Many managers profess they have objectives but never take time to write them down or have them understood. Thus, many considerations which should have been investigated are overlooked. Top managers of companies who have made major changes in their systems have indicated that their work would have gone more smoothly had they adopted a formal slate or objectives. In the data processing project, the statement of objectives is not a purely academic task. It is a task which, if done without bias, will in the end be very profitable.

The objectives indicate the various approaches to be followed and even the emphasis necessary to achieve the end results desired. The objectives normally revolve around the many types of economic advantages. Typical objectives that may encourage a firm to investigate the use of automation are:

to relieve management of routine decision-making

to increase productivity of available work forces

to reduce errors by reducing human involvement

to increase the value of information

to reduce per-unit processing costs

to reduce physical storage requirements

to make more effective use of human resources by replacing detailed tasks with review functions

to permit the use of specific scientific techniques

The basic objectives of the data processing project must center on cost-effectiveness. That is, management must orient the business objectives so that effectiveness is maximized at the lowest possible cost. The project team consistently must set its goals with cost-effectiveness as the basic objective from which all others flow. Cost savings accrue through savings in personnel and machines, while effectiveness increases through speedier reports, improved relations with customers, and greater efficiency in the processing of data.

The objectives of the data processing project form the basis for the scope of the project. Broad objectives create a problem in that the project activity becomes complex and unmanageable. Some project teams begin their work with the obvious problem areas, such as high volume operations or repetitive operations with high clerical costs. Most organizations are more subtle and complex than this.

The project team first develops a general overview of an organization's problem areas and needs. Evaluating tangible factors, they select areas which are likely to produce the largest benefits from using new procedures and equipment. The history of the particular function as detailed in literature, etc., helps to determine whether the areas should be considered for detailed study. Two important facets are the previous efforts to improve similar operations and prior project work for the area in question; an operation deserves study if other organizations have successfully automated similar procedures and methods. Management is more willing to venture into automation if success has been demonstrated. Previously unexplored areas, or areas where previous efforts had been unsuccessful, may with new and proper techniques prove to be rewarding areas for automation.

More important than the history of an operation are the benefits that can be derived. The present cost of data processing operations can indicate whether it is economically feasible to use new equipment. Such costs are either replaceable (they can be saved by new methods) or nonreplaceable (they continue despite the adoption of new methods). Cost balancing or savings of the replaceable may offer benefits by improving the results of an operation. These include accuracy, speed, flexibility, and increased decision-making capability. Automation can also produce results in the area of human behavior. That is, personnel benefit from a decrease in the laborious, routine work which characterizes clerical operations.

A third factor evaluated in determining the scope of the project area is the relationship of different operations. The functions within an organization may be independent, interdependent, or located on a continuum somewhere inbetween these extremes. If the operations are generally interdependent, the scope of the project will of necessity be initially great. The project team analyzes each operation by functional area; but, since they are interdependent, one functional area leads to another. This leads to a system-wide approach to the study/project.

The converse procedure is to select an area independent of other areas or isolated from them. This is the minimum area approach. A single functional area is the initial area of concern, but more can be added. The minimum area approach has merit if management desires to start new operations with a minimum delay, if personnel are not available for a large project, or if there is no reasonable basis for enlarging the project area.

The area chosen for a project should not be considered fixed. The study of problems in one area almost always leads into other areas, and large potential benefits may be discovered for an area not originally studied. On the other hand, the areas first selected may turn out to be too large to handle effectively. If important new factors are discovered, the project team should consider redefining the selected area. The scope of problem areas selected for study should be consistent with available resources. Demands for and limits on the organization's resources, whatever the reasons, must be considered in setting the scope of the data processing projects.

REFERENCES

Butler, Jr., Arthur G. "Project Management: A Study in Organizational Conflicts." *Academy of Management Journal*, March 1973.

Feingold, Carl. *Introduction to Data Processing* (3d ed.) Dubuque, IA: Wm. C. Brown Company Publishers, 1980.

Lord Jr., Kenniston W. and Steiner, James B. *CPM Review Manual Data Processing Handbook* (Second Edition). New York: Van Nostrand Reinhold Co. Inc. 1978.

Mixon, S. R. *Handbook of Data Processing Administration, Operations, and Procedures*. New York: AMACOM, 1976.

Chapter
6
PROJECT MANAGEMENT FUNCTIONS IN THE ORGANIZATION

The "project organization" and "functional organization" are inseparable; one cannot survive without the other. Much of the confusion and concern about project management centers around a failure to understand the complementary nature of the formal authority and responsibility relationship found in the project/functional (or matrix) organization.

Operational realizations of the matrix organization vary from the form in which the DP project manager has everyone associated with the project working directly for him in a "line" capacity, to the form in which the project manager is a coordinator or facilitator. Projects or tasks forces are essentially *horizontal* in nature; bureaucracies, the embodiment of the classical functional organization, are *vertical* in nature. The basic dichotomy found in matrix organizations centers around a project-functional interface reflected in Table 6.1. This table provides a simple set of key words as underlined.

The interface clearly describes how the project manager accomplishes his project ends by the managing of relationships within the total organization. There are few things which the project manager

TABLE 6.1. The project functional interface.

DATA PROCESSING PROJECT MANAGER	FUNCTIONAL MANAGER
What is to be done? *When will* the task be done? *Why will* the task be done? *How much* money is available to do the task? *How well* has the total project been done?	*How will* the task be done? *Where will* the task be done? *Who will* do the task? *How well* has the functional input been integrated into the project?

can do alone. He must rely on the support and cooperation of other people within the organization. He must look to functional managers for specific support. Indeed, the project manager "gets things done by working through others" in the classic sense of that phrase which is often used as a "definition" of successful management.

This managing of organizational relationships is three-dimensional. Upward, the project manager must relate to his boss, who is either a general manager or a manager of projects. Downward, he relates to members of his project team. Horizontally, he relates to functional managers and to representatives of other organizations—e.g., the customers.

Managing these sets of relationships is a most demanding task. It is nearly impossible if care has not been taken to describe the formal authority and responsibility relationships that are expected within the organization. This means making explicit the network of relationships that he has in each of the three dimensions. To whom does he have to relate? What are the key relationships? What is the work breakdown structure around which action is expected? Who works for whom? In other words, a systems view of an organization is essential for him to understand his role.

Project management functions embody four basic organizational types: centralized organization, decentralized organization, task force organization, and matrix organization. The full meaning of these organizations will be examined in greater detail below.

CENTRALIZED ORGANIZATION

The term "centralization" hinges on authority relationships rather than function. In a centralized organization, management is centered at one location to obtain the benefits of greater specialization and ease of coordination, communication, and top level decision-making.

Generally, if management is centralized, information processing is also centralized so as to support the staff. In fully centralized computer operations, all data to be processed are submitted or transmitted to one central location, the principal offices of the company. Information is provided to the staff agencies at the central location, and certain reports may be forwarded to field locations. Communications and data transmission costs are usually high. Centralized computer facilities ordinarily have larger scale computer and peripheral equipment than comparable decentralized locations.

The role of the computer has been envisioned by some as encouraging a swing to the centralized concept because unlimited amounts of data are readily available at the home office.

DECENTRALIZED ORGANIZATION

Just as the centralized organization revolves around authority rather than function, the term "decentralization" also hinges on authority relationships. In a decentralized operation, the authority and responsibility for results may be as far down the line as efficient management permits. Decentralization may imply that the size and volume of the organization's data processing needs are too unwieldy to control from a central point. It may take too long to send facts up the line and wait for the decision to return. The basic concept of decentralization is that facts are gathered and decisions are made at the scene of action.

TABLE 6.2. Comparison between centralization and decentralization.

FACTOR	FAVORING DECENTRALIZATION	FAVORING CENTRALIZATION
Cost of decision	Low cost	High cost
Policy	Uniform	Broad, vague
Economic size	Large	Small
History of expansion	External acquisition	Internal growth
Local environment	Dynamic	Stable
Output	Objective standards	Difficult to Measure
Subordinate managers	Well-trained	Inexperienced

Data processing is decentralized when placed with branch offices or locations to support the components of the company co-located with them. Generally, these facilities have smaller equipment than centralized facilities. Products are provided to local agencies, and a modest amount of data is submitted to higher echelons. Data transmission and communications costs are moderate.

Lower costs and higher processing outputs of newer computers encourage the decentralized concept. Data transmission costs are lower when decentralized units support widely separated branches or divisions.

TASK FORCE ORGANIZATION

The task force approach is essentially a team effort. A task force is created to accomplish some specific objective or mission. Its members are drawn mainly from within the organization—occasionally supplemented with outsiders—and are selected because of their potential contribution to successful attainment of the mission. Once the objective has been reached and the specific assignment finished, the members of the task force are returned to their original organizational unit. Relatively speaking, the task force enjoys only a temporary existence in the organizational life span.

Structural fluidity is the theme for any task force. The heart of the concept rests in the ability to add new members when their potential contribution is high and to subtract members from the core group when specific contributions have been secured and no further need of these particular talents is foreseen. In this way, the team approach permits rapid adjustment to changing demands and requirements. It provides the means whereby a company can take prompt and maximum advantage of significant changes or modifications in mission, technology, and market requirements. Diverse technical individuals and units are tied together by a common purpose. A sense of accomplishment is achieved as tangible results accumulate from team efforts.

This diversity in composition of membership permits cutting across traditional organizational lines which frequently act as impediments to communication and cooperation during periods requiring rapid changes in ideas, technology and implementation. Putting relatively small groups of complementary or supplementary functions together under a single administrator facilitates the interchange of skills represented as they are brought to bear on the problem at hand.

A team concept places primary emphasis on the objective. Because of its characteristics in assignment of personnel and in mission orientation, the members become a semi-sufficient group within the firm's structure. Thorough understanding of the nature of the mission to be accomplished gives the team a decided advantage over its more traditional divisional or departmental counterpart in that simultaneous efforts on various aspects of the problem are facilitated and phasing from one stage of development to the next is made more readily. The latter results in part from the continuous indoctrination and information about the progress of the project shared by all team members. No time is required by successive departments for indoctrination, for them to develop a "feel" for the project, or for these later units to explore avenues which have already been investigated during previous stages of inquiry and development.

However, many managers fail to appreciate the effectiveness of the task force because they see it merely as another committee. Actually, the task force and committee are by no means synonymous. It is true that the committee, especially the ad hoc committee, is similar to the task force in that it is a transitory device designed to solve a problem or accomplish some other specific undertaking and is disbanded on attainment of the objective for which it was appointed. However, there are significant differences between the two. Specifically:

The task force is a full-time assignment for the people making up the team. It is not something that is attended to in one's spare time away from normal duties. Each member concentrates his full attention on the problem at hand and is expected to make a positive contribution.

The task force is granted a different kind of authority and responsibility than is the ad hoc committee. It is seldom, if ever, created to act as a judiciary body. It is not primarily an educational device, nor is it a subtle sales gimmick. The task force has a mission, a leader, and a projected completion date. It is not in a position where it can "pass the buck," fail to reach a conclusion, or file majority-minority reports. It is established to take positive action, and it is given the authority necessary to implement this charge by a superior echelon.

Certain conditions are prerequisite to the satisfactory establishment and performance of a task force or project team. Awareness of these factors and an understanding of their implications are essential for a company to obtain satisfactory results from the team concept. For instance:

Problems must be such that they are project- or task-oriented. This criterion suggests that there be a specific mission to be accomplished, one that can be stated with some precision as to what and how it will be achieved. In other words, the ingredients in terms of time and specific talents can be determined with some degree of assurance that these factors will contribute toward attaining the objective. There must also be a specific, definite goal. The formulation of the goal may, for example, be in terms of a product to be developed to the point where introducing it to the market is commercially feasible. Because a definite objective can be established, the resultant necessary steps become more easily identifiable. In the case just cited, the team would then be charged with development of a workable set of product specifications, establishment of a proper production process, and creation of a suitable sales organization (including market testing, selection of dealers, preparation of advertising materials, and securing of adequate financing).

A corollary of this first proposition is the condition that there must be an end point to the project or assigment which can be both determined in advance and recognized in fact, once it has been attained. Without this distinguishable end point, the project team is in danger of becoming a permanent facet of the organizational structure. While in some cases this permanence may be a desirable condition, it controverts one of the basic reasons for turning to the task force concept. Therefore, some checkpoint must be established, at which time the entire team and its accomplishments should be reviewed by the initiating authority to determine whether attainments have been satisfactory, what steps or stages still remain to bring the project to operational status, and whether or not conditions justify further continuance of the team itself.

Events or results which constitute checkpoints or end points must be determined during the planning phases of the task or project. Examples of such points may include one or more of the following:

- The product under development reaches a preestablished rate of return on investment.

- A product or product line reaches a specified sales volume within a given calendar period.

- Progression is made from prototype, job-order production to large volume, long-run production requirements (this stage can be further determined by means of engineering-drawing release points, developmental budget review decisions, and similar well-established standard transition points).

- Completion of contractual obligations with the accompanying inspection and customer acceptance.

A third criterion of successful task force utilization is that the goal or completion date must be short-range; that is, the time interval from inception of the project to completion of the desired results must be of relatively short duration. This time limit may well be one year or less, or as long as several years. However, if the amount of time required for successful completion of an assignment is projected much farther into the future, the organizational arrangements reach a stage of permanence not characteristic of the temporary type of arrangements contemplated when discussing a task force device. This is not to prohibit a task force from becoming a permanent organizational unit should the need be demonstrated, but it does indicate that the conditions which justified a task force approach have changed and the solution no longer lies in a transitory device.

Basically, the task force organization provides for a transfer of skills and knowledge from planning specialists to operating executives with a maximum of effectiveness. Thus, the successful employment of the task force concept requires from management new approaches for delegating authority at all levels in the company, a definition of functional interrelationships and responsibilities, and the formulation and management of operating practices and procedures.

Consequently, management must exercise extreme care to build into the organizational structure both team and functional responsibilities in such a way that the company may capitalize to the maximum on the benefits and strengths of both.

MATRIX ORGANIZATION

The term "matrix" grew up in the United States aerospace industry, and has now become the accepted term in both business and academic circles. How can we best define it? I believe that the most useful definition is based on the feature of a matrix organization that most clearly distinguishes it from conventional organizations, such as "one man, one boss" or a single chain of command system.

So, a matrix organization employs a *multiple command system* that includes not only a multiple command structure but also related support mechanisms and an associated organizational culture and behavior pattern.

*Consider a company composed of two divisions. Division A is an operating entity which produces a standardized product in high volume. Within Division A are the functional departments through which the standardized work can flow. (Functional departmentalization is the traditional way of organizing in such an instance. A major functional department such as finance would normally be comprised of a number of minor functional departments such as credit, disbursements, fund control, and accounting.) Division A may be thought of in terms of four major functional departments—production, engineering, personnel and finance. The managerial emphasis in these departments would—because of the nature of the activities which they perform—be primarily on improving operating efficiency. Figure 6.1 shows Division A to be traditionally organized to achieve such efficiency.

Division B of the company is a "job shop" operation which performs contract work for the government. Their work is composed of various projects, each with rather specific objectives and well-defined points of completion.

The level of participation by various functional entities in each of Division B's projects is highly variable as each project progresses toward completion. In the early stages of a project, the emphasis may be on the choice of materials and components, while at a later stage this facet will be de-emphasized. This is due to the natural life cycle of a project. Thus, the combination of people and resources that can best jointly pursue project goals changes from time to time in each of Division B's projects. Here, then, the primary management emphasis must be on organizing and controlling the projects rather than on seeking greater efficiency.

The matrix organization of this hypothetical two-division company is illustrated in Figure 6.1. Division A needs no matrix concept because of its continuing standardized work load. Division B

*Reprinted by permission of the publisher from *Systems Analysis and Project Management*, David I. Cleland and William R. King. Copyright 1975 by McGraw-Hill Book Co.

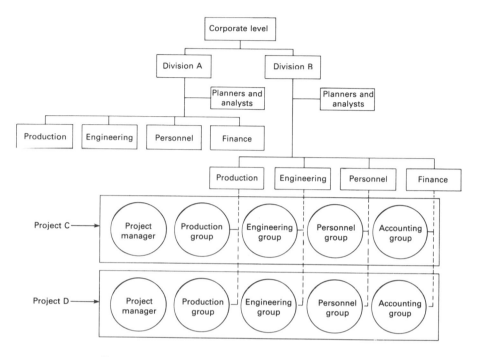

FIGURE 6.1. Illustrative matrix organization.

has all the same functional departments as does Division A, but each provides facilities and functional support to the two major activities of the division—projects C and D.

Each of the project organizations depicted in the lower portion of Figure 6.1 is comprised of a project manager and work groups from the various functional departments. The project manager is given the authority and responsibility for the achievement of project goals. The line organization is left to function by providing support for the various projects. Typically, the work groups for each project are assigned on a full-time basis from their various functional units to the project. When the project is completed, or when their services are no longer essential to it, they are assigned back to their functional units.

In view of this example, it can be ascertained that the matrix concept of organization has important implications for the myriad tasks of management. In matrix organizations, one finds a management philosophy which dictates that the organization shall reflect major work relationships rather than traditional work alignments. This new organizational structure contains four major elements:

1. functional support
2. project management
3. routine administration
4. research and development (strategic planning).

These are examined below.

FUNCTIONAL SUPPORT

Functional support consists of facilitative technology provided for the company by various groups. In a manufacturing organization this element would be supplied by three groups, designated "production," "marketing" and "finance". Functional support is provided for all projects in the organization as well as for the advancement of the state-of-the-art in a particular discipline.

PROJECT MANAGEMENT

Project management is carried out by managers acting as *unifying agents* for particular projects in respect to the current resources of time, funds, materials, people, and technology. The project managers act as focal points for their project activities through an organization superimposed on the traditional functional organization structure. They are, in effect, the general managers of the company for their particular projects. They actively participate in planning, organizing and controlling those major organizational and extraorganizational activities involved.

ROUTINE ADMINISTRATION

Routine administration involves the accommodating services provided for mission-related activities. These services include the centralized activities required to keep score on the business as a whole as well as the routine administration and accounting of funds, people, materials, and ideas. Examples are the personnel function and recurring logistical support.

RESEARCH AND DEVELOPMENT (STRATEGIC PLANNING)

Research and development activities are those concerned with advancing the strategic state-of-the-art in the functional areas and with developing system plans and products/services for the company's future. This group is less concerned with accomplishing current work than with obtaining future work and finding new uses for existing resources; consequently, its work is more conceptual and abstract.

Contemporary managers force the problem of keeping themselves up-to-date on the many ad hoc activities needed to complete a project within time, cost, and technological boundaries. These projects may be in varying degrees of maturity; some may be merely concepts, while others are nearing completion and phaseout. This stream of projects, encompassing a number of different products, each of which requires considerable effort and attention, often first manifests itself in the R&D function. The R&D functional manager cannot stay on top of all the development efforts for which he is responsible. To assist in these developments, a project engineer (project manager) is assigned to each of the major projects to achieve, first of all, unity of communication and coordination across the disciplines of the organization, as well as within the engineering discipline. He becomes a source of integrated information concerning his particular project and interaction point for coordinating the diverse organizational and extraorganizational activities involved. This communication function, coupled with the coordinative function, enables him to exercise control over many aspects of the project.

As more and more projects are added, the functional managers depend increasingly on the project managers to keep them informed, to manage their projects, and to coordinate action, as necessary, among the functional groups within the organization. The functional executive further depends on a "purposeful conflict" between project managers and functional managers as a means of evaluating relative trade-offs for the time, cost, and technical parameters of a particular project. The chief executive expects his project and functional managers to resolve daily operating problems among themselves and to bring only major unresolved questions to him. Management by exception is the objective.

Rarely does the project manager find that the project activities are limited to his own organization; he usually must work with participants (or contributors) outside the company. He therefore has superior knowledge of the relative roles and functions of the individual project, and so is a logical person to take part in major interorganizational decisions affecting the project.

We thus see that an alternative to the purely functional organization is both viable and potentially effective, and that the matrix organization has grown to be a significant force in modern management.

REFERENCES

Cleland, David I. and King, William R. *Systems Analysis and Project Management.* New York: McGraw-Hill, 1975.

Davis, Stanley M., Lawrence, Paul R., Kolodny Harvey and Beer, Michael. *Matrix.* Reading: Addison-Wesley Publishing Company, Inc., 1977.

Lord Jr., Kenniston W. and Steiner, James B. *CPM Review Manual Data Processing Handbook* (Second Edition). New York: Van Nostrand Reinhold Co. Inc. 1978.

Wickesberg, A.K. and Cronin, T.C. "Management by Task Force," *Harvard Business Review*, November-December 1962.

Chapter
7
IMPLEMENTING THE PROJECT MANAGEMENT ORGANIZATION

Producing a large data processing product or software system is fraught with all the problems inherent in any highly labor-intensive activity. A large workforce must be assembled and organized into a cohesive team whose sole purpose is to produce a data processing product within the limits of time and budget. Plans must be made and controls established. People must be trained, and they must be motivated to accomplish achievable goals that the entire team has agreed upon.

Data processing management therefore consists of all the technical and management activities required to implement an acceptable solution to a validated user's need within an agreed-upon amount of time and with agreed-to resources.

ESTABLISHING THE DATA PROCESSING PROJECT

To establish the data processing project, the charting authority should sign an appropriate announcement. As a minimum it should designate the purpose of the project, establish the general

71

organizational format for the project, appoint the data processing project manager, and state general management's support for the project. It may also include other appointments on an organization chart and in policy statements. However, it is more important to get out the fundamental information early rather than delaying its release until all detailed organizational and staffing decisions have been made.

The announcement should be in whatever format is used for major communications to the organization. Although it may be addressed only to senior executives, it should have a wide distribution. The outline presented below may be used as distinct steps for the establishment of a data processing project.

I. The project Charter should emphasize the following elements:
   A. Project goals
   B. Name of the project
   C. Estimate of resources needed (This may be omitted because it is sensitive; however, the estimate should somehow be recorded.)
II. The project Organization should emphasize the following:
   A. The Management responsibility for the project should include:
      1. Establishment of a project manager
      2. Directive authority
      3. Review authority
      4. The executive responsible for completing the organization phase
      5. Chartering authority (This is implicit in the signature of the charter and may be omitted.)
   B. The Organization affected (division, departments, etc., that will participate in the project) should be identified.
III. The Schedule to accomplish the project should be defined to encompass the following:
   A. General time frame of the project
   B. Schedule for completing the organization phase
   C. Interim reviews (if desired)
IV. The Resources Allocation needed to accomplish the project task should emphasize:

    A. Resources assigned to the organization phase
    B. Method of Cost Charging by Participating organizations. (The resources allocation may be omitted if adequate resources are under control of the given responsibility for the organization phase.)
  V. Statement of general management support for the project should be stated, so as to encourage wavering functional managers to give enthusiastic support to their counterparts on the project.
 VI. Finally, the establishment of the data processing project should be signed by the chartering authority.

PROJECT ORGANIZATION CHARTS

Preparing organization charts for data processing projects can become an unnecessarily time-consuming exercise. However, the charts should be issued soon after the data processing project is established and signed by the chartering authority.

It is easy enough to add the data processing project manager to the basic organization chart and as reporting to the directive authority; this is preferably accomplished in the initial charter. A problem arises when the chart for the internal organization is to be prepared, particularly when a matrix form of organization (see Chapter 6) is to be used. The old rules of chartmanship do not easily apply here. Early solutions may show horizontal rows of project managers with various managements of lines leading from both a functional and a project box to each project functional manager.

A much better practice may be to draw the organization chart of the project with all managers shown reporting in a conventional line to the project manager. Then, a symbol added to each box containing a project functional manager will refer to a footnote that might say, for example, "These managers report to the data processing project manager for project direction and to the respective functional division heads for policy direction."

Although project functional managers appear on the project chart, they should also continue to appear on their respective functional division charts. Both project and functional charts should contain identical or essentially similar footnotes so that different stories will not be told to different people.

ROLE OF DATA PROCESSING PROJECT MANAGER

Although the role of the data processing project manager is applied under a variety of different titles in different organizations, there are several salient factors which characterize most applicants.

1. The data processing project manager operates independently of the organization's normal chain of command; a "horizontal hierarchy" comes into being, reflecting an amalgamation of interfunctional resources directed toward a specific goal having time, cost, and technical parameters.

2. The data processing project manager negotiates directly for support from functional elements; normal line and staff relationships give way to a "web of relationships" directed to the beginning and completion of specific undertakings.

3. While the role of the data processing project manager may vary widely from one of a coordinating nature to the "general manager" function, he is the single focal point of contact for bringing together organizational effort toward a single project objective.

4. The data processing project manager assumes total responsibility and accountability for the project success or failure.

This manager is also responsible for reporting on project progress to the customer and to others outside the project who require information about its status. This is consistent with the project manager's responsibility for customer liaison. In a project done under a contract with an outside organization, the data processing project manager is responsible for reporting both to the customer and to upper management.

Although the data processing project manager is the full-time leader of the project, managing data processing projects is, without question, a difficult job. Not only does it require sophisticated tools and special organization design considerations, but also a different breed of manager. Five areas that require special managerial skills are often cited by project leaders as necessary conditions for project success:

1. Coping with a multidisciplinary project environment.
2. Dealing with problems across functional lines.
3. Building effective teams at various organizational levels.
4. Handling conflict effectively.
5. Managing change.

Specifically, the data processing project manager must be able to integrate various supporting disciplines in a continuous changing work environment. In his search for multidisciplinary problem resolutions, he must often cross functional lines to deal with personnel over whom he has limited formal authority. Moreover, he has to build teams at various levels of the project organization. This requires an understanding of interpersonal dynamics to make sure that various specialists contribute to the end objective of the project. Thus, the challenge is for the data processing project manager to provide an environment conducive to the motivational needs of his team members. Equally important to successful project performance is his ability to deal effectively with the inevitable conflict situation. Taken together, his role is a difficult one. His project's success often depends significantly on the ability to deal effectively with human behavior in a multidisciplinary environment.

However, to a large extent, management of a system's development will succeed or fail depending on decisions made at the outset, and such decisions are normally made by general management within the host organization structure—those to whom the data processing project manager will report. It is the buyer's organization and management that are most important at the outset of a project because they make the initial decisions and allocate project resources, and it is the host management that sets the tone and establishes the desire and impetus for attaining product integrity.

There are some elementary but important principles that management should adhere to when undertaking responsibility for the management of a system's development. They include the following:

> The selected data processing project manager must not only be responsible for the project that he is to lead, but also requires commensurate authority. There should be no question of accountability between the data processing project manager and his general manager. The project manager should be the "captain" of the project. If this is not the case, then general management becomes the *de facto* project manager and consequently should be held accountable for the project.
>
> There should be a single general manager to whom the project manager reports. If this is not the case, the effectiveness and accountability of the project manager may be diffused and the issue of who is "captain" leads to an indecisive management environment.

The earlier point about decisions at the beginning of a project affecting the prospect of success and the degree to which a system will possess the elusive attribute of "integrity" is most important. Selection of the buyer's project manager, the one highest in the direct responsibility chain, is an important early decision to be made by the buyer's general management.

PROJECT MANAGER SELECTION

Data processing project manager selection should be made according to the usual practices of the organization. One subtle criteria for such a selection may be derived from examining the value of project success and failure in both the long and short run. One would want a project manager who would succeed in the short run and leave behind a constructive atmosphere for future projects and related interpersonal relationships. However, some projects require such urgent attention for successful scheduled performance that the brilliant, heavy-handed driver is the right choice for project manager. Alternatively, the clear-thinking manager who can optimize costs and schedules and technical performance may not be the right choice, whereas the big spender who will get the job done better or faster under conditions of great urgency may be the right choice.

Good data processing project management in any sphere of activity seems to have three ingredients:

1. Technical ability, enough to judge the quality of the work of subordinates.
2. Leadership ability, a desire and ability to get results.
3. Conceptual thinking ability; able to take an objective stance; one step removed from the immediate problem.

During the *initial creative phase*, technical ability means having an understanding of the business problem together with a good understanding of systems solutions. Leadership ability is not project team management but handling user directors and staff: the ability to disagree constructively. Conceptual thinking ability is a vital ingredient if a good solution is to be found; the problem needs to be studied as one of a class of problems, anticipating growth and change.

During the *execution phase* of the project the emphasis shifts. Technical ability means not only a sound computer knowledge but also an awareness of people and systems—the human interface and what can be achieved with a computer system. Leadership ability means assigning tasks and checking that they get done: a systematic recording of all agreements and meticulous attention to detail. Conceptual thinking ability is the desire to look ahead, avoiding problems by forward planning.

It is not often that all these qualities are found in one person, but if we are aware of their need we can build a more balanced management team. A data processing project manager whose strength is attention to detail might best be supported by an experienced supervising manager who is good at forward planning.

Of all the qualities, the ability to assign tasks of the correct size and subsequently to check that they are completed is the one to prize most highly in a data processing project manager.

As previously stated, a data processing project manager's ability to perform effectively may depend on his or her leadership style, the task complexity, the required technological sophistication, and the climate of the organization in which he functions. Further, his overall influence may vary over the life of the project, since complexity, budgets, client demands, and functional interfaces change. Thus, effective leadership relates the human, technical, and situational variables of a project in a complex manner.

PERSONNEL SELECTION AND EVALUATION

Data processing project managers often interact with the various functional and staff departments in managing their programs. Depending on the type of project organization (see Chapter 6), the data processing project manager has different degrees of control over resources.

However, the failure of data processing project managers to address the personnel issue seems to be more widespread with the advent of microprocessors. This new technology has brought with it a new job description: the hardware/firmware engineer. Typically, these professionals have had training and job experience as digital electronic engineers and have had some involvement with interfacing microprocessors. They began programming by writing test programs for their hardware design and have gained some expertise in assembly language programming of microprocessors. With this background, data processing project managers have begun to consider them to be experts in both digital design and programming.

Unfortunately, these engineers have often not been exposed to formal computer science education. They have to learn by experience the need for high level languages, top-down design, and structured testing methodologies. Also, unfortunately, as these principles are being learned, the projects on which they are learned are often late, unreliable, and difficult to use.

What, then, are the important factors to consider when staffing a software or data processing project? Obviously, the proper mix of people is essential. A project consisting solely of experienced or inexperienced engineers will not have an adequate range of abilities and interests to take a project from conception through implementation. The subject of mixes of people has been studied, and it has been generally concluded that a good mix consists of experienced leaders to guide the architecture design, less experienced designers to deal with data structures and lower level design considerations, and implementors to handle coding and testing.

The actual types of backgrounds the engineers should have will vary with the nature of the project. Hence, a good tactic is to staff a data processing project with personnel who take a user perspective of the product.

However, for a data processing project, the representative elements of functional responsibility which might be integrated by the data processing project manager for the objectives of the project may include:

engineering

marketing

financial management

procurement

systems analysis

contracts

engineering operations, etc.

Because of the importance of the data processing project control function, the data processing project manager might have a staff of key individuals to assist him in this area, some assigned to him directly, and some supporting him from the functional organization. The remaining elements, however, are normally the responsibility of the appropriate functional managers. Each functional manager may assign a key individual within the organization for liaison with the data processing project manager and his staff. This individual, although reporting to the functional manager, represents the data processing project manager within that functional organization, and is the focal point for the activity on that project (see Figure 7.1).

One of this individual's main functions will be to plan all the or-

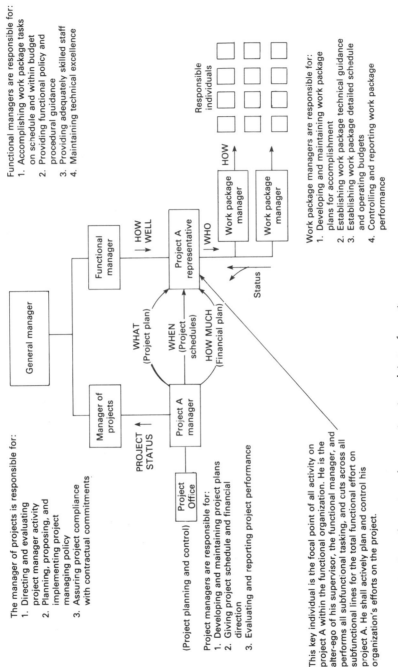

The manager of projects is responsible for:
1. Directing and evaluating project manager activity
2. Planning, proposing, and implementing project managing policy
3. Assuring project compliance with contractual commitments

(Project planning and control)

Project managers are responsible for:
1. Developing and maintaining project plans
2. Giving project schedule and financial direction
3. Evaluating and reporting project performance

This key individual is the focal point of all activity on project A within the functional organization. He is the alter-ego of his supervisor, the functional manager, and performs all subfunctional tasking, and cuts across all subfunctional lines for the total functional effort on project A. He shall actively plan and control his organization's efforts on the project.

Functional managers are responsible for:
1. Accomplishing work package tasks on schedule and within budget
2. Providing functional policy and procedural guidance
3. Providing adequately skilled staff
4. Maintaining technical excellence

Work package managers are responsible for:
1. Developing and maintaining work package plans for accomplishment
2. Establishing work package technical guidance
3. Establishing work package detailed schedule and operating budgets
4. Controlling and reporting work package performance

FIGURE 7.1. Project-functional organizational interface.*

*Reprinted by permission of the Publisher, from Systems Analysis and Project Management, David I. Cleland and William R. King (Page 246). Copyright 1975 by McGraw-Hill Book Co.

ganization's responsibilities for the project in consonance with the total project plan, and to ensure that all organizational effort satisfies the requirements of the project. He then becomes the alter ego of the functional manager for that project. His planning role is an important and continuous one since he is required to maintain and update his portion of the total project plan as the project matures. His inputs and changes to the total project plan must be through the data processing project manager who ensures that all plans and changes thereto are in harmony and consistent with the total project objectives.

Depending upon the nature, size, complexity, schedule, current phase, and potential of the project, certain specialized functional personnel may be organizationally assigned to the data processing project manager for the duration of his project, or for as long as required to ensure successful passage through its most critical phases. The "borrowed" members of the data processing project management organization represent their functional organization's responsibilities on the project, such as financial operations, contracts, etc. These personnel, who are provided by their functional "home" organizations on a loan basis, charge their time to the appropriate project, or overhead account, as specified by the project charter or as mutually agreed upon by the loaning (functional), borrowing (project), and financial organizations.

Assignment to a data processing project team may be too parochial for the person who wishes to maintain his technical status and identification with his technical reference group. These are important to the development of a technical capability in the organization since the functional organization is where functional knowledge is advanced, expertise is developed, standards of performance are established, and manpower and facilities assignments are made.

UNPLANNED PROJECT TERMINATION

Termination of a data processing project seems to be the last thing to think about while the project is underway. However, for many people working on the project, eventual arrival of the completion date is a continuous threat. It affects their morale and detracts from constructive activity at the time when a unified effort is most needed.

In data processing organizations where the project management concept is new, management must carefully evaluate the effect of project terminations and assure that such changes do not have adverse effects on the employees' progress in the company. It would be highly unfair for a system analyst to return to his or her functional department from a project assignment to find that his advancement had been impaired as a result of his absence. If this happens, management will find it exceedingly difficult to induce good people to participate in future project efforts.

PERSONNEL TRAINING

Personnel in the data processing organization are hired with specific educational criteria. They already possess the broad concepts of the nature of the data processing and systems functions and understand the specialized terminology of data automation. Their education should have prepared them to accept training.

Training, as differentiated from education, is more procedure-oriented than problem-oriented. It is short-range instruction on the precise steps necessary to perform a job. It includes instructions on the operational methods for a specific make and model of equipment. It describes the input, flow, processing steps, and output for an application and prescribes the terms and words of a specific language. Training enables the employee to perform a specific job in the organization.

There are two categories of training in most data processing organizations. On-the-job training involves learning by doing under the direct instruction of an immediate supervisor. Classroom training is conducted apart from the job, usually outside the organization.

To be uniformly effective, on-the-job training must be formalized or controlled. The steps, procedures, operations or skills to be mastered need to be identified and described on a permanent record of training. After the trainee has reached an adequate proficiency in a particular phase, the supervisor makes an appropriate notation on the training record and signs it. At periodic intervals, the trainee should demonstrate his proficiency by taking a test designed or endorsed by fully qualified or supervisory members of the organization. Achievement should be recognized by the award of a certificate, a change in title or level, a pay increase, or a combination of these. The training should continue until the trainee reaches the fully qualified skill level and is awarded the appropriate title and pay level.

Classroom training is sometimes held in conjunction with on-the-job training. More often, it is oriented to new equipment or systems and is conducted apart from the organization. Computer vendors have sponsored much of this type of training. Although vendor training treats students gently, as customers, the quality and benefits of this training are almost always good.

REFERENCES

Awani, Alfred O. *Project Management Techniques.* Princeton: Petrocelli Books, Inc., 1983.

Bersoff, E.; Henderson, V.; and Siegel, S. "Software Configuration Management: An Investment in Product Integrity." Englewood Cliffs: Prentice-Hall Inc., 1980.

Bruggere, Thomas H. "Software Engineering: Management, Personnel and Methodology." Proceedings, Fourth International Conference on Software Engineering, The Institute of Electrical and Electronics Engineers, 1979.

Cleland, David I. and King, William R. *Systems Analysis and Project Management.* New York: McGraw-Hill, 1975.

Lord, Jr. Kenniston W. and Steiner, James B. *CPM Review Manual Data Processing Handbook* (Second Edition). New York: Van Nostrand Reinhold Co. Inc. 1978.

Martin, Charles C. *Project Management: How to Make It Work.* New York: AMACOM, 1976.

Reifer, Donald J. "The Nature of Software Management: A Primer." Tutorial: Software Management (First Edition). The Institute of Electrical and Electronics Engineers, Inc., 1979.

Thamhain, Hans J. and Wilemon, David L. "Leadership Effectiveness in Program Management." *IEEE Transactions on Engineering Management*, Volume EM-24, Number 3. The Institute of Electrical and Electronics Engineers, Inc., August 1977.

Chapter
8
PROJECT MANAGEMENT PROCESS

After the project has been organized and staffed by general management, it will operate under the direction of the data processing project manager. The following discussion describes the DPPM process during its operational phase.

DPPM functions are discussed here more or less as though they occur that way. For any one single segment of the project, no one activity should take place before its predecessors: project decisions should not start before planning of the activity has been completed. On the other hand, after a project is launched, all the activities are likely to be going on simultaneously, but for different parts of the project. The model shown in Figure 8.1 is a useful way of looking at and thinking about DPPM and of bringing order into its execution.

CUSTOMER LIAISON

Every data processing project has a customer. It is essential to find out what the customer really wants and to let him know what they

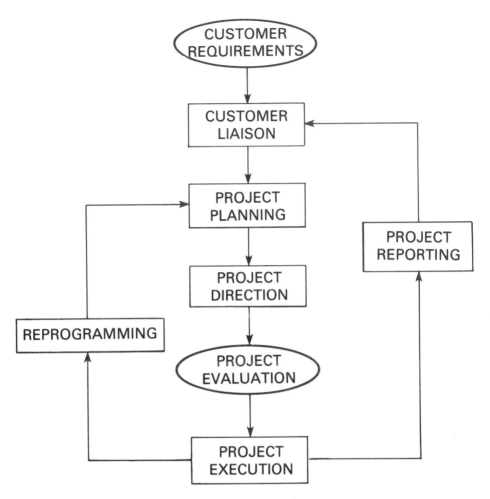

FIGURE 8.1. Project management functions.

are really getting, when and how he will get it, and how much to pay for it.

To accomplish this important communication assignment is a key task of the data processing project manager. If general management really wants him to manage the project, then they—not anybody else—will tell him what they want and how they want it done. Only then can he carry out the project to their liking. Furthermore, if he is really their agent, as he so often is in larger projects, he must know their viewpoint so as to reflect it accurately in his management of the project.

In short, the data processing project manager must lead the liaison with the customer. If the project is done under contract, and the identification of the customer is obvious, the necessity for assigning the data processing project manager the responsibility and authority to communicate with the customer is, if anything, even greater.

The primary objective of customer liaison is to reach clear agreements on what is to be done on the project, a definition of the characteristics of the project and products, key schedule dates, and the associated funding. Nearly as important is that all parties understand all constraints within the bounds of the project and the criteria that should be used in choosing between alternative ways of managing the project.

A word of caution: Although it has been asserted that customer liaison should be assigned to the data processing project manager, this does not mean that all other members of the project team should be excluded from customer liaison procedures. On the contrary, their selective participation should be encouraged on a controlled basis. Particularly in matters of contract administration, procurement specialists in the customer organization should work closely with the contract administrator of the project team. Similarly, technology specialists in both organizations should communicate directly.

Certainly, the data processing project manager should have the authority to establish the project position before such contracts are made and should be given full information about them, and agreements reached in these discussions should have his approval in advance or else be considered tentative until he approves them. In projects conducted within an organization, the data processing project manager has principal authority for liaison with the internal customer, and his office should be the primary channel of communication. However, this does not preclude contacts by other members of the team.

As in all business transactions, successful execution of a project is much more readily achieved when there is a clear agreement in advance about the intended scope and results of the project. The data processing project manager should have this responsibility.

PROJECT PLANNING

Planning is recognized as the fundamental and primary task of management and the foundation upon which all other management activities must be based. According to Yehezkel Dror in *The Planning Process: A Facet Design*, "Planning is the process of preparing a set of decisions for action in the future directed at achieving goals by optimal means." The three key concepts in this definition are that planning is future-oriented, requires the preselection of objectives, and necessitates the selection of rational and efficient strategies to achieve those objectives.

Planning can be defined from a different viewpoint. Peter Drucker points out that planning is not forecasting but rather needed because forecasts are inaccurate; planning does not deal with future decisions but rather with future actions and consequences associated with present decisions, and planning is not the elimination of risk but rather the recognition of the costs associated with future uncertainties.

Objectives in a project may be overlooked in the press of day-to-day operations. Planning forces project management to consider all project actions in terms of ultimate objectives. Planning also provides a basis for other functions of the project manager. Directing the project requires a plan to establish the normal or desired manner of performance for the efficient use of resources.

Planning techniques and systems vary in complexity from the simple Gantt Chart (Figure 8.2) which lays out task sequences against time, to the complex Planning Programming Budget System (PPBS) which provides the institutional framework for Federal government decisions. Regardless of complexity, newer techniques have several common characteristics: they are systematic, they tend to be quantitative in nature, and they become highly personalized as they are modified and adapted by each individual project or organization. The use of a budget (cash budget, sales budget, produc-

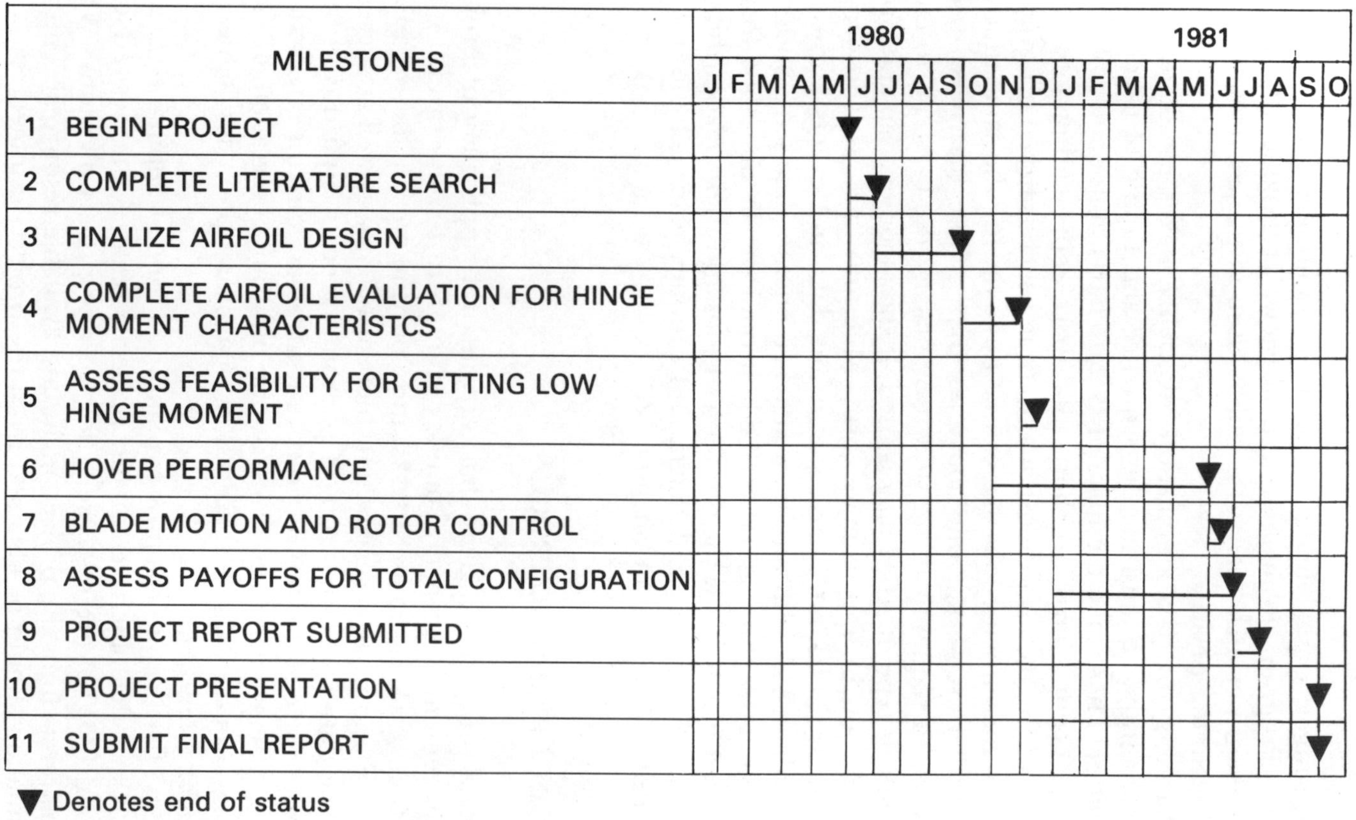

FIGURE 8.2. Gantt Chart.

MILESTONES	1980 / 1981

MILESTONES	J	F	M	A	M	J	J	A	S	O	N	D	J	F	M	A	M	J	J	A	S	O
1 BEGIN PROJECT				▶																		
2 COMPLETE LITERATURE SEARCH						▶																
3 FINALIZE AIRFOIL DESIGN								▶														
4 COMPLETE AIRFOIL EVALUATION FOR HINGE MOMENT CHARACTERISTCS											▶											
5 ASSESS FEASIBILITY FOR GETTING LOW HINGE MOMENT													▶									
6 HOVER PERFORMANCE																▶						
7 BLADE MOTION AND ROTOR CONTROL																	▶					
8 ASSESS PAYOFFS FOR TOTAL CONFIGURATION																		▶				
9 PROJECT REPORT SUBMITTED																			▶			
10 PROJECT PRESENTATION																					▶	
11 SUBMIT FINAL REPORT																						▶

▶ Denotes end of status

tion budget, capital budget, etc.) is a traditional planning technique. Program Evaluation and Review Technique (PERT), a time-event network analysis, is widely used in project management as a planning device.

Planning for data automation invariably makes use of network flow diagrams to illustrate the sequence and timing of events and activities. These take the form of Gantt charts, milestone tables, or PERT. Gantt charts are horizontal bars representing jobs; the length of the bars is proportional to time which is ticked off graphically in increments. Jobs that can be done during the same time or in parallel are shown one above another. Those that need to be performed sequentially are shown by placing the bars end to end. When this type of scheduling is used, it shows job overlap and project duration in approximate form. Milestones are used in charts similar to the Gantt Chart. Significant data and events are especially identified with an arrow marker on the time axis, and the milestones are listed and described chronologically in outline form. The best way to show the duration of jobs and their relationship to each other in intricate, detailed, and complex plans is by means of the PERT discussed in Chapter 12.

PROJECT PLANNING PROCESS

A data processing activity that warrants the application of project management is normally complex enough to require careful integration of its component tasks and coordination of the organizations. Planning is necessary to achieve efficiency as well as success.

The data processing project planning process is portrayed here in successive steps, but in practice it involves constant interactions back to earlier phases. This is not only an observation of how things work in the real world; it is a prescription for achieving proper integration.

The first step in the project planning is one of definition. *Exactly* what are the objectives of the project? What is the desired end product? What are the criteria for making project decisions? What constraints limit the project, including available resources? This information should be obtained from the project customer.

In a data processing project, a feasibility study should be undertaken to define the characteristics of the end product so that it can meet the specified requirements of the project. The output of this effort should be sufficiently detailed to permit project planning to proceed.

The next step is to develop a statement of the tasks that must be completed to accomplish the overall objectives of the project. These should be defined first in terms of the end products of the tasks, then according to the role each participating organization will play in each task. As parts of the work statement are completed, schedules and budgets can be developed for the corresponding tasks. These two activities can proceed more or less in parallel.

Finally, functional plans for execution of the project should be made. These outline how to accomplish the tasks defined in the work statement, and should be detailed enough so that the project goals can be achieved on schedule and within budget. Each plan should concentrate on the nonstandard demands of the project and how these relate to other project plans, rather than on the details of fairly routine activities.

The data processing project manager is responsible for project planning. He is the leader of the team. He may have his own immediate staff to integrate the planning, but the people who will head the project functional organizations must be fully active participants in planning.

To summarize, the data processing project manager and his team produce project plans that contain a work statement, end-product specifications, budgets, schedules, and implementation plans that will be the basis for project execution.

PROJECT DIRECTION

The data processing project manager should have authority to direct all members and organizations in the project team. The nucleus of this direction is a statement of the required project tasks and schedules for their completion. In addition, direction usually includes funding authority and budget constraints and, in the case of technical and hardware-oriented projects, a definition of the project end products. Constraints and ground rules are also part of the project's direction.

Ideally, project direction is merely an extension of project planning; the data processing project manager simply issues the project plans with a directive to execute them. In real life the matter is not that simple, for it is often desirable to issue direction for only a part of the period covered by the plans. Furthermore, it often turns out that a project's direction should be more specific and detailed than corresponding sections of the plans.

The nature and depth of the project's direction delegated to the data processing project manager is a major issue in the organization of a project. Primarily, he should concentrate on end products and related schedules and budgets—the *what* and *when* of the project. He or she should be less concerned with *how* the tasks are executed or the techniques and detailed resource allocations used to accomplish them. Often his directive authority on how to execute a project will be simply an approval of an organization's own plan to meet project objectives. However, when there is a definite need, perhaps a contract requirement, for a specific method of project execution, he of course issues such directions.

The appropriate depth of a project's direction is determined by two factors—success and efficiency. Obviously, such direction should be detailed enough to ensure that the objectives and goals of the project will be met. If the direction has been complied with and the end products do not meet its requirements, then the direction has been faulty.

Efficiency and proper resource allocation are the other keys to determining the optimal depth of a project's direction. In a complicated project, the tasks of the various organizational units must be coordinated very carefully; failure of one department to complete its task on time may pull all the others in an inefficient mode of operation.

In most cases, a project's direction should be issued through the normal authorization channels of the organization where it will be more readily understood and not be regarded as a complicating overlay system. In some instances, a streamlined direction system may be required to permit the degree of flexibility the project was established to achieve. In whatever manner it is given, a project's direction must be clearly visible and understood by all.

A data processing project manager should not be in a position to issue rapid-fire directions in a helter-skelter manner without enough formalization to permit accountability for performance. On the other hand, the data processing project manager needs the authority to issue emergency direction in any manner he deems appropriate, with the requirement that he follow it up rapidly with confirmation through the normal system.

PROJECT EXECUTION

Execution of data processing project tasks take place after planning has identified their scope and direction has authorized their accomplishment. During these phases the tasks are identified in such a way that they can be assigned to the departments of the organization. It is the responsibility of the individual department managers to manage and supervise their particular project tasks within schedule, within budget, and in accordance with definition and specifications.

The data processing project manager assigned full-line authority over the departments executing project tasks has full responsibility for the efficient performance of these departments in all things, including those tasks. In more complex yet often more efficient matrix organizations (see Chapter 6), the manager is still responsible for the successful completion of project tasks, but he must work through the department heads and their superiors.

PROJECT EVALUATION

Evaluation is the continuing process of assessing the progress of the project. The word "control" (see Chapter 15) is often used in this same sense, but sometimes that word takes on a fiscally-oriented and short-term flavor that makes it less appropriate than "evaluation" to describe this important part of the data processing project management cycle.

Evaluation is primarily concerned with the progress of the project in meeting its principal objectives. It assesses status at the moment and extrapolates from that assessment to forecast ultimate project success. Separate assessments should be made about schedules, budgets, and technical performance. The reasons for the variances should be identified not only by the people who generate the variance data but also by those responsible for doing the job. Managerial judgement should then be applied to combine them in developing forecasts regarding total project goals.

Ideally, project evaluation consists of comparing existing conditions and current results with project plans and with the specifics of a project's direction. Any deviation represents a possible problem that should be highlighted, analyzed, and understood. This guideline should be followed as the primary canon of project evaluation.

In practice, however, many problems appear that are real, potentially troublesome, but somehow unconnected with the quantitative variances produced by the control systems. These anomalies, particularly when associated with the judgments and interpersonal relationships of key project team members, may be more demanding of solutions than more formally stated variances.

"Project management" is sometimes associated by executives almost exclusively with the use (or misuse) of various control systems (CPM, PERT, and so on). Successful project management is far more than new control systems. However, the project management evaluation function will be considerably more effective if it judiciously uses the right mix of controls, and while the right set of control systems certainly varies from project to project, it also does so within the life cycle of any given project.

Successful evaluation of project progress should provide for both formal examinations of data from control systems and informal assessments by project team members. The leadership qualities of a data processing project manager are most important in this phase. He must carefully scrutinize the assessments both of his team and of his control systems, and only then should he form an evaluation of how the project is doing.

REPROGRAMMING

After its evaluation phase, DPPM usually requires changes in the project plan, in the basic resources assigned to the project, or even in the basic project concept and objectives. Encountering this need for change is not a reason for despair or inaction. Projects are set up to cope with situations of uncertainty and complexity. Project management is as much concerned with keeping the project moving after it is started as it is with the initial planning. Reprogramming is the term used here to designate this part of the project management cycle.

Reprogramming proceeds directly out of the evaluation phase in which accomplishments to date and estimated future progress are compared with project plans and directives. Variances are analyzed during the evaluation activity to determine their magnitudes and causes. Reprogramming can then correct them.

A first approach of correcting variances may be to call for better performance on the part of an executing department, perhaps bringing this about by eliminating misunderstandings concerning what is desired, or it may be to ensure the availability of intended information and resources. This is simply a matter of clarifying the project's direction and improving performance so that the original plan can be followed.

If it is simply not possible to carry out the details of the original plan or if there is a schedule problem in a department, the plan may be extended. If the problem is a budgetary, additional budget may be provided out of reserves or by transferring funds from some other less critical part of the project. In these solutions the original project objectives are maintained but the project plans change.

If the problem is a major one, it may be impossible to meet all the project objectives: cost, schedule, and end-product performance. The program must then be replanned to meet the most important project objectives while minimizing adherence to the others. In doing this, a clear understanding of criteria, discussed above, is most important.

Another reason for reprogramming stems from customer liaison rather than evaluation. The customer almost always requires some change in the project after it is planned and executed. Each change should be defined carefully and its impact on project plans analyzed in the general sequence just described.

Changes in project planning and direction should be accomplished as changes or additions to existing plans and direction, not through different means. It is imperative that the communications and administrative channels used for initial plans and direction be used for changes. Failure to follow this procedure will result in chaos.

Project management is often looked on as a complicated planning exercise followed by a period in which the data processing project manager and his team sit around half-occupied, waiting for results. This is far from the truth, for coping with the constant changes in the project as it proceeds is often the biggest challenge to project success.

PROJECT REPORTING

The data processing project manager is responsible for reporting on project progress to the customer and to others outside the project who require information about its status. This is consistent with his responsibility for customer liaison. In a project done under a contract with an outside organization, he is responsible for reporting both to the customer and to general management.

It is important that the internal management and external reporting of the project be based on a common set of data. Maintaining more than one set of books is uneconomical and leads to misunderstandings among those who should be working together cooperatively. This does not mean that every piece of data available to the data processing project manager should be given to the customer, but it does mean that customer reports should be clearly traceable to project data. Further, it does not mean that every early indication of project difficulties should be reported immediately and in detail to the customer, but that no false or misleading impression should be created by the omission of data in reporting. The nature of arm's-length commercial negotiations may influence the timing and detail of the data released to a customer, but they should never influence its basic honesty.

The data processing project manager's data for reports should be based on any special project control systems, on the information systems of the overall organization, and on reports from departments executing project tasks. Departmental reports to him should be based directly on the data the department uses to manage its work. In the case of a matrix organization, any departmental reports to higher functional management that reflect on project tasks should be made available to him. Assessments should concern themselves with departmental tasks and status, and should not be independent judgments on overall project status.

Although reporting is logically the outcome of the evaluation and reprogramming activities, it really takes place from the beginning of the project and should be approached on a positive basis by all members of the project team. It should be looked on as a constructive opportunity to describe project successes and to get understanding and help from project problems.

REFERENCES

Lord Jr., Kenniston W. and Steiner, James B. *CPM Review Manual Data Processing Handbook* (Second Edition). New York: Van Nostrand Reinhold Co. Inc. 1978.

Martin, Charles C. *Project Management: How to Make It Work*. New York: AMACOM, 1976.

Chapter
9
WORK BREAKDOWN STRUCTURE

The work breakdown structure (WBS) is a vehicle for breaking a data processing project down into subproject, tasks, subtasks, work packages, and so on. It is an important planning tool which links objectives with resources and activities in a logical framework. It becomes an important status monitor during the actual implementation as the completions of subtasks are measured against the project plan.

The WBS is an enumeration of all work activities in hierarchic refinements, it organizes work to be done into short, manageable tasks with quantifiable inputs, outputs, schedules, and assigned responsibilities. It may be used for project budgeting of time and resources down to the individual task level, and later, as a basis for progress reporting relative to meaningful management milestones. A data processing management plan based on a WBS contains the necessary tool to estimate costs and schedules accurately and to provide visibility and control during production.

Such a plan may be structured to evaluate technical accomplishments on the basis of task and activity progress. Schedules and CPM/PERT networks (see chapters 11 and 12 respectively) may be built upon technical activities in terms of task milestones (i.e., accomplishments, outputs, and other quantifiable work elements). Projected versus actual task progress can be reviewed by technical audit and by progress reviews on a regular basis. Formal project design reviews are major checkpoints in this measurement system. However, knowledge of what a WBS is, what its goals and benefits are, and what its structure is supposed to be like does not necessarily instruct one in how to apply that knowledge toward developing a WBS for a particular project.

In this section, we shall review some of the characteristics and benefits of the WBS and discuss how these can be developed and applied in data processing/software implementation projects. This material will be oriented principally toward new-software production tasks, although many of the concepts will be applicable also to continuing maintenance and operations tasks.

ESTHER SOFTWARE WBS PROJECT

The Esther Company has been given the task of writing a program, such as that structurally illustrated in Figure 9.1, in which the target language instruction set was not intended to be executed by computer, but, instead, by human beings. However, this job is much more difficult for a number of reasons, among which are ambiguities in the English language and a multitude of human factors. Nevertheless, such a program, often named the PLAN (Figure 9.2), is an essential part of almost every industrial project.

One of the difficulties in writing this program is to supply enough detail so as to execute without allowing ambiguity. Another is getting the right controls into the program so that the programees perform as stated in the PLAN. Still another is making the PLAN complete, with all contingencies covered and a proper response to each supplied. One final problem of note here is making the plan bug-free, or reliable, so that once execution starts, if everything proceeds according to the PLAN, there is no need to deviate.

Programmers well-schooled in modern techniques would approach the writing of this PLAN in a structured way, using

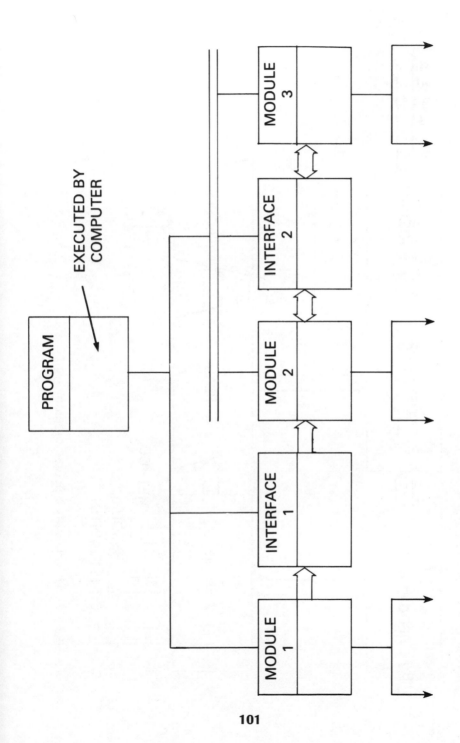

FIGURE 9.1. The modular hierarchy of a program.

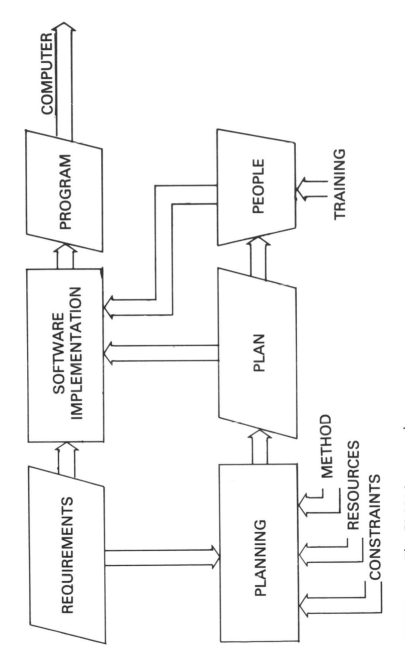

FIGURE 9.2. The PLAN is a people program.

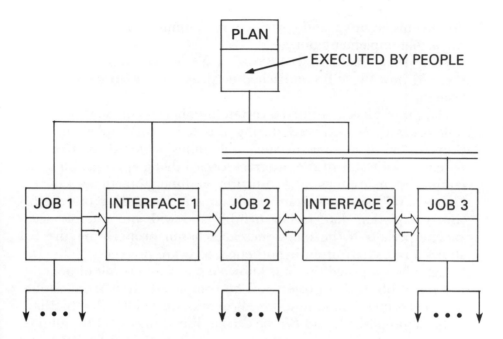

FIGURE 9.3. The work breakdown structure.

top-down design methodology, modular development, step-wise refinement, hierarchic layering of detail, structurally sound constructions, and semantically definite documentation. Such an approach would tend to bring a measure of organization to the PLAN, understandability to its documentation, and reliability to its execution. If created in this way, the resulting format of the PLAN work tasks would have the attributes of what is known in the engineering industry as a "work breakdown structure" illustrated in Figure 9.3.

SOFTWARE WBS

The goals assumed here for generating the software WBS are to identify work tasks, needed resources, implementation constraints, and so on to that level of detail which yields the accuracy stipulated in the original PLAN, and to provide the means for early calibration of this accuracy and corrective replanning, if required, during the actual implementation.

How refined should this WBS be? Let's answer this question by showing how the WBS and schedule projection accuracy are interrelated.

If a project has identified a certain number of equal-effort "unit" milestones to be achieved during the course of implementation, then the mere number of such milestones achieved by a certain date is an indicator of the progress toward that goal. A graph of accumulated milestones as a function of time, sometimes called a "rate chart," permits certain predictions to be made about the future completion date rather handily and with quantifiable accuracy, especially if the milestones are chosen properly. Figure 9.4 shows a rate chart of an hypothetical software project.

Let it be supposed that it is known *a priori*, as a result of generating the WBS, that a project will be completed after M milestones have been met. These milestones correspond to all tasks that have to be accomplished, and can be accomplished once and for all (i.e., some later activity does not reopen an already completed task; if one does, it can be accomodated by making M larger to include all such milestones as separate events). The number M, of course, may not be precisely known from the first, and any uncertainty in M will certainly affect the accuracy of the estimated completion date. Such uncertainties can be factored in as secondary effects later when needed for the refinement of accuracy.

Now, let it be further supposed that it has been possible to refine the overall task into these M milestones in such a way that each task is believed to require about the same amount of effort and duration to accomplish (Figure 9.5.). Viewed at regular intervals (e.g., biweekly or monthly), a plot of the cumulative number of milestones reported as having been completed should rise linearly until project completion.

More quantitatively, let m be the average number of tasks actually completed during each reporting period, and let σ be the standard deviation of the actual number of milestones completed each reporting period about this mean value (the values of m and σ are presumed to be constant over the project duration). The value of m is a reflection of the team average productivity and σ is a measure

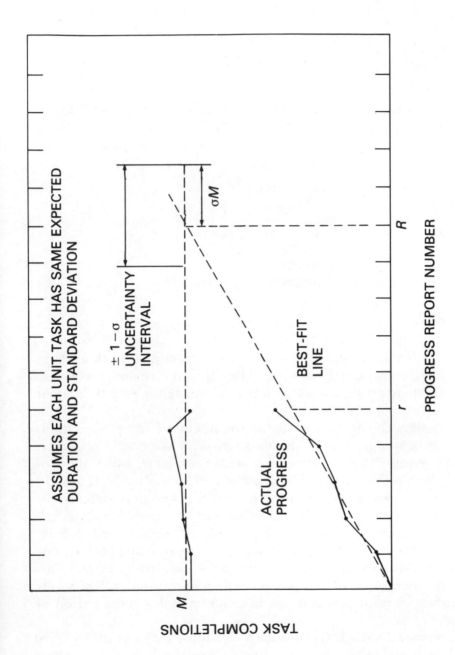

FIGURE 9.4. Conceptual progress rate chart.

105

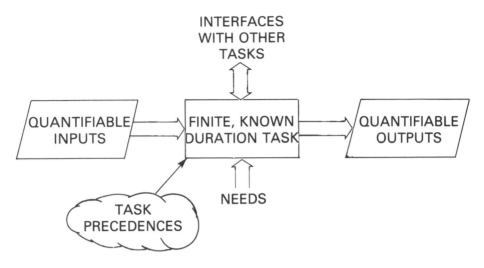

- SIZED FOR SINGLE INDIVIDUAL
- NO FURTHER BREAKDOWN INTO SUBTASKS

FIGURE 9.5. The unit task.

of the ability to estimate the team's production rate. Both attest to team effectiveness: first, in their ability to produce and, second, in their ability to create a work plan that adequately accounts for their time.

By design, the mean behavior of the milestone completion status is linear, a straight line from the origin with slope m. The project should require M/m reporting periods to complete, which time, of course, should not depend on whether a WBS was made. (I am discounting in this discussion whether WBS generation increases or decreases productivity.) Thus, M/m should be a constant value, relatively speaking. If M is made large, tasks are smaller and shorter, so proportionately more are completed each reporting period. The project schedule will, in fact, assume some productivity or mean accomplishment rate, but an actual performance value will generally be unknown until progress can be monitored for some period of time.

However, although the numbers M and σ may not affect team productivity, they do directly influence the effectiveness with which a project can monitor its progress and predict its future accomplishments. Generation of a WBS, of course, gives (or estimates) the parameter M. Monitoring the completion of milestones provides estimates for m and σ. From these, projections of the end data and calculations for the accuracy of this prediction can be made. Based on such information, the project can then divert or reallocate resources to take corrective action should progress not be deemed suitable.

In this simplified model, a least-square-error straight-line fit through the cumulative milestone progress over the first r reports (of an expected $R = M/m$ reports) at regular ΔT intervals will predict the time required to reach the final milestone. It will also provide an estimate of m and σ. The normalized predicted completion date may be expected to deviate from the projected value (as a one-sigma event) by no more than

$$\sigma_M \leqslant 1.48 \, \sigma_1 \, (R/rM)^{1/2}$$

within first-order effects. The value

$$\sigma_1 = \sigma/m^{1/2}$$

represents the normalized standard deviation of an individual task milestone (it is limited to values of less than unity in the underlying model), and σ_M represents the deviation in time to reach milestone M.

The bound permits the specification of WBS characteristics that enable accurate early predictions of future progress. High overall accuracy depends on a combination of low σ_1 and large M. One may compensate for inaccurate appraisals of productivity only by generating a very detailed WBS.

As an example, suppose that a 10 percent end-date prediction accuracy is required (i.e., $\sigma_M = 0.1$) by the end of the first quarter ($r/R = 0.25$) of a project. Then, as shown in Figure 9.6, the trade-off figure is

$$M/ \, \sigma_1^2 = 876.$$

Hence, if the WBS is highly uncertain ($\sigma_1 = 1$), that WBS should contain 876 unit milestones. If the project is confident that it can

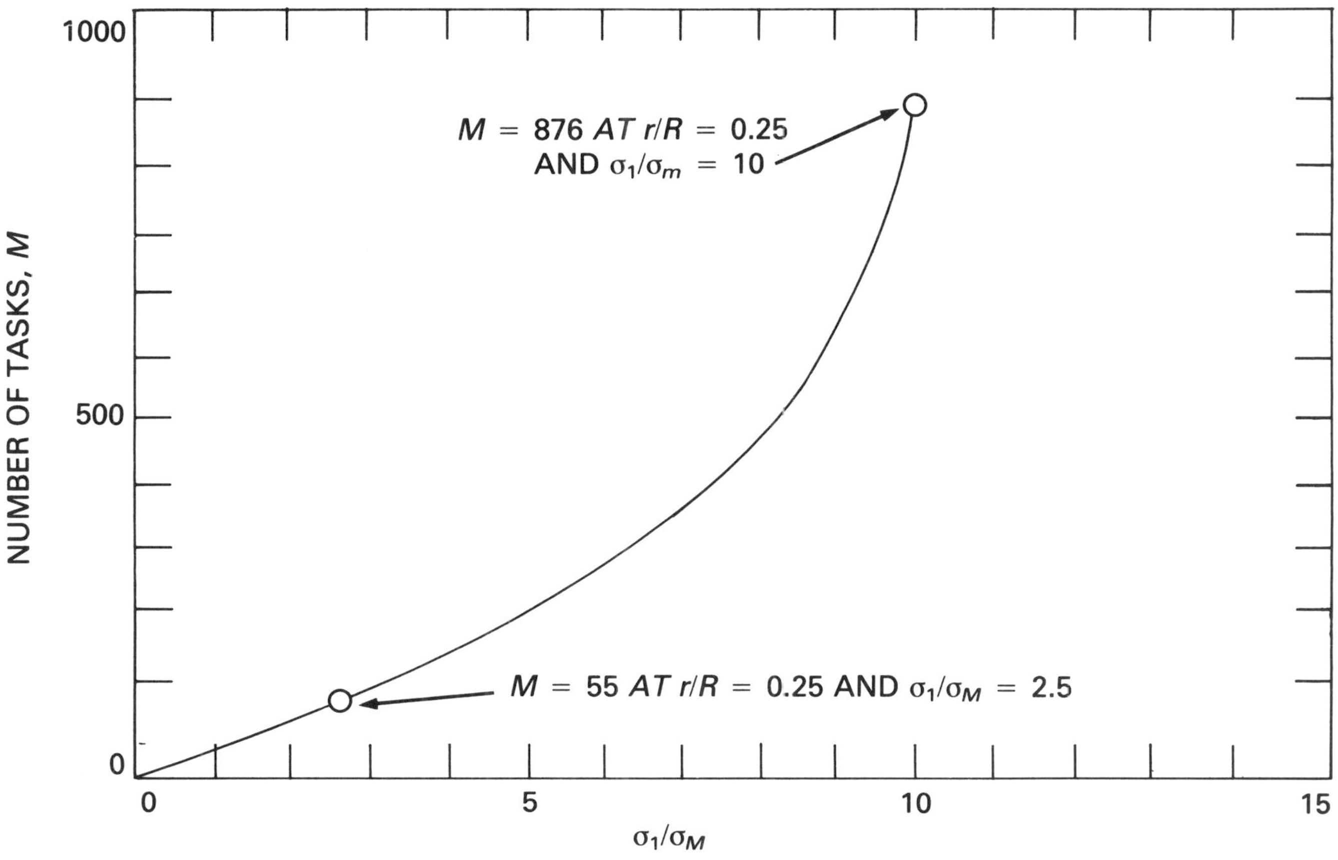

FIGURE 9.6. WBS unit milestones and variance ratio.

hold more closely to its average productivity (and has most contingencies provided for) with $\sigma_1 = 0.5$, then it needs only about 220 milestones. A one-person-year project with biweekly reporting, one milestone per report (26 milestones in all), must demonstrate a $\sigma_1 = 0.17$ level of task prediction accuracy.

It is therefore both necessary and important to generate a detailed WBS rather carefully and to monitor milestone achievements relative to this WBS very faithfully, if accuracy in predicting the future progress of a project is of great importance.

REASONABLE SCHEDULE ACCURACY

A data processing project manager on a two-year, 10-person task may perhaps be able to manage as many as 876 subtasks, each formally assigned and reported on. That amounts to about one subtask completion per week from each of the other nine workers; but the generation of the description for the subtasks will require considerable effort. Moreover, it is unlikely that such a detailed plan would have a σ as large as one week. If the project manager is able to break the work accurately into 876 week-long subtasks, task deviations can probably be estimated to well within a week.

The ability of the data processing project manager (or planning staff) to generate a clear and accurate WBS will determine the level to which the WBS must be taken. Greater accuracy of the work breakdown definition produces greater understanding and clarity of the actions necessary to complete task objectives. If the work is understood, readily identified, and achievable as discerned, the confidence of reaching the objectives is high. Thus, the further the subtask descriptions become refined, the better the estimator is able to check the individual subtask durations and uncertainties. Refinement ceases when the appropriate M / σ_1^2 is reached.

Practically speaking, a work plan with tasks shorter than one week in duration will usually require too much planning and management overhead to be worthwhile. On the other hand, a work plan with tasks longer than one or two weeks will probably suffer from a larger σ_1. Thus, a breakdown into one- or two-week subtasks is probably the most reasonable target for planning purposes.

A work year consists of about 47 actual weeks of work (excluding vacations, holidays, sick leave, etc.). Therefore, a project of w workers can reasonably accomodate only about 47 w/d tasks per year (including management tasks) each of duration d weeks. Spread over y years, the total number of milestones can reach $M = 47wy/d$, so that the practical accuracy limit one may reasonably expect at the one-quarter point in a project ($r/R = 0.25$) is about

$$\sigma_M \leqslant 0.432\sigma_1(d/wy)^{1/2}$$

Note that accuracy is related to the total person-year effort in a project, other things being equal. A three-person-year project completing one task per person-week can expect to have $\sigma_M \leqslant 0.261\sigma_1$. With a $\sigma_1 = 0.4$ ($\pm$ 2 days per weekly task), the end-date estimation accuracy is within 10 percent.

GENERATING THE WBS

The general algorithm for generating a WBS goes somewhat like this:

1. Start with the project statement of work and put this TASK on top of the "working stack".

2. Consider the TASK at the top of the working stack. Define technical performance objectives, end-item objectives, reliability and quality objectives, schedule constraints and other factors as appropriate; inputs and materials required for starting the task; accomplishments and outputs that signal the completion of the task; know precedent tasks or milestones; known interfacing tasks; resources required, if known. Determine whether this task can be accomplished within the duration (or cost) accuracy goal.

3. If the goal is achieved, skip to the next step; otherwise, partition the current TASK into a small number of comprehensive component subtasks. Include interfacing tasks and tasks

whose output is a decision regarding substructuring of other subtasks. Mark the current TASK as a "milestone," pull it into the "finished stack", and push each of the subtask descriptions onto the working stack.

4. Repeat from step 2 until the working stack is empty.
5. Sequence through all items from the "finished" stack and accumulate durations (costs) into the proper milestones.

The steps in this algorithm are not always simple to perform and cannot always be done correctly without sometimes referring to items already put into the "finished" list. The process is one of creation and thus requires judgement, experience, identification of alternatives, trade-offs, decisions, and iteration. The last is required since, as the project statement of work is refined, eventually the implementation of the program itself appears as one of the subtasks to be refined. When this subtask is detailed into component parts, the work descriptions begin to follow the influences of the program architecture, or organizational matters, chronological constraints, work locations, and "whatever makes sense".

Therefore, the formation of the WBS, the detailed planning, and the architectural design activity are all mutually supportive. The architecture indicates how to structure the tasks, and the WBS goals tell when the architectural phase of activity has proceeded far enough. Scheduling makes use of the WBS as a tool and in turn influences the WBS generation by resolving resource conflicts.

There are many subtasks in a software project, however, that are not connected with the architecture directly, such as requirements analysis, project administration and management, and preparation for demonstration and delivery. The structure of these subtasks, being independent of the program architecture, can be made fairly standard within a given organization for all software productions. However, since there is no automatic or closed-loop means to guarantee that all the planning factors needed in the WBS actually get put into it, a Standard WBS Checklist can be a significant boom to proper software project planning to decrease the likelihood of something "dropping through the cracks".

STANDARD WBS CHECKLIST

A typical Standard WBS Checklist should include many factors gained from previous successes and should contain items to avert some of the identified shortcomings. Table 9.1 shows a typical upper-level structure of this WBS checklist. Detailed task descriptions are also in the process of documentation and evaluation. A short application guidebook is planned to instruct cognizant individuals in the method, approach, and practice.

Such a checklist and guidebook, together with useful automated WBS entry, update, processing, and report generation aids, impose standards on software projects that are intended to facilitate the project management activity and make it more effective. Initial scheduling and downstream rescheduling of subtasks are aided by a WBS database that contains precedence relationships, durations, costs, resource requirements, resource availability, and similar constraints on each subtask. PERT (see Chapter 12) and CPM (see Chapter 11) are applied directly to the WBS database, resulting in a preliminary schedule. Alterations of this schedule are then effected by editing the WBS via additional constraints recorded into the database. Actual production progress is measured by marking milestone completions. These are then plotted into a rate chart (Figure 9.4) and all significant milestones are projected to a best-estimate completion date.

LIMITATIONS OF WBS

Although the WBS is a well-known, effective project management tool, it has not been applied to data processing/software projects as often as to hardware and construction. This is probably because the planning and architectural design tasks in software have not always been sufficiently integrated, to be mutually supportive, for several reasons: all of the management, support, and miscellaneous tasks were seldom able to be fully identified and detailed during the planning phase; because separation of work into manageable packets quite often requires design decisions as a part of the detail design phase; because the basis for estimating subtask durations,

TABLE 9.1. Software implementation project: outline of detailed work breakdown structure.

1. ANALYZE SOFTWARE REQUIREMENTS
   1.1 Understand functional and software requirements
   1.2 Identify missing, vague, ambiguous, and conflicting requirements
   1.3 Clarify stated requirements
   1.4 Verify that stated requirements fulfill requestor's goals
   1.5 Assess technology for supplying required software
   1.6 Propose alternate requirements or capability
   1.7 Document revised requirements

2. DEVELOP SOFTWARE ARCHITECTURE
   2.1 Determine architectural approach
   2.2 Develop external functional architecture
   2.3 Develop software internal architecture
   2.4 Assess architected solution vs. requirements
   2.5 Revise architecture and/or renegotiate requirements
   2.6 Document architecture and/or changed requirements

3. DEVELOP EXTERNAL FUNCTIONAL SPECIFICATION
   3.1 Define functional specification standards and conventions
   3.2 Formalize external environment and interface specifications
   3.3 Refine, formalize, and document the architected external operational view of the software
   3.4 Define functional acceptance tests
   3.5 Verify compliance of the external view with requirements

4. PRODUCE AND DELIVER SOFTWARE ITEMS
   4.1 Define programming, test and verification, QA, and documentation standards and conventions
   4.2 Formalize internal environment and interface specifications
   4.3 Obtain support tools
   4.4 Refine and formalize the internal design
   4.5 Define testing specifications to demonstrate required performance

TABLE 9.1. (Continued)

4.6 Define QA specifications

4.7 Code and check the program

4.8 Demonstrate acceptability and deliver software

5. PREPARE FOR SOFTWARE SUSTAINING AND OPERATIONS

   5.1 Train cognizant sustaining and maintenance personnel

   5.2 Train cognizant operations personnel

   5.3 Deliver sustaining tools and materials

   5.4 Deliver all software and data deliverables to operations

5.5 Install the software and data into its operational environment

5.6 Prepare consulting agreement between implementation and operations

6. PERFORM PROJECT MANAGEMENT FUNCTIONS

   6.1 Define project goals and objectives

   6.2 Scope and plan the project

   6.3 Administrate the implementation

   6.4 Evaluate performance and product

   6.5 Terminate the project

---

costs, and other constraints has not existed or been known; and because software managers have not been trained in WBS methodology. Modern software engineering studies of phenomenology and methodology are beginning to close the gaps. However, the existence of useful tools and methods does not ensure their acceptance, nor does their acceptance ensure project success. The WBS is a planning, monitor, and control tool whose potential for successful application within a software project has been demonstrated.

REFERENCE

Tausworthe, Robert C. "The Work Breakdown Structure in Software Project Management", *The Journal of Systems and Software*, 1, Copyright 1980 by Elsevier/North Holland, Inc.

Chapter
10
PROJECT NETWORK

The need for procedures which allow simulation of the possible future stages of a project through to completion led to the adoption of the network as a desirable means of depicting the elements of a project and the relationships among them. This network idea is the basis of all critical path analysis schemes and is used to depict a project plan.

Data processing projects usually consist of a number of interrelated tasks or activities. Certain tasks can be executed simultaneously. Some tasks can only be started after other tasks have been completed, i.e., precedence relationships exist between the various tasks. Each task takes a given time to complete, and tasks may require scarce resources, such as manpower or funds. The data processing project manager may be interested in finding the earliest time that the project can be completed with the resources available. A number of other planning and scheduling problems, such as construction projects, periodic overhaul or maintenance of large installations, most capital expenditure projects, or the introduction of new products or procedures all require a coordinated plan that involves the sequencing of interrelated ordered tasks and the deployment of limited resources.

In the late 1950s a number of closely-related approaches based on network analysis were developed to deal with such problems. Two of the best-known techniques, CPM and PERT, have proven themselves not only as tools of planning but also as tools for controlling the execution of the plans.

NETWORK CONCEPT DEVELOPMENT

The network concept involves the graphical representation of activities and their precedence requirements. Activities are elements of the project which represent logical subdivision of the work to be done. The level of detail used depends upon the degree of control desired. For example, if the control is desired only on the start of a project, the entire project may be described as a single activity.

To illustrate the network event representation, let us consider the inventory control project shown in the flowchart in Figure 10.1 which lists the various tasks to be undertaken to complete the project. Figure 10.1 shows the order in which the tasks have to be undertaken. For instance, task C (formulate a mathematical model for the proposed inventory control system (ICS)) can only start when task A (detailed analysis of environment for proposed ICS) has been completed. Task H (formulate forecasting model) can only start after the detailed analysis of the environment for the proposed inventory control system and of the demand data sources, i.e., after tasks A and G have been completed. Similarly, the computation of the control limits for the products stored in inventory (task Q) can only start if both the input forms for the ICS program have been filled in (task N) and the demand forecasting base file, from where the ICS program obtains demand forecasts, has been created (task P). Table 10.1 lists the precedence relations and estimates for the durations of the 17 tasks.

*Let us assume that we can draw on a sufficient number of people to have any number of tasks executed simultaneously. If the project is given the go-ahead, what is the earliest project completion date? This is one of the questions we would like to have answered.

For small project problems, such as ours, the answer can easily be found by enumerating all possible sequences of tasks. In our example, there are 14 different sequences. The project is only completed when the sequence with the longest time has been completed.

CPM provides an efficient technique to find the longest time sequence. In Figure 10.1, we use blocks (or nodes) to represent each activity. The arrows between the nodes simply indicate the precedence relations. Although this flow (Figure 10.1) could be used directly to perform the computations of the CPM, there are certain advantages in reversing this convention and drawing a network where directed lines or links represent tasks and nodes indicate precedence relationships. With each link we associate a number that represents the duration of the task. Since each'link starts and ends at a node, nodes also represent the event of starting or completing a task. Nodes are therefore often referred to as events.

Figure 10.2 depicts the network associated with the tasks listed in Table 10.1 using this principle. The nodes are numbered consecutively in such a manner that each link always leads from a lower order to a higher order node. Node 1 represents the start of the project. The length of the link is usually not drawn proportionally to the duration of the tasks. The number under each link is the duration of the corresponding task.

In this representation each task is uniquely defined by the two nodes where the corresponding link starts and ends. For instance, task A can be denoted by (1,2). The duration of task A is denoted by t_{-12}. In general, a task is identified by nodes (i,j) and its duration the t_{ij}. If the problem is solved on a computer, this is a convenient way to specify tasks and task durations.

Figure 10.2 shows several links as broken lines. They are introduced to avoid ambiguities in the network logic or to allow proper representation of precedence relations. Consider, for instance, the sequence of tasks C,D,E, and F as shown in Figure 10.1. Tasks D and E both follow C, and F requires both D and E to be completed. This ordering could be represented as shown in Figure 10.3.

Tasks D and E both start and end at the same nodes. If tasks are

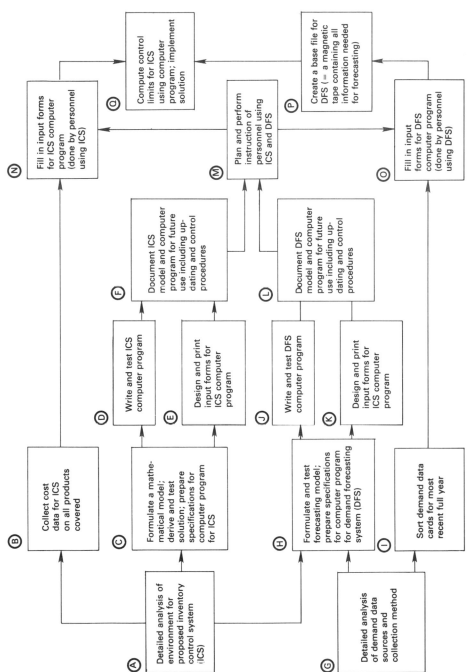

FIGURE 10.1. Flow of tasks for an inventory control project.

TABLE 10.1. List of tasks for Inventory Control Project.

TASKS	PRECEDENCE	DURATION IN WEEKS
A	—	3
B	A	12
C	A	4
D	C	10
E	C	2
F	D,E	3
G	—	2
H	A,G	4
I	G	3
J	H	16
K	H	2
L	J,K	2
M	F,L	2
N	B,M	2
O	I,M	1
P	O	2
Q	N,P	3

referred to by the starting and ending nodes, then both are denoted by (5,7). To avoid this we would introduce a dummy task
with a zero duration which leads to a new node. In Figure 10.2 the
dummy task gives rise to link CE (connecting tasks C and E) which
leads from node 5 to node 6. Task E is then started from this new
node 6. Each task is now again uniquely defined by two node
numbers. Exactly the same reasoning leads to the introduction of
dummy task HK. Note that the dummy task could precede task D
rather than task E, or it could follow either task D or E rather than
precede it. (However, whenever possible, the dummy task should
precede a task that gives rise to it. Otherwise, the computations of
free float—described in a later section—are less straightforward).
   A somewhat different situation gives rise to the remaining four
dummy tasks. For instance, the dummy tasks AH and GH are re-

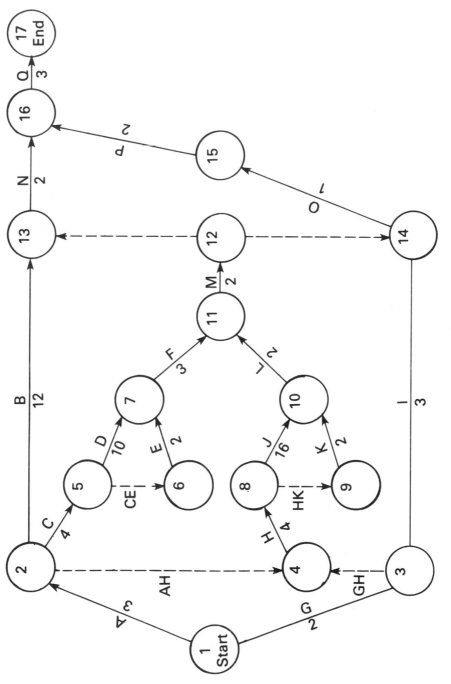

FIGURE 10.2. Network diagram for an inventory control project.

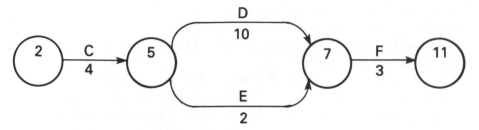

FIGURE 10.3. An ambiguous representation of tasks.

quired because task H has both A and G as predecessors, whereas tasks B and C only depend on task A, but not on task G, and task I only requires task G, but not task A. The dependence of task H on tasks A and G is indicated by the dummy tasks AH and GH.

As an exercise, explain why dummy tasks MN and MO are needed.

In terms of this network, the earliest project completion date is equivalent to finding the longest path through the network.

TIME ESTIMATES

When a network drawing has progressed to the point where the data processing project manager is satisfied that he has a workable plan, the next concern is the assignment of activity responsibilities and the making of resource-time estimates. The process of resource-time estimation is directly dependent upon the degree of detail of the activities in the network. As the process of estimation proceeds, it may become necessary to redefine some of the activities to reflect shorter intervals of time that can be accurately and independently estimated.

All time estimates are directly related to the resources to be used for the activity. All estimates must be based on a normal level of work effort with respect to manpower assigned, shifts worked per day, and days worked per week.

Estimates should generally be made by considering each activity a separate, independent effort, completely isolated from preceding and succeeding activities. It is helpful to have it clearly understood that an estimate is not an inflexible commitment but is simply the individual estimator's experience reflected in a numerical statement and, therefore, may be wrong. The real committment is to the completion of the project.

Since resources directly influence the time consumed, and the resources available have a direct effect upon the length of time required, it must be assumed that the normal resource level will prevail throughout the span of the activity. This may appear to be a rather broad assumption but it is a reasonable one. The estimator must make his jdugment as if the activity in question were the only work before him. Future conflicts may require re-estimates.

Since time estimates are commonly posted directly onto the network, it is easy for the estimator to see the critical path developing. Knowledge of the critical path is almost certain to cause the estimator to consciously or subconsciously modify his estimates to obtain some preconceived total duration time.

Thus, the object of time estimation is to predict problem areas. If the activities are properly subdivided into short, controllable elements, and one gets out of hand, timely corrective action can be taken before the problem becomes widespread. It is better to be 100 percent wrong on a three-week job than to be 15 percent wrong on a 52-week job. Poor time estimates on small jobs are simply not as dangerous as poor estimates on jobs of long duration where knowledge of the existence of a problem may not be indicated until the project is in serious trouble.

EARLIEST PROJECT COMPLETION TIME

Assume that we are able to determine that the *earliest finish times* for tasks N and P are the end of week 29 and the end of week 30, respectively. Thus, the *earliest time* at which all tasks prior to node 16 are finished is the end of week 30. Only at that time can task Q be started. The *earliest start time* of a task is therefore defined to be equal to the earliest time of the node where the task starts, i.e., the latest of the earliest finish times of all preceding tasks. In our case, this is the end of week 30. The duration of task Q is 3; hence, we find that the earliest finish time of task Q is the end of week 33.

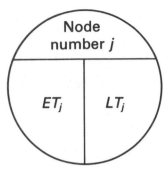

FIGURE 10.4. Use of node circles in computations.

Task Q being the last task to be performed, the end of week 33 is also the earliest completion time of the entire project.

In fact, we do not yet know the earliest finish times of tasks N and P. They can be determined if we know the earliest times of nodes 13 and 15. These in turn could be found if we had the earliest finish times of the preceding tasks, etc. This gives us the idea to begin at the starting node and systematically evaluate the earliest times for each node until we reach the final node.

For this evaluation, it is convenient to divide each node circle into three parts as shown in Figure 10.4.

Initially we are only interested in the ET_j portion. Here we insert the earliest time (ET) that node j can be reached. At least that many periods (weeks in our case) must have elapsed since the beginning of the project before any task following node j can be started. The earliest time thus refers to the end of period ET_j.

EARLIEST TIME *ET* OF NODE *j*

ET is equal to the latest of the earliest finish times for all tasks preceding node j; i.e.

$$ET_j = \text{maximum } (EF_{i,j}, \text{ all } i_k) \qquad [10\text{-}1]$$

where

$$(i_k, j)$$

is a task ending at node j, and

$$EF_{ikj}$$

is the earliest finish time of task (i_k, j).

EARLIEST FINISH TIME OF TASK (i, j)

Let t_{ij} be the duration of task $((i, j))$; then the earliest finish time of task (i, j) is

$$EF_{ij} = \mathrm{ET}_i + t_{ij} \qquad\qquad [10\text{-}2]$$

The complete evaluation for our project is shown in Figure 10.5. If the nodes have been properly numbered, i.e., no higher numbered node leads to a lower numbered node, then the nodes can be evaluated in numerical order. The following simple algorithm evaluates the earliest completion time:

1. SET $ET_1 = 0$

2 Go to next higher numbered node. Evaluate earliest finish times of all tasks that end at that node. Find the earliest time for that node, using equation [10-1].

3. If there remain any nodes that have not been evaluated, return to step 2; otherwise terminate iterations.

We can now test our understanding of this algorithm by working out the earliest times of all nodes using Figure 10.2, and also, verifying the result with the solution shown in Figure 10.5.

It is usually convenient to have only one terminal node. If the original problem has more than one terminal node, simply introduce dummy tasks as needed. In this case, the earliest time of the last node evaluated gives the earliest project completion time.

RESOURCE TIME ESTIMATES

Since resources directly influence the time consumed on a project, and the resources available have a direct effect upon the length of

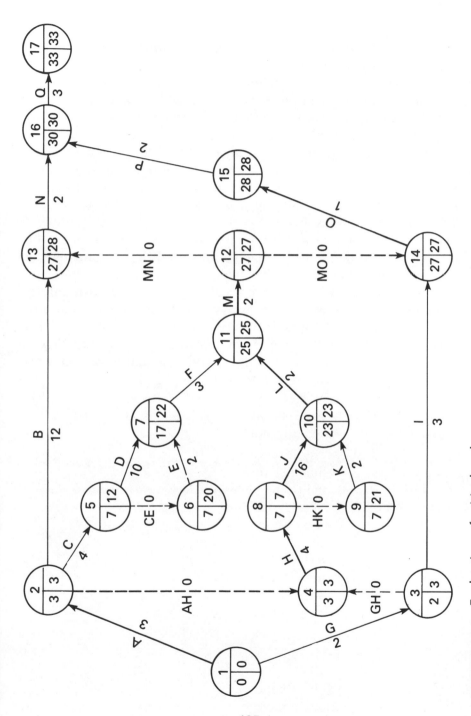

FIGURE 10.5. Evaluation of critical path.

time required in estimating manpower expenditure, the standard should be a normal working interval such as hours, days, or weeks. One method of estimating activity durations is to estimate the man-hour, or skill-hour, requirements for the activity and divide that figure by the expected work crew size. However, an activity will often include several skills or crafts so that the skill hours included become difficult to convert to a total activity or duration time. Generally, the finer the activity breakdown, the more accurate the time estimate can be. It is usually better to have more detail than required than to risk errors arising from partial dependency relationships and inaccurate estimates.

The resource-time estimating phase is an ideal time to collect the data that will be needed for analysis and modification during the progress of the project.

To obtain fullest value from critical path planning, scheduling, and control procedures, it is necessary to express time estimates in terms of dollars, man-hours, work crew sizes, and equipment. This information will enable the project manager to make intelligent time-cost trades, reallocate resources, and reschedule activities effectively during the course of the project.

REFERENCES

Awani, Alfred O. *Project Management Techniques*. Princeton: Petrocelli Books, Inc., 1983.

Daellenbach, Hans G. and George, John A. *Introduction to Operations Research Techniques*. Newton, MA: Allyn and Bacon, 1978.

Chapter
11
CRITICAL PATH METHOD

CPM is a network-based procedure developed to assist in the scheduling and control of multiactivity projects. CPM provides the important capability of allowing the data processing project manager to allocate additional resources to critical activities so that the critical path and thus the project duration can be shortened. CPM uses only a single estimate of activity times and thus does not consider the effects of uncertainty or variability in activity times. Because of this, CPM is perhaps most applicable to repeating or recurring projects where experience and historical data provide good estimates of actual activity times. Projects involving construction and maintenance programs have been typical areas for CPM project management applications.

Let us digress to the inventory control project discussed in Chapter 10. *Our next problem is to find which path of the tasks has the longest completion time.* Any delay in these tasks will delay the earliest project completion time. Thus, the tasks on this path are the critical ones, and this path is referred to as the *critical path* of the network. There may be several paths that all have the same longest completion time. Each such path is a critical path.

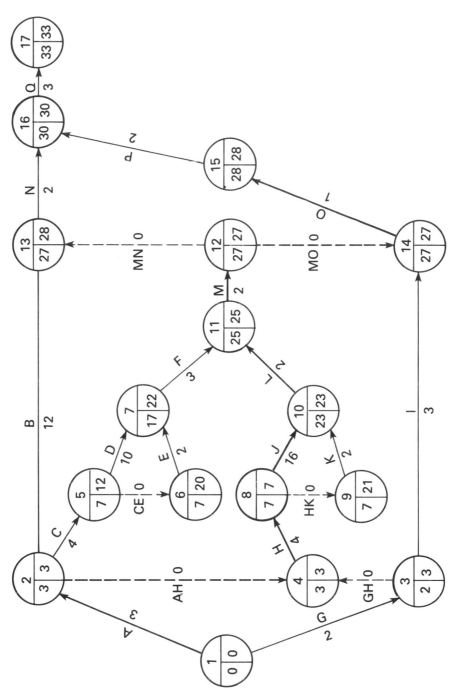

FIGURE 11.1. Evaluation of critical path.

How can we identify a critical path? Consider node 13 in Figure 11.1. The earliest time all tasks preceding it can be finished is ET_{13} = 27. (Remember that it denotes the end of a period). This is also the earliest start time for task N. However, since task N takes only two weeks and the earliest time of node 16 is ET_{16} = 30, task N can be delayed by at least one week without delaying the completion time of the entire project. The *latest start time* for task N is the end of week 28. If any tasks preceding task N are delayed such that the start time for tasks from node 13 is later than the end of week 28, the project completion time is also delayed. In other words, the *latest time, LT,* all tasks preceding node 13 have to be finished without delaying the whole project is the end of week 28.

On the other hand, task P can be started, at the earliest, by the end of week 28, the earliest time of node 15. Given that task P takes two weeks to complete, and the earliest time of node 16 is 30, the latest start time of task P is also the end of week 28. There is no leeway. Unless all tasks preceding node 15 are finished by this time, the project completion will be delayed. In other words, the latest start time of task P is the same as the earliest time of node 15. This property holds for all tasks on a critical path.

CRITICAL TASKS AND CRITICAL PATHS*

A task for which a latest start time is equal to the earliest time of its starting node is a crictical task. Each path from the start node to the end node of the network that consists of critical tasks only is a critical path.

Thus, we found a simple way to identify the critical tasks of a network and all critical paths.

To determine the latest times of all nodes, we use an algorithm similar to the one used on an earlier section to find the earliest time.

*From H. G. Daellenbach and J. A. George, *Introduction To Operations Research Techniques.* Copyright © 1978 by Allyn and Bacon Inc. Used with permission.

LATEST TIME LT_i OF NODE i

LT_i is equal to the earliest of the latest start times for all tasks following node i, i.e.;

$$LT_i = \text{minimum } (LS_{ij_k}, \text{ all } j_k) \qquad (11\text{-}1)$$

where (i,j_k) is a task starting at node i, and LS_{ij_k} is the latest start time of task (i,j_k).

LATEST START TIME OF TASK (i,j)

The latest start time of task (i,j) is

$$LS_{ij} = LT_j - t_{ij} \qquad (11\text{-}2)$$

Here's the algorithm for finding latest times:

1. Set $LT_i = ET_i$, where i is the terminal node.
2. Go to the first lower numbered node. Evaluate latest start times of all tasks beginning at that node. Find the latest time for that node, using equation (11–1).
3. If the starting node has been evaluated, terminate iterations; otherwise, return to step 2.

These computations are also shown in Figure 11–1 in the right-hand-side portion of the node circles labeled by LT_j in Figure 10.4. Verify the results!

We can now identify the critical path by the nodes with $ET_i = LT_j - t_{ij}$;

nodes 1→2 → 4→8→10→11→12 → 14→15→16→17

tasks A dummy H J L M dummy O P Q

This path is identified by the heavy line in Figure 11.1.

Any task not on the critical path can be delayed, within limits. If we consider each task by itself (neglecting any interactions with preceding or subsequent tasks), then the difference between the ealiest time of the node from which the task starts and its latest start time is the largest amount by which the task can be delayed without affecting the earliest completion time of the project. This difference is called the total slack or total float (*TF*) of the task. Thus, critical tasks have zero total float.

TOTAL FLOAT OF TASK (*i,j*)

$$TF_{ij} = LS_{ij} - ET_i = LT_j - ET_i - t_{ij}. \qquad (11\text{-}3)$$

For example, the noncritical task B = (2,13) has a

$$TF_{2,13} = LS_{2,13} - ET_2 = (28 - 12) - 3 = 13$$

If task B is delayed by more than 13 weeks, then the earliest completion time of the entire project will be delayed. However, delaying one task may affect the amount by which subsequent tasks can be delayed.

For example, tasks C, D, and F all share the same float of 5. The largest amount by which a task may be delayed without affecting the earliest start time of any subsequent tasks is called *free slack* or *free float (FF)*. Free float is the amount of float available when all other tasks take place at their earliest times. For instance, noncritical task B may be delayed by up to 12 weeks without affecting task N. Its free float is thus 12. On the other hand, noncritical task G cannot be delayed at all without delaying any of the subsequent tasks. Free float can never exceed total float. Along any segment of the network where all tasks have the same total float, only the latest task has a positive free float. For example, of tasks C, D, and F, which have the same total float of 5, only F has a free float and its free float is 5.

FREE FLOAT OF TASK (*i,j*)

$$FF_{ij} = ET_j - EF_{ij} = ET_j - ET_i - t_{ij}. \qquad (11\text{-}4)$$

Again for task B = (2,13)

$$FF_{2,13} = ET_{13} - EF_{2,13} = 27 - (3 + 12) = 12.$$

Both free float and total float are useful for planning decisions. The DP project manager has some choice as to when to start tasks with float. This may allow him to schedule such tasks in a manner that reduces the amount of manpower needed. For instance, tasks E and K are similar in nature and thus require the same professional training. Both could be started after week 7. Since both have float, they can be scheduled in such a manner that the same person can do both tasks consecutively.

ACTUAL PROJECT PLANNING AND CONTROL THROUGH CPM

The computations for determining the critical path and the amount of total and free float are so simple that projects with up to a few hundred tasks can still be performed by hand. Any self-contained segments of the network that have only a beginning and ending node in common with other parts can be analyzed separately. By inserting only the final results of this analysis into the total project structure, the whole segment can be regarded as a single task. Using this trick, a complex network can be broken down into a number of smaller networks, each of which is analyzed for its critical paths.

Larger projects are best analyzed by computer. The computer can handle projects with several thousand tasks and automatically keep track of the amount of various resources required during the project. Some programs allow the input to be in the form of Figure 11.2, i.e., tasks are attached to nodes rather than to links, eliminating the translation process. The program may contain a calendar covering up to 25 years which includes all official holidays. All start and finish dates are assigned by the program to their projected calendar dates. The program may also allow special work and shift patterns to be specified.

The practical use of CPM is twofold. It is a tool for detailed planning and scheduling of projects made up of a large number of interconnected tasks, and is also a highly useful aid in continuously measuring the actual progress of the project according to the plan. Such continuous control allows DPPM to predict delays or pinpoint situations that could lead to delays—often well ahead of their ac-

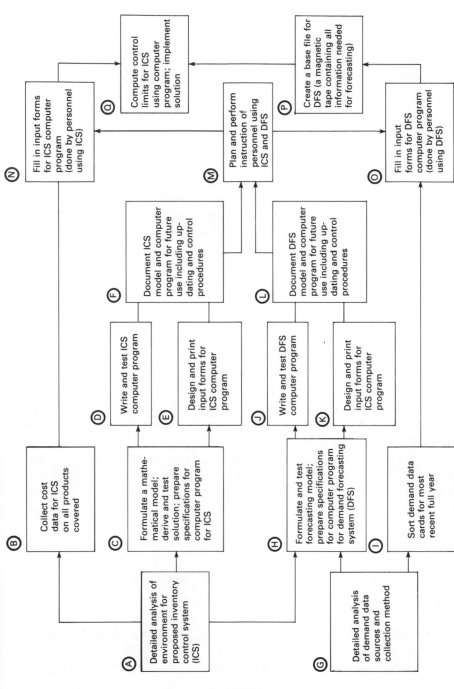

FIGURE 11.2. Flow of tasks for an inventory control project.

133

tual occurrence. Corrective and remedial action can thus be taken early enough to counteract some of the consequences of late project completion. Furthermore, by using the current progress status as the starting point, DPPM can work out the new projected critical path and earliest completion time in light of the latest information.

Continuous control is more effectively achieved if we redraw the CPM network as a *schedule graph,* on which the horizontal projection of all links is drawn to a time scale representing their task duration. Usually, we also have to plan the starting dates for noncritical tasks. Figure 11.3 shows a possible schedule graph for the inventory control project studied earlier. Actual task times are drawn as solid lines, and float times as dotted lines.

In this project, tasks that require the same professional training are scheduled, as far as possible, in such a manner that the same person can perform them. For example, task H (formulate forecasting model) is followed by task C (formulate inventory control model). The former is on the critical path, the latter has considerable float.

As the project progresses, the data processing project manager can continuously monitor the actual execution by marking the progress of each task on the schedule graph. When he observes or predicts any irregularities, such as late starts or excessive task duration, he can immediately determine whether they will cause a delay in project completion. Self-contained segments of a project can be controlled individually.

For large projects, this control is best done directly by computer. Some CPM programs are specially designed for control purposes by keeping the current status of a project on a random access memory file, such as a disk. Progress on task completions, as well as any new estimates of task durations for tasks not yet started or completed or any other changes in the project, can be fed into the computer at any time. The program can also be instructed to provide a new status report, flag present and predicted delays in task completion, and update the critical path and float times.

DISADVANTAGE OF CPM IN DATA PROCESSING PROJECTS

CPM has one grave disadvantage: it tends to encourage activities to begin at their latest start date—and with data processing projects

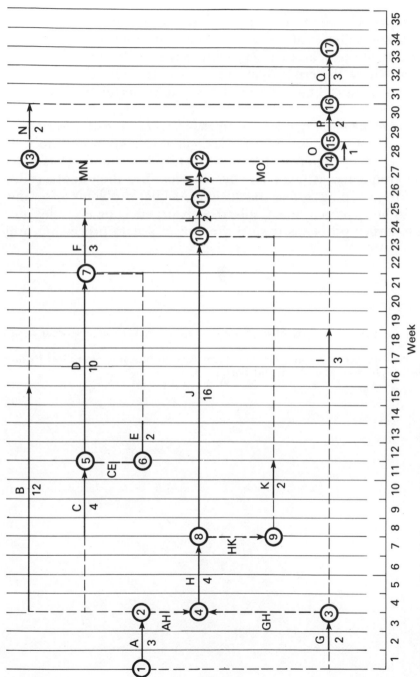

FIGURE 11.3. Schedule graph of a CPM network.

135

that approach is entirely wrong. We are not dealing with exact science; there is almost always some degree of innovation in the data processing project, and consequently it is very difficult to know in practice where the critical path really lies. It is almost worse if we do get the plan right—for every job will have become critical at the end.

The right approach is to bring every activity forward to its earliest possible start date. In this way a buffer is created to absorb any shock. In the data processing environment, the attitude of putting off problems to tomorrow is fatal. The big decisions are the ones to reflect on before reaching a final conclusion. As little problems arise, they need to be explored and resolved with urgency, or else they may lead to larger problems toward the end of a data processing project.

REFERENCES

Awani, Alfred O. *Project Management Techniques*. Princeton: Petrocelli Books, Inc., 1983.

Daellenbach, Hans G. and George, John A. *Introduction to Operations Research Techniques*. Newton, MA: Allyn and Bacon, 1978.

Chapter
12
PROGRAM EVALUATION AND REVIEW TECHNIQUE

PERT is another network-based procedure developed to assist management in planning and controlling many programs and projects that consist of numerous specific jobs or activities, each of which must be completed in order to complete the entire project.

PERT is partially evolutionary—drawing from Gantt charting, line of balance, and milestone reporting systems—and partially a new creation. The concept of task interrelationships and their graphic representation is old; but time and cost concepts, the critical path, and the computerized reporting systems used in the technique are new. The merger of the old and new in PERT has been called a breakthrough in the art and science of management.

PERT is used to facilitate the planning and control of complex data processing programs involving considerable uncertainty. With it, data processing project managers can quickly identify schedule problems and allocate resources to overcome them. By cutting across organizational lines of a business it permits an examination of the entire system of activities encompassed in a company's programs. Because of its enormous power, PERT was made mandatory in 1964 on larger Department of Defense and NASA contracts. It has also found wide usage in nondefense industries, a development which has been accompanied by PERT programs by most computer equipment manufacturers.

ORIGIN OF PERT

PERT was developed in 1958 by a special study group composed of C. E. Clark, D. G. Malcolm and J. Roseboom of Booz, Allen and Hamilton; R. Young and E. Lenna of Lockheed's Missile Systems Division; and W. Fazar of the Navy's Special Projects Office (SP). It was developed for the Polaris Submarine weapon system because, by the fall of 1957, it was clear that the various management tools adopted or developed for Polaris did not provide certain information essential for effective program evaluation and decision-making. Not one of these tools, nor all in combination, furnished the following vital information:

appraisal of the validity of existing plans and schedules for meeting program objectives;

measurement of progress achieved against program objectives;

measurement of the outlook for meeting program objectives.

It was felt by those managing complex projects that the existing state-of-the-art—reflected by bar charts and milestone reports—when applied to complex research and development projects did not ferret out impending trouble spots quickly and was not adequate for control. The study team formed by SP improved upon the existing technology, particularly the Critical Path Method used for project planning at DuPont, and added statistical considerations to allow for uncertainty. The result was PERT. While the government has always been concerned with predicting program outcomes in terms of time, cost, and technical performance, the PERT used in 1958 was clearly concerned with time. This aspect of PERT generally became known as PERT/Time. PERT/Time is a method for planning and control distinguished by four characteristics:

1. PERT network
2. time estimates
3. determination of slack and critical path
4. taking corrective managerial action, if necessary.

Although PERT was developed concurrently and independently of CPM, it can be approached as an extension of CPM to deal with uncertainties in task durations. All of our computations to find the critical path were based on estimated or expected duration times. PERT is an attempt to determine not only the expected length of the critical path but also to obtain some measure of the variability of the earliest project completion time. (We say *attempt* because PERT does not fully succeed in this objective.)

PERT/TIME

In PERT, task durations are assumed to be independent random variables, each with an expected value of t_{ij} and a variance of σ_{ij}^2. Thus, any path through the network represents a sum of independent random variables. In particular, the length of the critical path as determined by CPM is such a random variable with

$$\text{expected value } \mu = \sum_{\substack{\text{all } (i,j) \text{ on} \\ \text{critical path}}} t_{ij} \qquad [12\text{-}1]$$

and

$$\text{variance } \sigma^2 = \sum_{\substack{\text{all } (i,j) \text{ on} \\ \text{critical path}}} \sigma_{ij}^2 \qquad [12\text{-}2]$$

Equation (12-2) follows from the fact that the variance of the sum of independent random variables is equal to the sum of the variances of the random variables. (See Appendix A).

Traditionally, PERT assumes that the individual tasks follow a particular form of the *beta distribution* which lends itself to an intui-

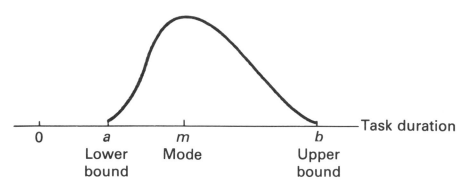

FIGURE 12.1. Beta distribution and task duration.

tively appealing interpretation for the task duration as shown Figure 12.1. The use of the beta distribution serves three purposes. The first is that an "expected elapsed time" for an activity can be determined from the three time estimates. The three time estimates are:

1. Optimistic time (a)—the activity time if everything progresses in an ideal manner.
2. Most probable time (m)—the most likely activity time under normal conditions.
3. Pessimistic time (b)—the activity time if we encounter a significant breakdown and/or delays.

Second, probabilities of completing an activity may be completed from the three time estimates. Thus, in programs with high uncertainty, data processing project managers may be able to speak of meeting schedules in terms of probability statements. Third, the use of the beta distribution provides a statistical foundation for the PERT network. The beta distribution is, of course, dependent on subjective time estimates of people.

To make statistical inferences about the timing of future events, it is necessary to typify the intervals between adjacent events in terms of their expected values (equation 12-1) and variances (equation 12-2). The expected value is a statistical term that corresponds to the mean. Variance (the square of the standard deviation) relates to the uncertainty associated with the process. If the variance of an activity is large, there is great uncertainty connected with the activity, and vice versa.

Two simple equations will produce the estimate of mean and variance for the ranges of distribution encountered. The expected task duration, or the mean of the distribution, is given by:

$$t_{ij} = \tfrac{1}{3}(2m + \tfrac{1}{2}(a + b)) \tag{12-3}$$

Equation 12-3 is based on the PERT assumption that the uncertain activity times are best described by a *beta probability* distribution; that is, the equation provides the average time for the special case of a beta probability distribution as the best description of the variability in activity times. The distribution assumption, which was judged to be reasonable by the developers of PERT, provides the time distribution shown in Figure 12.1.

For uncertain activity times we can use the common statistical measure of the *variance* to describe the dispersion or variation in the activity time values. In PERT we compute the variance of the activity time from the following equation:

$$\sigma_{ij}^2 = (1/6(b - a))^2 \tag{12-4}$$

As we can see, the difference between the pessimistic b and the optimistic a time estimates will greatly affect the value of the variance. With large differences in these two values, DPPM will experience uncertainty in the activity time. Accordingly, the variance given by equation (12-4) will be large.

ILLUSTRATIVE EXAMPLE*

The diesel motor of the emergency power generating plant of the DeVoe Factory needs an extensive overhaul job. At the same time, the cracked concrete base also has to be remade. Project manage-

*From H. G. Daellenbach and J. A. George, *Introduction To Operations Research Techniques.* Copyright © 1978 by Allyn and Bacon, Inc. Used with permission.

TABLE 12.1. Diesel motor overhaul.

| TASK | PRECEDENCE | In Days | | | t_{ij} | σ^2_{ij} |
		MODE m	MINIMUM a	MAXIMUM b		
A. Dismantle motor	—	2	2	2	2	0
B. Overhaul motor	A	7	6	14	8	$\frac{16}{9}$
C. Rebuild motor base and cure	A	9	8	10	9	$\frac{1}{9}$
D. Test and adjust motor	B	2.5	2	6	3	$\frac{4}{9}$
E. Mount motor on base	C,D	2	2	2	2	0

ment plans to have this job performed during the annual vacation closing of DeVoe. DeVoe remains closed for only three weeks or 15 working days. Project management would like to know whether the overhaul job can be finished during the closing. Table 12.1 summarizes the various tasks of the job.

The t_{ij} and σ_{ij}^2 are found using equation (12-3). Note that if the minimum and maximum times are equal, there is no variability in the task duration, and hence the variance is zero. This is the case for tasks A and E. For task B we obtain:

$$t_{ij} = \tfrac{1}{3}\,(2m + \tfrac{1}{2}\,(a + b)) = \tfrac{1}{3}\,(2(7) + \tfrac{1}{2}\,(6 + 14)) = \tfrac{24}{3} = 8$$

and

$$\sigma_{ij}^2 = (\tfrac{1}{6}(b - a))^2 = (\tfrac{1}{6}(14 - 6))^2 = (\tfrac{4}{3})^2 = \tfrac{16}{9}$$

The t_{ij} values so computed are now used as input in finding the critical path in the same manner as for CPM. Since the t_{ij} values are estimates of expected values, the duration of the critical path is also an estimate of an expected value. For our simple illustrative example, the critical path can be found by inspection. It consists of tasks A, B, D, E. By utilizing equations (12-1) and (12-2) respectively, we can find the following statistics for the expected length of the critical path and its variance or standard deviation as follows:

Expected length of critical path $= 2 + 8 + 3 + 2 = 15$ days
Variance of duration $= 0 + \tfrac{16}{9} + \tfrac{4}{9} + 0 = \tfrac{20}{9}$
Standard deviation $= \sqrt{\tfrac{20}{9}} = 1.49$ days

Thus, the expected length of the critical path is just equal to the closing period.

What is the probability distribution of the length of the critical path? From probability theory we know that no matter what the form of the individual probability distributions, the probability distribution of a sum of independent random variables is approximately normal for a sufficiently large number of variables. We also assume that the contribution of each random variable is small in comparison to the total. If the individual distributions are not highly skewed and none of the tasks dominate all others as to length, this property holds approximately for as few as $n = 10$ tasks. (Obviously, if the individual distributions are close to normal, it holds for even smaller numbers). Therefore, we can use the normal distribution to make probability statements about the duration of any path through the network and, in particular, about the length of the critical path.

For the sake of demonstrating the principle, let us assume that for our illustrative example problem the normal distribution is a sufficiently good approximation. We can then state that with a probability of 0.9099 the duration of the critical path does not exceed 17 days, and with a probability of 0.9778 the duration does not exceed 18 days, as shown in Figure 12.2.

Since the expected earliest project completion time is equal to the length of the critical path, it is easy to fall into the trap of concluding that the probability of an earliest project completion time of no more than 17 days is 0.9099. This would be a fallacy! Let us see why.

Although noncritical tasks will not affect the *expected* earliest project completion time, they may affect its variability. Tasks with a small amount of slack but large variability may have a significant probability that the length of the paths on which they lie may turn out to be longer than the critical path. PERT simply ignores these

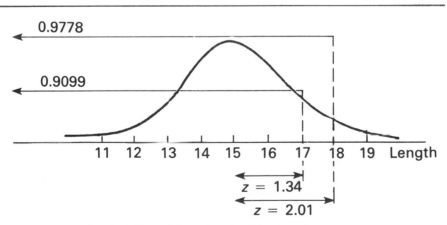

FIGURE 12.2. Probability of length of critical path.

effects and, therefore, tends to underestimate the variability of the earliest project completion time. Unfortunately, there exist no analytic methods to deal with this problem. *Stochastic simulation* is the only way to derive the empirical distribution of the earliest project completion time. (For more information, refer to a text on management science or operation research).

In our particular example, a probabilistic statement about the length of the critical path is practically equivalent to a statement about the earliest project completion time. The reason for this is the very small variance of the only noncritical task (task C).

Since the variability of the earliest project completion time depends on the variability of all tasks on the critical path, as well as on tasks of "near" or "close-to-critical" paths, any action that can reduce the variance of these tasks reduces the variability of the earliest project completion time, and therefore increases the probability of meeting project target dates.

COPING WITH PROBLEMS

An important development like PERT naturally is attended by a certain amount of confusion and doubt. PERT does indeed have its problems. However, they are not always what businessmen think they are, and often there is an effective way of coping with the restrictions. In any event, it is time to compare the situation in which PERT works best with situations in which real (or imagined) troubles occur.

UNCERTAIN ESTIMATES

One key question concerns the unknowns of time and resources that data processing project management frequently must contend with.

In PERT methodology an available set of resources including manpower and facilities is either known or must be assumed when making time estimates. For example, it is good practice to make special notations directly on the network when some special condition (e.g., a 48-hour rather than 40-hour week) is assumed. Experience has shown that when a well-thought-out network is developed in sufficient detail, the first activity time estimates made are as accurate as any, and these should not be changed unless a new application of resources or a trade-off in goals is specifically determined. A further caution is that the first time estimates should not be biased by some arbitrarily established schedule objective, or by the assumption that a particular activity does not appear to be on a critical path. Schedule biasing of this kind, while it obviously cannot be prevented, clearly atrophies some of the main benefits of the technique—although it is more quickly "discovered" with PERT than with any other method.

Because of the necessity for assumptions on manpower and resources, it is easiest to apply PERT in *project-structured* organizations where the level of resources and available facilities are known to the estimator. PERT does not itself *explicitly* resolve the problem of multiprogram planning and control, but there is general recognition of this problem, and considerable effort is being devoted to a more complete approach to it. Meanwhile, in the case of common resource centers, it is generally necessary to undertake a loading analysis, making priority assumptions and using the resulting data on either a three-time or single-time basis for those portions of the network which are affected. It should be pointed out, however, that in terms of actual experience with PERT, the process of network development forces more problems of resources constraint or loading analysis into the open for resolution than do other planning methods.

PERT has perhaps been most usefully applied in those situations where there is a great deal of interconnection between the activities of a network, or where there are interface connections between different networks. Certainly, network development and critical path analysis are not very appropriate for the pure research project where the capabilities of small numbers of individuals with highly specialized talents are being utilized at a "constant rate" and where activities have no significant dependence on other elements of the organization.

USE OF STANDARD NETWORKS

Because of the considerable impact of PERT on many organizations where detailed planning has not had a major emphasis, a trend has developed which can be characterized as "standard networking". This has to do with efforts to use the typical or established pattern of carrying out a new program in a particular industry. Standard networking has many advantages (particularly in handling the large amount of data involved in PERT), but it may also compromise one of the real objectives of PERT, i.e., *obtaining a valid network meaningful to the person(s) who will execute the work.* In the area in which PERT is used most effectively, no two programs are exactly the same, and no two individuals have exactly the same approach to the development of a network. Therefore, standard networks should be introduced with this caution: DPPM should always allow for the possibility of modifications which will match the realities of the program.

APPLICATION TO PRODUCTION

A final problem, and one often viewed as a disadvantage of the PERT technique, is the system lack of applicability to all of the manufacturing effort. As has been stated, PERT deals with the time domain only and does not contain the quantity information required by most manufacturing operations. Nevertheless, PERT can and has been used very effectively, through the preliminary manufacturing phases of production prototypes or pilot model constructions and in the assembly and test of final production equipment still "high on the learning curve". After these phases, established production control techniques which bring in the quantity factor are generally more applicable.

Note, however, that many present-day programs never leave the preliminary manufacturing stage, or at least never enter into mass production. Therefore, a considerable effort has been made to integrate the techniques of PERT within some of the established methods of production control, such as line-of-balance.

STRENGTHS OF PERT

A system which has been made mandatory in large military and NASA projects must have great managerial advantages. The major ones seem to be as follows.

First, it forces careful planning of the projects to which it is applied. In complex projects it is impossible to see how events and activities can be planned without fitting the pieces together in a network. When PERT is used it assures that planning is done in an enterprise. PERT also forces the development of concrete and specific plans and provides a solid basis for evaluating the results of plans.

Second, PERT permits simulation and, therefore, experimentation. In more complex and uncertain programs PERT can, when automated, permit data processing project managers to determine very quickly and with considerable precision the estimated time and cost implications of taking alternative courses of action. For a complex program such as the Space Shuttle, for example, the human mind would be completely incapable of encompassing the many details required for planning. With the successive summations permitted by the computer, project managers are able to look at the entire program and determine appropriate changes in sequencing events and resources.

Third, PERT forces participation in the planning process and pushes it down the managerial line. Operating people make time estimates and, in effect, help to set objectives and goals in the plan.

Fourth, it permits effective control. Most progress reporting techniques provide project management with historic information, but PERT lays a base for anticipatory project management action against troublespots by looking ahead at potential problems. Being forewarned, DP project managers can take action to shift resources or undertake other measures to assure the necessary degree of control. By an appropriate summation of data, PERT can provide different levels of management the needed information for each to exercise the proper control. PERT provides a much improved information system for project managerial control, and permits concentration of action on the most critical problems because it identifies current and future problems.

Finally, the major strength of PERT is its adaptability to many different management needs. The management planning and control concepts upon which it rests are important and valuable in different situations.

REFERENCES

Awani, Alfred O. *Project Management Techniques.* Princeton: Petrocelli Books, Inc., 1983.

Daellenbach, Hans G. and George, John A. *Introduction to Operations Research Techniques.* Newton, MA: Allyn and Bacon, 1978.

Miller, Robert W. "Managing Projects and Program Series," pages 155–157, *Harvard Business Review,* March-April 1962.

Steiner, George A. *Top Management Planning.* New York: Macmillan Publishing Co., Inc., 1969.

Chapter
13
PROJECT COSTS

Data processing project management is responsible for accurately estimating the costs of the data processing project before undertaking the assignment. The addition of cost and manpower to the basic time-oriented network system discussed in earlier chapters provide cost and manpower data directly related to the work sequence and time schedule. Such an addition is aimed at making it possible to predict overruns or underruns in costs and manpower expenditures and to have sufficiently supplementary information concerning critical areas.

TYPES OF PROJECT COSTS

The total cost for any feasible project duration is the sum of the direct and indirect costs. Both costs vary with time.

INDIRECT PROJECT COSTS

Indirect costs traditionally are project overhead charges that continue for the life of the project. These costs cannot be associated directly with an individual activity. The bulk of indirect costs is made up of expenses for supervision, general-purpose equipment, administrative staff, interest taxes, and selling. If bonus or penalty clauses exist in a contract, they usually are included in the indirect cost category since they apply to the total project rather than to one activity. Usually, indirect costs are derived from historical records of costs. Often, indirect costs can be expressed as dollars per unit of time; with an indirect cost of $150 a day, a project of ten days duration incurs a total indirect cost of $1,500, whereas a nine-day project duration would incur a total indirect cost of $1,350—assuming the resources can be used productively if released early. Thus, we normally expect indirect costs to decrease if project duration is expedited.

DIRECT PROJECT COSTS

The direct cost for the project is simply the summation of all the individual direct activity costs for the project. The sources of direct costs are direct labor, materials, equipment; so, direct costs can be tied directly to an activity. Direct costs vary with time; that is, it costs money to buy time off the critical path. Of course, the key is to shorten those individual activities that cost the least to shorten. Note that we can reduce critical activities only by compressing project duration. Without a project network plan, the tendency is to expedite all activities in the project to reduce project duration; this is equivalent to a blanket across-the-board increase in costs, which is indeed a waste.

Recall that in setting activity-time estimates for the project, the network planner assumed that normal operating methods would be used to accomplish the activity. Implicit in "normal operating methods" is the assumption that the task will be performed efficiently and that the method represents the lowest direct cost. Hence, if we wish to shorten project duration by shortening the activity time of an activity on the critical path, it will require more resources (money). For example, if the critical path consisted of only two activities and the costs of expediting the respective activities by one day are $400 and $150 respectively, we would select the second

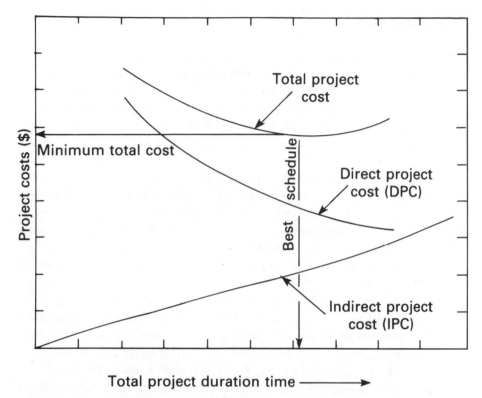

FIGURE 13.1. Determination of best project schedule.

activity to compress project duration because it costs the least. Shortening the critical path by one day adds $150 to the total direct cost of the project. This process of shortening an activity duration time is called "crashing". By computing the least total direct cost for several different feasible project durations, it is possible to derive the curve for the total direct cost of the project shown in Figure 13.1. Note also that the indirect project cost curve is plotted and these two curves are then summed to produce the total project cost curve. The best project schedule can be selected and established from this final curve. This model is impractical to the extent that it assumes the given network is the best way to plan the project. Actually, revision of the network to reflect improved plans is almost always the way time is saved.

CPM COST MODEL

The cost of completing a data processing (DP) project usually can be divided into costs directly related to individual tasks (such as manpower and equipment) and costs related to the duration of the DP project as a whole (such as managerial services and other overhead items). Most tasks can be expedited if more resources are applied to them. Figure 13.2 illustrates such relationships. In simplest form, they are linear.

Direct costs are lowest at a normal level of b_{ij}. Any slowdown beyond this level does not produce further cost savings. The duration cannot be cut below the *crash* level a_{ij}. The data processing project manager's objective is to find a schedule of task durations that minimizes total direct and indirect costs.

For small problems the following heuristic reasoning will usually find the optimal schedule. The data processing project manager start out with an initial schedule using normal duration times for all tasks, yielding, in some cases, the maximum-length critical path. The DP project manager now attempts to step-wise reduce the total project duration by expediting one or more of the critical tasks. As critical tasks are shortened, the float of parallel noncritical tasks decreases and ultimately vanishes. Therefore, further decreases in the earliest project completion time may entail reducing several

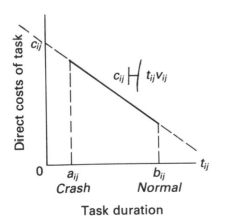 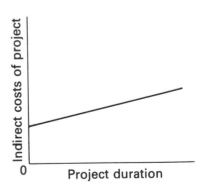

FIGURE 13.2. Costs associated with a project.

critical tasks on parallel critical paths simultaneously. Any critical task or combination of parallel critical tasks are candidates for being expedited when the combined rate of increase of direct costs as measured by their components σ_{ij} is less than the rate of savings of indirect costs. At each step-wise reduction or iteration, the critical task or combination of critical tasks with the smallest total rate of increase of direct costs is chosen as the candidate for being expedited. At least one candidate task is shortened to its crash level, a_{ij}, in each iteration unless a noncritical task becomes critical on a parallel path prior to reaching this level. For small data processing projects these computations are best done on a schedule graph.

ILLUSTRATIVE EXAMPLE

Consider the data processing project shown in Table 13.1. Indirect project costs amounts to $500 per week.

Part (a) of Figure 13.3 shows the schedule graph of the critical path for normal task duration, $t_{ij} = b_{ij}$. Its length is 11 weeks. The total cost is found by summing tasks, the direct costs—$c_{ij} - t_{ij}v_{ij}$—and adding the indirect project costs. The latter amount of $500 is multiplied by the length of the critical path, or $5500. The direct cost for task A is $3,200 - 8(300) = \$800$. Verify that direct costs for the remaining tasks are $600, $1,000, and $100. The total for normal task duration is thus $8,000.

The data processing project manager now find the task on the critical path with the lowest rate of increase of direct costs, v_{ij}. This

TABLE 13.1. CPM cost project.

TASK	PRECEDENCE	NORMAL TIME	CRASH TIME	DIRECT COSTS	
A	—	8 weeks	4 weeks	3200	300
B	—	4	3	1000	100
C	B	2	1	1800	400
D	A,C	3	2	700	200

Week

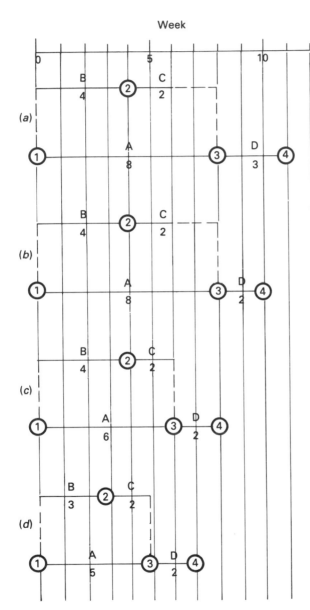

Critical path for normal times:
Total cost $8000
Task D has lowest v_{ij} =
$200 \leqslant 500$ and is a
candidate for expediting.

First iteration:
Task D reduced to $a_{ij} = 2$;
new total cost $7700
Task A now has lowest
$v_{ij} = 300 \leqslant 500$
and is a candidate for
expediting.

Second iteration:
Task A reduced to $t_{ij} = 6$; B
and C now become critical.
New total cost $7300
Tasks A and B together
have sum of v_{ij} of
$300 + 100 \leqslant 500$ and
are candidates for
expediting.

Third iteration:
Task B reduced to $a_{ij} = 3$,
task A reduced to $t_{ij} = 5$.
New total cost $7200
No combinations of tasks
on critical paths have rates
of direct costs totalling less
than 500. Minimum cost
schedule reached.

FIGURE 13.3. Interations of CPM cost model.

is task D with $v_{ij} = \$200$. Since this is less than the weekly rate of indirect project costs, task D is expedited, in this case to its crash time of $a_{ij} = 2$. Costs go up by \$200 in direct costs and down by \$500 in indirect costs. The next critical path has a length of 10 weeks and a total cost of \$7700. This is shown in part (b) of Figure 13.3. At the second iteration, task A is expedited by two weeks. At that point, the total float for tasks B and C have been reduced to zero and become critical tasks. The new critical path of length 8 is shown in part (c). The DP project manager now searches for combinations of tasks on parallel critical paths for simultaneous time reductions. Tasks A and B have a rate of increase of direct costs of \$300 + \$100, or \$400 which is less than the rate of indirect project costs. The maximum reduction possible is one week, at which point task B reaches its crash time. The new critical path of 8 weeks is shown in part (d). No further time reduction can be made now without increasing total costs. Why? The optimal project duration is thus 8 weeks at a cost of \$7,200.

Although this method is fairly effective for small data processing projects, it becomes cumbersome for even moderate-size projects of several dozen tasks, and at that point an optimal solution can no longer be guaranteed. More powerful approaches, such as the linear programming formulation of scheduling problems are then needed to tackle the problem. (This is the topic of Chapter 14.)

PERT/COST

PERT/Cost is an extension of PERT/Time, wherein a cost dimension is added. PERT/Cost is distinguished by seven features:

1. a work breakdown structure
2. work packages
3. networks
4. time/cost interrelationships
5. periodic updating of networks and estimates
6. program evaluation
7. taking corrective managerial action, if necessary.

In PERT/Cost, overall costs are broken down into successively smaller pieces of hardware, services, equipment, or facilities until manageable units for planning and control are derived. These units are called work packages (e.g., wing or fuselage). Cost accounting numbers serve to summarize costs of packages at all levels within the work breakdown structure.

Networks that interrelate activities and events for work packages are constructed as in PERT/Time (see Chapter 12). Either the program schedule or the cost of the entire program may determine the amount of the physical resources assigned to a particular work package. The critical factor here is how any particular work package fits into the entire program. There is a trade-off between cost and time; generally, however, the schedule considerations of the entire program dictate the cost of an individual work package.

Once the time constraints for a work package are defined, the corresponding resources in terms of manpower, equipment, etc. are calculated. The latter in turn determine the time estimates of the network describing the work package. Time and cost estimates of the work package are then calculated, and each work package is assigned a budget on the basis of these estimates. Thus, a comparison of actual and budgeted amounts for the work accomplished can later be made at the work package level. By the same token, the summation of work package costs throughout the work breakdown structure determines the estimated cost of the program within the time constraints used.

Periodically, an estimate-to-complete is made for each work package in progress. The sum of costs already incurred plus the estimate-to-complete determines the estimate at completion for the work package. A comparison may then be made between planned versus actual (including estimate-to-complete) costs as shown in Figure 13.4.

The networks and cost estimates are revised periodically to conform to actual and to planned changes in the program. From them, summary reports showing a breakdown of planned versus actual costs are constructed, and this will help a data processing project manager to see where corrective action is necessary and possible. Furthermore, he should be able to forecast future bottlenecks because the time network can predict schedule slippages, and displays

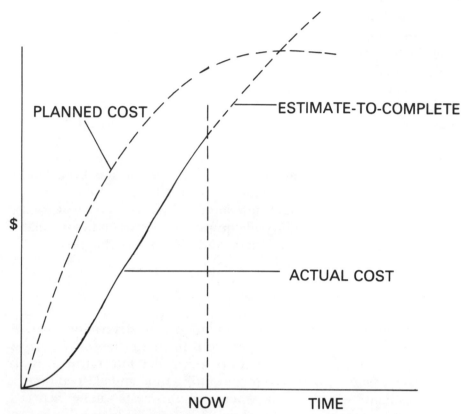

FIGURE 13.4. Planned versus actual costs.

such as Figure 13.4 can predict cost overruns. The data processing project manager now has the tools to plan and simultaneously control the time and cost dimensions of his project.

COST ACCOUNTING

The total cost for any feasible data processing project duration has already been discussed in some detail in the preceding section. In this case, the two basic accounting methods available are job costing (project or direct cost accounting) and standard cost accounting (indirect cost accounting).

The first establishes a job number; each project and all labor and machine rentals are charged accordingly. This simple system is helpful in product profit-and-loss accounting. In data processing this method has some disadvantages; for example, the cost of a re-run would be directly charged to the project whose work was being redone even though the basic cause was machine or operator failure. Similarly, the costs of testing, set up, assembly, and the like would be charged directly, and operator or programmer inefficiency would be charged to the project on which it occurred.

Standard cost accounting avoids this kind of situation. Under this method, established performance standards are converted by the accounting department into standard job costs on which basis charges are made, including all equipment rentals and costs related thereto (operators, programmers, and all indirect charges).

SOFTWARE COST ESTIMATING

The objective of software cost estimating is to determine what resources will be needed to produce and maintain the software associated with a product. Resources of particular interest in software cost estimating are manpower, computing time and elapsed time. A good estimate will also show when and how costs will be incurred, so that the estimate can be used not only to provide justification for software development but also as a management control tool.

PROBLEMS IN SOFTWARE COST ESTIMATING

Software cost estimating is a complicated process because projected development is influenced by a large number of variables, many of which are subjective, nonquantifiable and interrelated in complex ways.

Some reasons for not obtaining a good estimate are:

1. A lack of understanding of the process of software development and maintenance.
2. A lack of understanding of the effects of various technical and management constraints.

3. A view that each project is unique, which inhibits project-to-project comparisons.

4. A lack of historic data against which the model can be checked.

5. A lack of historic data for calibration. The process by which a model is fitted to a given cost-estimating situation is called "calibration". The calibration of a model may be performed using formal curve-fitting methods on a representative historical data set by selecting values from experience, or, with some models, by running the model in calibration mode to assign values to selected parameters using appropriate historic data.

In addition, current estimating techniques suffer from:

1. Inadequate definition of the objective of the estimate (whether it is intended as a project management tool or as a decision-making aid) and at what stage the estimate is required so that inputs and outputs can be chosen appropriately.

2. Inadequate specification of the scope of the estimate (what is included and what is excluded).

3. Inadequate definition of and understanding of the premises on which it is based.

SOFTWARE ESTIMATING METHODS

Broadly, there are five methods of estimating the cost of developing and maintaining a software system:

1. personal experience, using analogy with similar historic projects and extrapolation based mainly on size and difficulty

2. the constraint method

3. percentage-of-hardware method

4. simulation

5. parametric modelling.

The first method, sometimes referred to as "Wildly Aspiring Guess (WAG)," has been and is still very popular because no better method has been proven. One of its problems is that each estimate is based on different experiences and therefore different estimates of cost of a single project may vary widely. A second problem is that the estimator must have experience of a similar project of a similar size. Experience does not work on systems larger than those in the base used for comparison nor on systems with a totally different content.

The constraint method is equivalent to taking an educated guess. Based on schedule, cost or manpower constraints, a data processing project manager agrees to develop the software within the constraints. The constraints are not related to the complexity of the project. In general, this method will result in delivery of the software within the specified constraints, but with the specification adjusted to fit the constraints.

The percentage-of-hardware method is based on two assumptions:

1. software costs are a fixed percentage of hardware costs;
2. hardware cost estimates are usually reasonably accurate.

However, other studies have shown that the first of these assumptions is not justified.

Simulation is widely used in estimating life cycle support costs for hardware systems, but is not appropriate for software costs estimating because it is based on a statistical analysis of hardware failure rates and spares logistics for which there is no software equivalent.

The parameric models (sometimes called SWAG, or "Scientific WAG") may be divided into three classes:

1. *Regression models*—The quantity to be estimated is mathematically related to a set of input parameters. The parameters of the hypothesised relationship are arrived at by statistical analysis and curve-fitting on an appropriate historical database. There may be more than one relationship to deal with differ-

ent databases, different types of applications and different developer characteristics.

2. *Heuristic Models*—In an heuristic model, observation and interpretation of historic data are combined with supposition and experience. Relationships between variables are stated without justification. The advantage of heuristic models is that they need not wait for formal relationships to be established describing how the cost driving variables are related. A given model can become very effective in a stable predicting environment. If the model fails it is adjusted to deal with the situation. It therefore becomes a repository for the collected experience and insights of the designers.

3. *Phenomenological Models*—The phenomenological model is based on an hypothesis that the software development process can be explained in terms of some more widely applicable process or idea. For example, the Putnam model is based on the belief that the distribution of effort during the software life cycle has the same characteristics as the distribution of effort required to solve a given number of problems given a constant learning rate. This has been shown to follow the Rayleigh distribution.

It should be noted that the models considered do not necessarily fit tidily into one or other of the three classes, but if a model fits more into one class than either of the others, it will be regarded as a member of that class.

SOME FACTORS INFLUENCING SOFTWARE COSTS

The factors which influence the cost of a software project may be divided into those which are contributed by the development and maintenance organization—many of which are subjective—and those inherent to the software project itself. Current models differ in respect of the factors that are required as specific inputs. Many different factors may be subsumed in a single parameter in some models, particularly the more subjective parameters.

SIZE OF THE SOFTWARE

A favorite measure for software system size is the lines of operational code, or deliverable code (operational code plus supporting code, such as for hardware diagnostics) measured either in object code statements or in source code statements. It is rarely specified whether source code statements include nonexecutable code such as comments and data declarations. Other measures are lines of code including nondeliverable code (i.e. all code written during project development, whether deliverable or not, including support software and test software), the number of functions to be performed or number of modules (where function and module are intuitive measures), or the number of inputs and outputs.

Parametric cost estimating models relate cost in some way to the size estimate and are therefore heavily dependent on the accuracy of the size estimate. In some models a reasonableness check of the size estimate is included. The size is indicated in more than one way and the different estimates are checked for consistency. One way to do this is by indicating the class of function to be performed by the software system and the languages to be employed. A database of past projects is then searched to see what range of sizes have previously been achieved for that type of software. (Most databases do not include the size or cost of nondeliverable software.)

Another size indicator sometimes used is related to the size and structure of the database to be handled by the operational software.

Some models include algorithms for computing project size, either by splitting the project into smaller parts or by analogy with other similar software. Other models use size estimates as the starting point.

Studies have showed that size estimates can vary by as much as 10 times if the units are not well-defined. Since some support software, test software and diagnostic software may be nondeliverable although developed on the project, size estimates for the same project will be very different if such software is included in one size estimate and not in another. Similarly, if a model makes an assumption about the proportion of the total software included because it assumes a certain percentage of software for simulation of the environment or other nonoperational software, this should be clearly stated. Other studies have found that deliverable code averaged 70 percent of total code developed, with a standard deviation of about 30 percent.

QUALITY

Quality, documentation, maintainability and reliability standards required are all included in a single factor. This factor is sometimes called the platform type, reflecting the fact that the documentation and reliability requirements for software in a manned spacecraft are higher than in a stand-alone statistical package. The documentation and reliability requirements may be given a defined numeric scale from 1 to 10. In some estimating models there is also a parameter for the number of different locations at which the software will be run.

Prior study found that as the number of pages of external documentation required per thousand lines of source code increased by 10 percent, programmer productivity decreased by 63 percent. If independent validation and verification were required, then the cost of the software increased by about 20 percent.

LANGUAGES TO BE USED

The class of programming language used affects the cost, size, timescale and documentation effort. Some models require the percentage of software in each language, others merely require input of the language to be used in the majority of the software. Some models only apply to projects using assembler code.

Prior study estimates that the ratio of the total life cycle cost of a project programmed entirely in assembler to the total life cycle cost of the same project programmed entirely in a high level language could be as high as 5:1.

COMPUTING RESOURCES

Many models ignore the cost of computing (hardware and computer time). Others assume a fixed percentage of the total cost will be consumed by this item, while yet others take an average cost per man-month with different average costs for each phase in the development.

LABOR RATES

If the model estimates costs in terms of money rather than man-hours, the relationship of labor costs of man-hours within the development organization may be required by the model. The model may be capable of reflecting increased rates for personnel required to work unsocial hours due to decreases in the development time-scale or a lack of availability of development tools.

INFLATION

Costs estimated in terms of money rather than man-hours may take inflation rates into account, as well as the costs in a base year. If inflation is not built into the model, the rate of inflation may be required as an input.

PERSONNEL

The personnel assigned to a project contribute to the cost depending on manpower levels.

Most projects are resource limited in that the number of people with a given skill available to the project is limited. The level of manpower available at any stage in a project will affect the time-scale, and hence the cost, but it is not a required input for most models.

DEVELOPMENT ENVIRONMENT

The adequacy of the development environment, both in hardware and software, depends largely on the management of the development organization. This factor is not usually requested as an explicit input to a model, but may be implicit in the calibration of the model or in a general management parameter. Three aspects of the development environment which are sometimes required as inputs to models are:

1. *Development machine.* The adequacy of the development machine as a host for developing software for the selected target, and the availability of the development machine to the software development personnel, will affect both the schedule and cost of software development. Prior study shows that time-sharing, where the development machine is constantly available, is 20 percent more productive than batch systems for software development.

2. *Availability of associated software and hardware.* Projected late delivery of some item of associated hardware or software can affect schedules and costs. Models which use development schedules cater to this by rerunning with different input parameters.

3. *Software tools and techniques to be used during system design and development.* That newer tools and techniques properly applied can reduce development effort has been demonstrated. Prior study estimates that savings of up to 40 percent can be achieved by the application of modern techniques. Among techniques to be considered are:

    a. host/target development systems; (Prior study indicates that development on a different machine from the target has an adverse effect on cost unless the target has inadequate facilities for software development.)

    b. high level languages;

    c. MASCOT or a similar design and test methodology;

     d. prototyping;

     e. development libraries;

     f. development database;

     g. word processors for documentation;

     h. adequate programming support environment.

(This list is not complete.)

ESTIMATE SOFTWARE SIZE

Most models start from an estimate of project size, although some models include algorithms for computing size from various other system characteristics, such as units of work.

CONVERT SIZE ESTIMATE TO LABOR ESTIMATE

Some models convert from size to labor, other go directly from size to money estimates. In regression models, these conversions are either derived from productivity measures using the "cost per instruction" type of equation or are derived using the "general summing equation". The "cost per instruction" equation has the form

$$e = a*s* *b + c$$

    where:

* is multiply

** is raise to the power

e = effort needed, for example, man-months of effort or cost to develop the program

s = size of project, for example, number of machine level instructions; values are chosen for a, b and c by curve-fitting on as large an historic database as possible. Different values of a, b, and c are appropriate to different development organizations, different project types, different sets of units for measuring e and s, and different items included in the estimate.

The "general summing equation" has the form:

$$e = a1*f1 + a2*f2 + a3*f3 + \cdots + aifi + \cdots + am*fm$$

where ai are input parameters derived from the description of the software characteristics (including size) and the characteristics of the development environment, and the values fi are chosen by curve-fitting on a suitable historic database.

In heuristic models, the relationship of size estimate to labor estimate is not necessarily based on a statistically derived expression. In a phenomenological model the relationship would derive from the underlying theory.

ADJUST ESTIMATE FOR SPECIAL PROJECT CHARACTERISTICS

In some models an effective size is calculated from the basic size estimate discussed earlier, while in others from an effective labor or cost estimate. The effective estimate is an adjustment of the basic estimate intended to take account of any special project characteristics which make it dissimilar to the pattern absorbed in the underlying historic database. Such variations (which include the effect of volatility of the requirement, different software tools, difficulty above the level of projects in the database, or a different method of dealing with support cost) are frequently based on intuitively derived relationships, unsupported by statistical verification.

The adjustment may precede amalgamation of the costs of the different phases, or a single adjustment may be applied to the total.

DIVIDE THE TOTAL ESTIMATE INTO DIFFERENT PROJECT PHASES

Each model which deals with a project's schedule makes assumptions about the allocation of effort in the different project phases. The simplest assumption defines a percentage of the effort for each phase, such as the much-quoted 40 percent design, 20 percent code, and 40 percent test rule. It should be noted that this rule is not universally agreed. Some research shows that other percentages may be more appropriate, and the percentage in each phase may depend on other software characteristics. Some models assume that manpower allocation with respect to time follows a rectangular distribution, others that it follows a beta distribution (PRICE-S) or a Rayleigh distribution (Putnam). In general, the assumptions on manpower allocation with respect to time are based on historic data. The effect of deviating from the historic patterns has not been considered.

ESTIMATE NONTECHNICAL LABOR COSTS AND COSTS OF COMPUTER TIME

Where these costs are explicitly included, they are often calculated as a percentage of the technical labor costs. Sometimes such costs are included implicitly because they were included in the database from which the model was derived.

SUM THE COSTS

The nontechnical labor costs and the cost of computer time where these are included in the estimates are added to the technical costs of the different phases of the software life cycle to obtain an aggregated cost estimate.

REFERENCES

Awani, Alfred O. *Project Management Techniques*. Princeton: Petrocelli Books, Inc., 1983.

Brandon, Dick H. *Management Standards for Data Processing*. New York: Van Nostrand Reinhold Company, Inc., 1963.

Daellenbach, Hans G. and George, John A. *Introduction to Operations Research Techniques*. Newton, MA: Allyn and Bacon, 1978.

Gray, Clifford F. *Essentials of Project Management*. Princeton: Petrocelli Books, Inc., 1981.

Steiner, George A. *Top Management Planning*. New York: Macmillan Publishing Co., Inc., 1969.

Stanley, M. "Software Cost Estimating," Royal Signals and Radar Establishment, Memorandum 3472, Controller HMSO London, May 13, 1982.

Chapter
14
LINEAR PROGRAMMING FORMULATION OF SCHEDULING PROBLEM

$\mathbf{A}$s we have seen in Chapter 11, one could use a trial-and-error approach to making crashing decisions, but in large CPM networks one will probably need mathematical procedure to arrive at the optimal decision. Some network problems can be formulated as linear programs.

Linear programming problems are concerned with the efficient use or allocation of limited resources to meet desired objectives. These problems are characterized by the large number of solutions that satisfy the basic conditions of each problem. The selection of a particular solution as the best solution to the problem depends on some aim or overall objective implied in the statement of the problem. A solution that satisfies both the conditions of the problem and the given objective is termed an "optimum solution".

ILLUSTRATIVE EXAMPLE

While several solution procedures and variations exist for the CPM crashing procedure, the following linear programming model will

TABLE 14.1. Normal and crash activity data for the hypothetical data processing project.

ACTIVITY	NORMAL TIME (τ)	CRASH TIME (τ')	TOTAL NORMAL COST (C_n)	TOTAL CRASH COST (C_c)	MAXIMUM CRASH DAYS $(M = \tau - \tau')$	CRASH COST PER DAY $K = \dfrac{C_c - C_n}{M}$
A	7	4	$500	$800	3	$100
B	3	2	200	350	1	150
C	6	4	500	900	2	200
D	3	1	200	500	2	150
E	2	1	300	550	1	250
			$1,700	$3,100		

be used to analyze the hypothetical data processing project (see Table 14.1) for the CPM network shown in Figure 14.1. First we define the decision variables. Let:

X_i = time of occurence of event i, $i = 1,2,3,4,5$
Y_i = amount of crash time used for activity j,
$j = A,B,C,D$, or E.

Since the total normal time project cost is fixed at $1,700 (see Table 14.1), we can minimize the total project cost (normal cost plus crash cost) simply by minimizing the crashing costs. Thus our linear programming objective function becomes

$$\min \textstyle\sum_j K_j Y_j \qquad [14\text{-}1]$$

or

Note that the X_i variables indicating event occurrences do not result in costs; thus they have zero coefficients in the objective function.

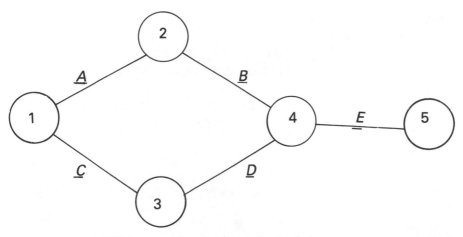

FIGURE 14.1. CPM network of a hypothetical data processing project.

$$\min 100_{Y_A} + 150_{Y_B} + 200_{Y_C} + 150_{Y_D} + 250_{Y_E} \qquad \text{[14-2]}$$

The constraints on the model involve describing the network, limiting the activity crash times, and meeting the project completion date. Of these, constraints used to describe the network are perhaps the most difficult. The constraints are based on the following conditions:

1. The time of occurrence of event i (X_i) must be greater than or equal to the activity completion time for all activities leading into the node or event.
2. An activity start time is equal to the occurrence time of its preceding node or event.
3. An activity time is equal to its normal time less the length of time it is crashed.

Using an event occurrence time of zero at node 1 ($X_1 = 0$), we can create the following set of network description constraints:
Event 2:

$$X_2 \geqslant \tau_A - Y_A + 0$$

where

$$X_2 = \text{occurrence time for event 2}$$
$$\tau_A - Y_A = \text{actual time for activity A}$$

$$0 = \text{start time for activity A } (X_i - 0)$$
$$X_2 \geqslant 7 - Y_A$$

or

$$X_2 + Y_A \geqslant 7 \qquad\qquad [14\text{-}3]$$

Event 3:

$$X_3 \geqslant \tau_c - Y_c + 0$$
$$X_3 + Y_3 \geqslant 6 \qquad\qquad [14\text{-}4]$$

Since two activities enter node 4, we have the following two constraints:

Event 4:

$$X_4 \geqslant \tau_B - Y_B + X_2$$
$$X_4 \geqslant \tau_D - Y_D + X_3 \qquad\qquad [14\text{-}5]$$

or

Event 5:

$$X_5 \geqslant \tau_E - Y_E + X_4$$
$$-X_4 + X_5 + Y_E \geqslant 2 \qquad\qquad [14\text{-}6]$$

The constraints [14-3] through [14-6] are necessary to describe our CPM network (Figure 14.1).

The maximum allowable crash time constraints are:

$$Y_A \leqslant 3 \qquad\qquad [14\text{-}7]$$
$$Y_B \leqslant 1 \qquad\qquad [14\text{-}8]$$

$$Y_C \leq 2 \qquad\qquad [14\text{-}9]$$
$$Y_D \leq 2 \qquad\qquad [14\text{-}10]$$
$$Y_E \leq 1 \qquad\qquad [14\text{-}11]$$

and the project completion date provides another constraint:

$$X_5 \leq 10 \qquad\qquad [14\text{-}12]$$

Adding the non-negativity restrictions and solving the above nine-variable, 11-constraint ([14.3] through [14.12]) linear programming model provides the following solution:

$$
\begin{array}{ll}
X_2 = 5 & Y_A = 2 \\
X_3 = 6 & Y_B = 0 \\
X_4 = 8 & Y_C = 0 \\
X_5 = 10 & Y_D = 1 \\
 & Y_E = 0
\end{array}
$$

Objective function = $350

This solution requires that we crash activity A for two days ($200) and activity D for one day ($150). Thus the total crashed project cost is $1,700 + $350 = $2,050. The crashed activity schedule for the data processing project is given in Table 14.2. Note that all activities are critical.

TABLE 14.2. Crashed activity schedule for the hypothetical data processing project.

ACTIVITY	CRASHED TIME	EARLIEST START	LATEST START	EARLIEST FINISH	LATEST FINISH	SLACK
A	5	0	0	5	5	0
B	3	5	5	8	8	0
C	6	0	0	6	6	0
D	2	6	6	8	8	0
E	2	8	8	10	10	0

Resolving the linear programming model with alternate project completion dates (constraint [14.12]) will show the data processing project manager the cost associated with crashing the project to meet the alternate deadlines.

Due to the substantial formulation and computational effort associated with scheduling and controlling large projects, most applications of PERT and CPM involve the use of computer programs developed to perform the appropriate network analysis. (For more information on linear programming, refer to a text on operation research or management science).

REFERENCES

Awani, Alfred O. *Project Management Techniques*. Princeton: Petrocelli Books, Inc., 1983.

Anderson, David R., Sweeney Dennis J. and Williams, Thomas A. *An Introduction to Management Science*. St. Paul: West Publishing, 1976.

Chapter
15
PROJECT CONTROL

Project control is the process which evaluates project performance toward predetermined goals. Efficiency is evaluated in the sense of optimum output for a given input and effectiveness in the sense that the specific performance contributes to achievement of project goals in the desired manner. The critical factor in the control process is timely action to modify operations so that they coincide with predetermined standards or goals. This means that the control system must include the following:

A logical description of goals, objectives, or standards in quantitative and qualitative terms.

A means of measuring current operations in terms of the same units of measure in which goals or standards are established.

An adequate information system to transmit operational performance data to the decision-maker for comparison purposes.

An action system to adjust the operations to conform with original standards.

Each of these elements is essential. For example, the best possible system on on-line sampling and analysis is of little value to the data processing project manager if he is unable to influence or adjust the production process in a timely fashion.

The control process may be treated as a series of distinct steps:

1. Set standards.
2. Define the performance criteria or limits of acceptable deviation
3. Measure actual performance.
4. Compare actual versus standard performance.
5. Take corrective action and re-evaluate standard if required.

It is apparent that the control process overlaps the planning function. This overlap is shown schematically in Figure 15.1.

The setting of standards is accomplished in the planning process, most frequently in the budget where general objectives or programs are translated into specific measureable units such as cost, revenue, time or items. Quantitative standards may be set by the evaluation of historical data (as in the use of raw material per unit of output) or by design (as in piecework output per man-hour.)

A system which controls all factors within tight limits is prohibitive in cost, as well as unnecessary. Some long-range objectives may require no defined control limits but rather a simple comparison of planned and actual performance on an annual or semi-annual basis. Other objectives, such as those in quality control, may require constant monitoring and close control limits. However, the preciseness of these limits should give consideration to tolerances of the measuring process and the cost of making adjustments.

The measurement of performance is the easiest task of the entire control process in that units of measure were established when the standard was set and only a physical count of time, units, labor hours or other measurements are required. Special measurement problems, if any, are technical rather than managerial in nature.

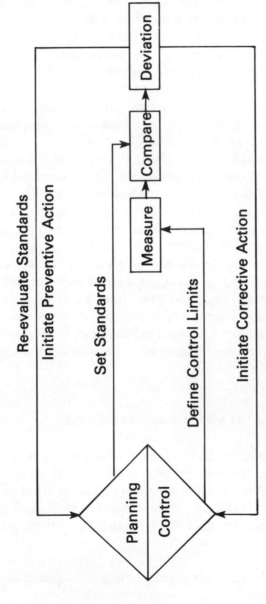

FIGURE 15.1. Interrelationship of planning and control.

179

The final step in the control process is preventive action. This is basically a planning process. It requires careful analysis of the actual rather than the apparent causes of the deviation, consideration of future courses of action which will adhere more closely to standards, and a decision as to any changes required in goals, processes, sensors, or standards. This preventive action may require major changes and call for a repetition of the entire planning process.

There are many control systems: finance, procurement, manufacturing, quality control, project/program management, and so on. To some extent, these control systems can be categorized as management (decision) systems or operational (technical) systems. Ideally, all DPPM control systems are fully integrated to permit the reconciliation of various accomplishments and failures. While fully integrated systems can seldom be achieved, a most effective common denominator is dollars—cost, profit, expenditures. For this reason, the integrated budget is a universal control device.

Time/Cost event network analyses such as PERT and CPM are also powerful tools for control. As a control device, the network indicates deviations from predicted times or costs for specific program events (milestones). These identified deviations immediately focus on current and future problems and, through an analysis of the network, permit an examination of alternate courses of corrective action.

MONITORING AND MEASURING PROGRESS

Let us start by putting PERT/Cost (discussed in Chapter 13) in context with a program management system called Program Appraisal and Review (PAR). Unlike operating reports used in many businesses, PAR is specialized for development work and applies to the program manager level. A PAR report on a program has the following sections:

1. Customer's and program manager's appraisal of program performance

2. Program performance information

    a. Cost (program budget)

    b. Time (program schedule)

    c. Technical performance (product specification conformity)

    d. Reliability insurance performance

3. Analysis of critical problems

4. Accomplishments to date

5. General program information

It will not come as a surprise to anyone that two of the key performance variables in PAR are cost and schedule performance. What may not be widely understood is the futility of trying to judge true development program cost performance from only a cost performance report. If one of our programs is reported behind schedule but on cost budget, not only is the final development article likely to be delivered late, but also the final program cost is likely to exceed budget, or to "overrun". This is particularly likely on development programs performed for the government where, very often in the past, at the desire of the government, cost and schedule estimates have been based on first-time success.

Time lost on a development program represents work not done, work that will cost additional money to complete. To put this in perspective, project managers of nondevelopment businesses can imagine their horror if they were to discover that when their financial reports showed an operation to be on budget, it often meant only that the budgeted (planned) amount of money had been spent while the planned amount of work (for that money) had not been accomplished.

This is where PERT/Cost comes in. The PERT/Cost system provides a general operating report for a development program with a cost and schedule performance section that stands on its own. Only through a management system that directly relates (a) development work vs. schedule performance to (b) development work vs. cost performance can the data processing project manager obtain meaningful answers to the following questions:

How much overrun in cost is this program now?

How far behind schedule is this program now?

What parts are causing the schedule and cost problems?

Are the customer and I both getting the same schedule and performance information on this problem?

Are the program team and I getting the same schedule and cost performance information on this program?

Most data processing project managers will agree that these are fundamental questions, but I suspect that many will argue that satisfactory answers were available prior to PERT/Cost. To see if this is really so, let us apply the questions just mentioned to an hypothetical data processing project made up of typical elements drawn from several projects.

OVERRUN IN COST

On how many data processing projects have the DP project managers received all of the cost performance information shown in Figure 15.2? I would like to call particular attention to Curve E, labeled "overrun" (read on the right-hand scale).

This curve indicates the percentage by which the total costs "today" are exceeding the original costs budgeted for this date plus the costs being lost, in effect, because work is not being accomplished on schedule. This overrun curve goes beyond the usual forecast of what the excess of actual overbudgeted costs will be at project completion. The curve shows what the overrun has been in past months, tells what is now (49 percent) and what it is estimated to become at project completion (24 percent). The curve thus provides a complete profile on overrun from project inception to completion.

This overrun profile is calculated from the actual cost to date

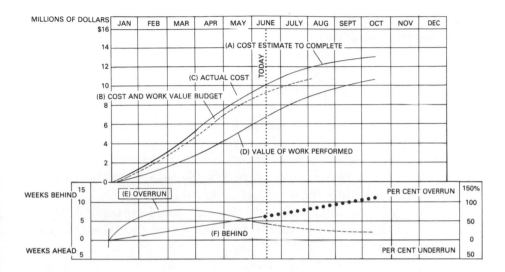

FIGURE 15.2. Cost-of-work curves.

(Curve C) and the value of work performed to date (Curve D), each measured through the PERT-Cost information system. The actual cost figure is a widely understood term deriving from the usual accounting summation of the total expenditures to date. The value-of-work-performed figure, however, is less widely understood, so let me explain.

As a part of the original contract negotiation, the proposed cost of each work task is negotiated. For example, on an aerospace development program each preliminary design, each "black box" development, each system design, procurement, fabrication, and environmental test, each launch and flight data analysis task is cost-estimated, negotiated with the government, and then made into task budgets. It follows that if "today" 265 of these discrete tasks (segments of work) have been completed, then—according to the PERT-Cost rules—the value of work performed to date is the originally budgeted cost of those specific 265 tasks. And if the money spent to date is greater than the negotiated cost of those 265 tasks, then we have overrun.

The foregoing explains why the budget curve (Curve B) is called the "Cost and Work Value Budget". This emphasizes that a budget provides not only the target for the costs to be spent but also the target for the simultaneous "value of work" to be created.

EVALUATING PERFORMANCE

On how many projects have the data processing project managers received a single, cost-weighted measure of schedule performance, with the schedule status of each work element weighted according to its value? In my experience, on practically none. Yet the PERT-Cost system can supply this very valuable measure.

Curve F in Figure 15.2, labeled "Behind" (read on the left-hand scale), shows just this information, indicating that the schedule status is now six weeks behind and that it is estimated to become 11 weeks behind at project completion. It provides an inception-to-completion schedule-status profile.

The data processing project manager who has not been able to place a value on the work performed now, the overrun (or under-run) now, and the overall schedule status now, will find that a new dimension has been added to his understanding of development project/program performance. The ability to provide a measure of the value of work output at each point of the project is PERT/Cost's strongest asset, and derives from the product and responsibility work breakdown structures through which all work is costed and scheduled.

IDENTIFYING PROJECT PROBLEMS

A key feature of the PAR system mentioned earlier is the structure of the charts used to provide the project manager with project/program information. Each status chart (cost, schedule, technical performance, and reliability assurance performance) is carefully designed to display the overall program along with supporting details that pinpoint sources of problems. Thus, with PERT/Cost, the product and responsibility work breakdown structures make it possible to determine which end-item subdivisions (i.e., parts of the product being developed) and which organization components are causing whatever status in the overall program picture, whether good or bad. These breakdowns, while useful for initial estimating and budgeting of cost and schedule, can also be used for subsequent reporting of cost and schedule. Here they can be particularly helpful in locating sources of problems.

For such use, a set of curves similar to Figure 15.2 can be constructed for each end-item subdivision and for each organization component. The first level breakdown (e.g., subsystems of a space vehicle system) is the one in which the project/program manager is primarily interested, although the PERT/Cost work breakdown structures may go to the component and part level for the product, and to the lowest level of management for the organization. To condense the overall space vehicle system curves, the curves for each subsystem of the space vehicle system, and the curves for the development managers reporting to the project manager all onto one sheet, and thus to put the total program in perspective, we use a bar summary to represent the system and each "first level" subsystem and organization curves.

Figure 15.3 demonstrates how such a bar summary is constructed, in this case for the overall program. It is an orthogonal projection of selected portions of the curves at the top of the figure (the same A, B, C, and D curves shown in Figure 15-2) onto the horizontal bar-summary shown below the "overrun" and "behind" curves. So constructed, the bar summary emphasizes:

(G) *How late today?* (The hash bar spans six weeks on the calendar-time scale).

(H) *How overrun today?* (The figures next to the vertical today line indicate a 49 percent overrun).

(I) *How late at completion?* (The time span between the terminal points of the upper and lower scale is 11 weeks).

(J) *How overrun at completion?* (The figures in parentheses at the right of the bar summary indicates 24 percent).

In addition, the actual costs to date can be read on the horizontal scale for C where the triangular pointer indicates actual costs to date of $10 million. The value of work performed to date can be

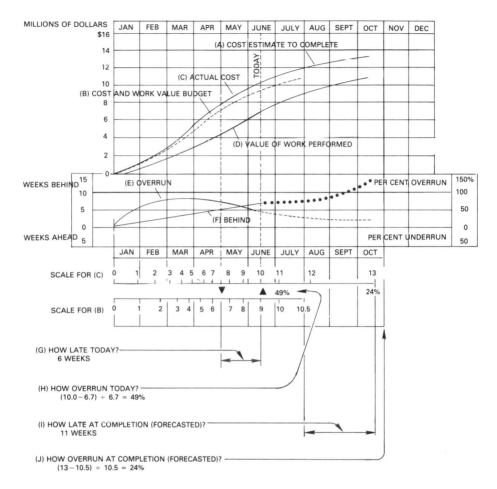

FIGURE 15.3. Construction of bar-summary of the cost-of-work curves.

read on the scale for **B**, where the triangular pointer shows a value of work performed to date of $6.7 million. We can construct bar summaries for the appropriate subdivisions which permits us to extend our viewpoint to the sources of interrelated schedule and cost problems and to make an important step toward understanding program schedule and cost trade-offs.

Figure 15.4 is an example of all this on one sheet. It happens to be an actual PERT/Cost summary chart designed for use in PAR.

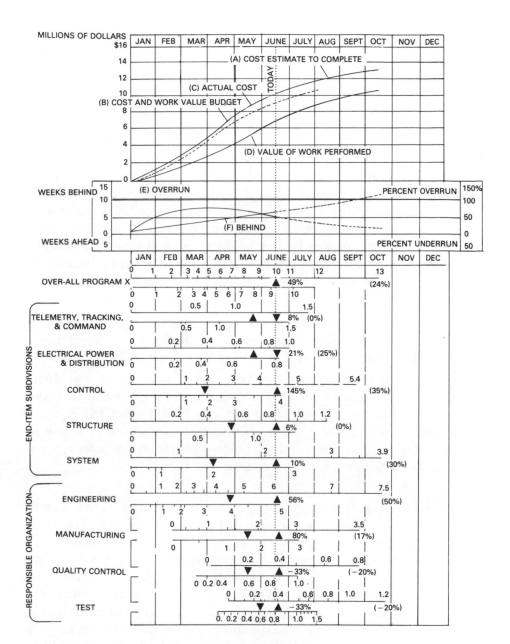

FIGURE 15.4. Report for general management.

At the top are, again, the same overall program curves seen in Figure 15.3. Then comes the bar summary for the overall program as developed in Figure 15.3, and for the subdivisions. The chart is essentially the PERT/Cost Management Summary Report called for in the Department of Defense and National Aeronautics and Space Administration Guide—PERT-Cost Systems Design (June 1962)—except that it has been translated into a different kind of graphic summary.

In this instance, having discerned an overall problem in terms of cost overrun and schedule slippage in the top portions of the chart, we examine the major program subdivisions in the lower portion to determine the sources of this problem. We can do this from two points of view because in Figure 15.4 one grouping of subdivisions covers schedule and costs by end-item, and the other by the responsible organizations. Thus, the chart shows that:

> From the length of its hash marked bar in the figure, engineering is the responsible organization with the most problems—overall 7½ weeks late and 56 percent overrun ($2.2 million).

> The "control" end-item subdivision represents a major problem area. With a slippage of 11 weeks (length of hash bar in terms of time scale at top of chart) and a "today" overrun of 145 percent (figure immediately to the right of the hash bar), it is apparent that this part of the product being developed has contributed heavily to "engineering's" cost and schedule difficulties.

Evidently, the engineering organization is experiencing serious difficulties in controls development. If we wish, we may follow up on this program clue by examining a cost-of-work summation of controls engineering across the engineering organization's several programs and from these determine if the problem is local or general. Conversely, by looking at another level of breakdown on the program, we might discover that the difficulty is predominantly in drafting (or some other subfunction). Either way the message is clear: action is needed. We have a measure of where our problem is and the degree of that problem.

ILLUSTRATIVE EXAMPLE

Six weeks after the initiation of an experimental re-entry vehicle program, it was noted that a cost trend showed the advanced technologies organization to be 150 percent overrun on the program, as contrasted with more reasonable costs from the other organizations (engineering, manuacturing, and so on).

Anyone associated with development work knows how difficult it is to show, early in a program, that an advanced technologies effort is overrunning. When the project/program manager of such an effort is criticized for being over budget, his response often is "yes, we are over budget, but we are also farther ahead than we had thought we would be by this time."

In this case, however, since PERT/Cost was measuring not only the over budget amount but also how much over value-of-work-performed we were, this answer could not be used.

Upon investigation, it was learned that, as an economy measure during the planning phases of the program, the systems analysis work previously planned had been drastically cut back over the objections of the manager of advanced technologies who now was overspending to accomplish other work he believed was necessary to minimize program risk.

Thus it is that PERT/Cost that was the basis for finding an early overrun and for pointing out what might be a flaw in the program plan.

FUTURE PROBLEM

One additional discernment can be made from reading the pointers and scales in Figure 15.4. The control subsystem has to date cost $4.4 million—for which expenditure only $1.8 million of work has been completed (145 percent overrun). In terms of the budget there is a $2.2 million value of work yet to be done ($4 million total budgeted value minus $1.8 million value completed).

Let us suppose, as the figure shows, that it is now estimated that this $2.2 million value of remaining work will be finished for $1 million cost ($5.4 million estimated cost to complete minus $4.4 million cost spent to date). In the author's experience, this is a most improbable occurrence, and it is therefore improbable as to whether the controls job can be completed for only the 35 percent overrun shown in September—in light of "today's" picture.

CONTROL OF THE PLAN

The final step in the planning process is the control of the approved plan. The control system compares actual performance against the plan. To the extent possible, the system should filter out insignificant deviations and report only the significant ones requiring management attention. This can be done by establishing control tolerances for each relevant variable. Exception reports then identify deviations that exceed their limits.

The feedback information provided by the control system serves three important functions. For one thing, it encourages more realistic initial planning and closer adherence to approved plans. There is ample evidence to suggest that without adequate control, planning tends to become a superficial exercise. Of course, encouragement to meet plans should not be so great as to motivate the lower levels to plan too conservatively or to persevere doggedly with an outmoded plan. The system should be such that it greatly discourages failure to acknowledge highly probable future deviations.

Secondly, the control system guards against excessive deviations from current plans that cause a partial breakdown in coordination. As deviations grow larger, the myriad interrelated activities throughout the organization are soon out of mesh. Furthermore, the cost of getting a plan back into control (for example, by the use of overtime to recover schedule slippage) may become large as deviations accumulate. The tighter the control limits, the sooner deviations are detected.

The control system should provide an hierarchy of responses to reported deviations. The lowest level response is simply to ignore the deviation. Owing to the relatively unsophisticated nature of most control limits, a deviation might be tagged as an exception when in fact the current plan should be retained (because the penalty of keeping it is less than the cost of any revision).

Alternatively, the current plan might be modified "locally" to the extent necessary to bring it back within control limits. The cost of such local replanning tends to be small. The disadvantage, however, is that once a deviation has occurred the current plan ceases, in general, to be the optimal one.

The highest level form of response is a complete replanning that involves the same sequence of steps used in the creation of the existing plan. Such planning examines the current situation anew, constrained only by higher level plans and the consequences stemming from past actions. Close scrutiny may, of course, reveal that the existing plan is still the best one currently available (even if, on hindsight, the existing plan should not have been adopted in the first place). If replanning indicates that the current plan should be revised, and if this then causes a deviation at the next higher level in the planning hierarchy, appropriate error signals should be sent to a higher level planner. Such exception reporting should continue on up the planning hiearchy to the point where deviations can be contained within existing control limits.

The level of response to an error signal depends on the seriousness of the deviation. The data processing project manager is clearly faced with a trade-off decision aimed at balancing the cost of ignoring the deviation against the cost of revising the plan. The more serious the deviation, the more resources one should devote to replanning. The decision in most cases must be based on a subjective evaluation of the trade-offs because, paradoxically, the penalty of not revising the plan can only be established once the revised plan has been determined.

For example, suppose that a monthly production schedule has been determined for the next six months. Such a schedule is based on (among other things) predicted sales. If, at the end of the first month, sales are 1,000 units less than predicted, the planer is faced with the following alternatives:

1. Stick with the existing production schedule over the remaining five months.

2. Cut back the second month's schedule by 1,000 units to bring inventories to their planned level at the end of the month.

3. Completely replan (including, perhaps, revision of the sales predictions) to determine the best schedule in light of current information. The proper response depends, of course, on the data processing project manager's estimate of trade-offs involved.

The final important function of the control system is to provide feedback information for adaptation. The control system should, when feasible, identify sources of (and resposibility for) deviations from plans in such a way that continual improvement can be made in the planning process. The identification and correction of deficiencies in the planning process provides the primary means by which the organization can achieve fundamental improvement through adaptation.

PROJECT DOCUMENTATION AND REVIEW

Project documentation has a special meaning in data processing. It is an orderly written record of the history of systems design and application programming. Documentation is the first step in a data processing system or an application program because it records the detailed fact-finding and subsequent analysis leading to the programming and coding. Changes to a system or application and the reasons for changes are added to the documentation.

Documentation is not a make-work project that merely records events after they happen. It should indicate alternate courses of action, record the decision, communicate this information to the personnel involved, and then become an historical reference.

It is sometimes difficult to distinguish between documentation and written policies, directives, standards, procedures, and run books maintained in a data processing organization. Documentation includes them all, as well as the record of their development.

Documentation should be developed and maintained in a data processing project. The data requirement or data automation proposal may be filed as a record with systems analysis. Source documents, flowcharts, system outputs and related records for the systems design should be maintained there. The programming unit should maintain a file including the basic specifications, flowcharts, coding sheets, tests, source program listings and related records. The operations division should maintain run books, procedures, instruction sheets and related records.

Modern integrated on-line, or real-time, systems are so large and complex that evaluation, constructive criticism, review or revision cannot be done properly without tracing through the documentation. Documentation makes it possible to go back and alter the original design or programming with the assurance that all pertinent facts are available to make all necessary changes easily and successful.

REFERENCES

Emery, James C. *Organizational Planning and Control Systems: Theory and Technology.* London: The Macmillan Company Collier-Macmillan Limited, 1969.

Lord Jr., Kenniston W. and Steiner, James B. *CPM Review Manual Data Processing Handbook* (Second Edition). New York: Van Nostrand Reinhold Co. Inc. 1978.

Paige, Hilliard W. "How PERT/Cost Helps the General Manager," *Harvard Business Review* (No. 63611), November-December 1963.

Chapter
16
MULTIPROJECT
INTEGRATION

INTERDEPENDENCE BETWEEN PROJECTS

Few, if any, actual data processing projects are carried on in complete isolation; most are constrained by external factors, such as the receipt of parts or the use of personnel, machines and facilities. One great benefit of the network-based system is its ability to integrate the plans of related data processing projects to show the effect of these interdependencies. The aim in this chapter is to indicate how the network-based system can bring it about. The integration of data processing projects which are all related to a larger program, as well as the integration of those related only because they are carried out by the same organization, will be discussed. In the latter case, the system enables a company to sum up all project business using the common denominator of time to provide relatively accurate status reports and forecasts.

TYPES OF INTERDEPENDENCE BETWEEN PROJECTS

Projects can be interdependent or related in several ways.

RESULT-OF-ACTION DEPENDENCY

This is a condition in which an activity must be completed in one project before another activity in a second project can begin because the result of the action in the first must be made available to the second. An example of this is a process in which a component part is completed and shipped to another company for final assembly, where the part fabrication is treated as one project and the assembly as another.

COMMON RESOURCE UNIT DEPENDENCY

In this relationship an activity must be completed in one project before another activity can be started in a second project because they both use the same skilled person, piece of equipment, or facility.

COMMON RESOURCE RATE-OF-USE DEPENDENCY

Activities in different projects using the same common resource (certain labor skills, for example) can proceed simultaneously unless the rate of use of the common resource exceeds the available supply. For example, work in one data processing project requires three system analysts; in a second, similar work requires four. There are nine system analysts available, and so these activities can proceed at the same time. However, if a third data processing project requires five system analysts, that activity will be constrained because the rate of use of a common resource is restricted. Limitations in working capital or specified types of funds can often create such a dependency between projects.

SEPARATE PLANNING OF PROJECTS

Because it is difficult to determine these interproject dependencies, each data processing project is usually planned and scheduled by itself, without specific consideration of the dependencies. Much of the difficulty comes from the fact that the dependencies are all caused by time, and so the planner does not know if a constraining or delaying dependency exists until all the projects are scheduled. Even when scheduling is complete the conflict is frequently not identified until trouble crops up on the project; by then, any solution is expensive. By use of the network-based system, the planner can overcome or at least anticipate problems of this nature which are not identified when data processing projects are planned separately.

When different organizations work on parts of the same total effort, a broad overall plan should be initially established to correlate the various parts and provide a starting point from which each group can develop its plan. After all the detailed individual plans have been prepared, they must be tied together so that the total effects of the interactions and interdependencies can be determined; each individual plan may be sound and valid by itself, and yet when all are integrated into an overall scheme serious conflicts may be revealed. The network plan with interface events gives the planner a means of evaluating these interrelationships simply and effectively.

INTEGRATING PROJECTS THROUGH COMMON EVENTS

The first two types of dependencies described above—the result-of-action and the common resource unit dependencies—can be represented by using common events to link the data processing project network plans together. The term "network integration" designates the process of linking previously separate network plans by common or interface events. An "interface event" is the point at which responsibility for a given action changes hands. Integration thus means meshing plans by joining them at well-identified points to denote a transfer of responsibility.

It is important for the reader to note the reference to interface events, *not* interface activities. Occasionally, one sees references to "interface activities" as some find it easier to understand the concept of interfaces if a line is drawn from one network (or subnet) to another. If a planner considers this carefully, however, he will realize that the activity must be included in one network or the other, not both.

PRIOR IDENTIFICATION OF INTERFACES

Before networks can be integrated the interface events must be identified; the same event must be present on each of two networks if the two occurrences are to be joined. It is desirable to identify such events before preparing the network, although it is often not possible to do so. When the planner identifies an interface while preparing a network, he must notify the planners preparing the other affected networks of the exact identity of the event so that all networks will contain all of the interface events.

PROBLEMS INVOLVED IN NETWORK INTEGRATION

Two basic problems are encountered when integrating networks by the use of interface events:

1. Identification and control of interfaces
2. Processing very large networks.

IDENTIFICATION AND CONTROL OF INTERFACES

The importance of identifying interfaces before drawing networks, if possible, has been discussed. However, interfaces are often not evident until the networks are fairly well-developed. It is a real problem to maintain interface-event control as the networks change and evolve; this problem has led some planners to use rather formal methods and procedures.

INTERFACE-EVENT NETWORK CONSTRUCTION RULES

The rules guiding construction of interface event networks are as follows:

1. The originating or performing project component will include in its network as activities, prior to the interface event, all activities leading to and including delivery to the user.

2. Interface events will appear as the same event (have the same number) in the detail network of the involved contractors/agencies.

3. All incoming interface events will have no immediate preceding activity in the user's network.

MILESTONE EVENTS

Milestones are key events which occur in a project network. These events are selected through discussions among the directors or project managers of all the affected elements of the organization.

DIFFICULTIES IN PROCESSING VERY LARGE NETWORKS

Because the planner has the ability to integrate a number of networks and will use this ability, he will encounter the difficulties involved in processing or analyzing the resulting integrated network. This may be very large.

The major difficulty is caused by the total number of activities in the network. Most network analysis computer programs can handle a limited number of activities, and these usually are a function of the size of the computer memory. The limits range from 200 to 5,000 for many computers, although one widely-used program will handle 75,000 (with some restrictions on the network structure). Some programs now available even have "unlimited" network-size capability. The final limit is, of course, one of economy.

Even if the planner is using a computer program which handles "unlimited" size networks, he quickly learns that the human ability to prepare error-free data falls far short of the machine's capacity to process them. Preparing huge networks and trying to keep them up-to-date is an expensive operation.

ANALYZING LARGE NETWORKS

A total integrated network can be analyzed by computer if it is within the network size limitations imposed by the particular computer and program. If the network size exceeds the capacity of the machine, several alternatives are possible:

The planner can manually reduce the network size by eliminating or consolidating activities and events.

He can cut the network into blocks or treat the subnet separately.

He can prepare a summary network showing major events (milestones), determine the time span between milestones from the detailed networks, and then analyze the summary network.

He can condense the subnets while retaining all interfaces and milestones, and can then integrate the condensed subnets into an integrated network, analyze this, and feed the results into the detailed subnets.

REDUCE NETWORK SIZE

Reducing network size can result in more practical networks if it is done properly. If the planner combines detailed activities in series, for example, he can improve the network by eliminating excess details provided no interfaces are adversely affected and only one authority has responsibility for the activities.

SEPARATE ANALYSIS OF SUBNETS

If a network can be halved at one interface event, then the planner can easily analyze the first portion by making the forward pass, use the resulting earliest expected completion date as the start of the second portion, and then go through the forward and backward pass in the second part. He would then have to feed the resulting latest allowable time for the connecting interface into the first portion to calculate the latest allowable times and the critical path for it (see Chapter 10). However, this procedure is impractical if several subnets are involved or if a number of interfaces tie the subnets together at different points in time. To illustrate the difficulties, it is suggested that the reader perform this analysis on three simple subnets of his own creation.

USE OF A SUMMARY NETWORK

Use of summary networks has proved to be confusing to many planners because lines drawn between milestone events or even major interface events on these networks do not represent actual activities. Such a network may have some value when used to display the results of a detailed analysis, however. Although it is theoretically possible to transfer span times derived from subnet analyses to a summary network to make an analysis, it is very difficult. One must be sure that all interfaces appear on the summary network and that all interfaces changed on the detailed networks are reflected in the summary one.

NETWORK SUMMARIZATION

The procedure of network condensation is to identify the milestone or key points in the network and then to reduce all direct and indirect restraints between each pair of key points to a single restraint. The condensation procedure is essentially the systematic application of the following steps:

1. Identify the key activities or milestone points in the network.
2. Insert a new activity node identifying the key points determined in step 1.
3. Identify all possible paths connecting each pair of status activities.
4. Select the longest time duration value between each pair of status activities.
5. Designate a new single activity having the duration of the longest connecting path between status activities.
6. Connect each pair of status activities with the new condensed single path activities.

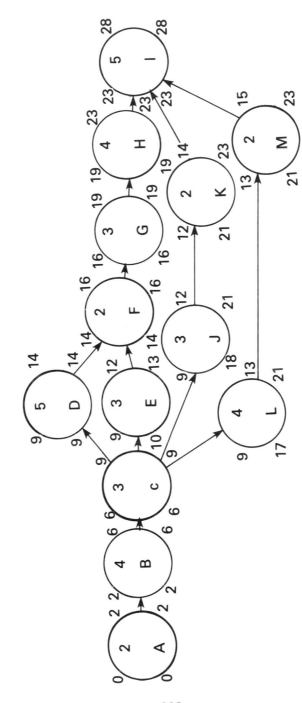

FIGURE 16.1. Detailed network.

ILLUSTRATIVE EXAMPLE

For the sake of demonstrating the principle discussed in this chapter, let us assume that Figure 16.1 represents a detailed network
for a typical data processing project. Now, from the detailed network, it is necessary to specify the point at which each key activity is
to be identified—beginning or end. If we specify the beginning of
activity A, the end of activity C, the end of activity F, and the end
of activity I as designated key points or interface events, as represented by Figure 16.2, then one could see from Figure 16.2 that:

1. a) Only one path connects Start A and End C.

    b) There are two paths, DF and EF, connecting End C and
       End F.

    c) One path, GHI, connects End F and End I.

    d) Two paths, JKI and LMI, connect End C and End I.

2. a) The only path between Start A and End C is the longest
       path.

    b) The length of path DF is $5 + 2 = 7$, and of EF is $3 + 2 = 5$.
       Path DF is selected as the longest path.

    c) Path GHI has a length of $3 + 4 + 5 = 12$.

    d) Path JKI has a length of $3 + 2 + 5 = 10$ and LMI extends
       to $4 + 2 + 5 = 11$.

3. The net activities are:

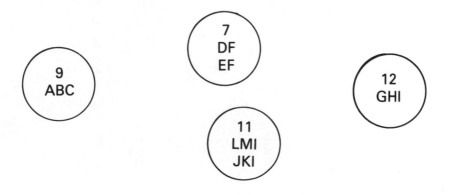

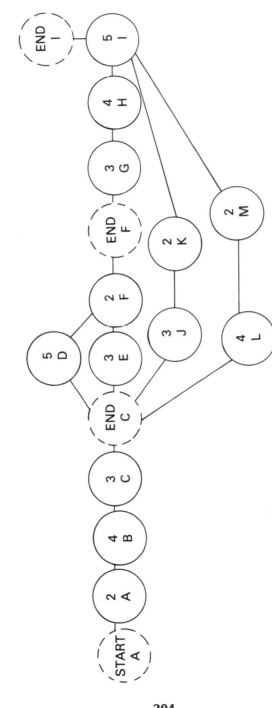

FIGURE 16.2. Inserted key points.

We can now see that no precedence relationships are changed and the condensed network is:

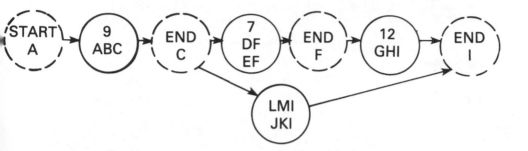

All status activities (key points or milestone events) not required for network closure can be eliminated to further compact the network without loss of information.

The condensed network shown in Figure 16.3 should have the same time data pertinent to the key points as the original network. A comparison of the original network (Figure 16.1) and the condensed network (Figure 16.3) is given in Table 16.1.

Note that in every instance the key point time values are the same.

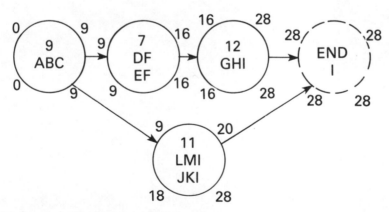

FIGURE 16.3. Condensed network.

TABLE 16.1. Comparison of original and condensed networks.

KEY POINT	ORIGINAL NETWORK TIME	CONDENSED NETWORK TIME
Begin A	ES = 0	ES = 0
	LS = 0	LS = 0
End C	EC = 0	EC = 9
	LC = 9	LC = 9
End F	EC = 16	EC = 16
	EC = 16	LC = 16
End I	EC = 28	EC = 28
	LC = 28	LC = 28

REFERENCE

Buchan, Russel J. and Davis, Gordon J. *Project Control Through Network Analysis and Synthesis.* Atlanta: DDR International, 1976.

Chapter
17
SOFTWARE MAINTENANCE PROJECTS

Software maintenance is defined as the process of modifying existing operational software while leaving its primary function intact. This definition *excludes* the following types of activity from the category of software maintenance:

major redesign and redevelopment (more than 50 percent new code) of a new software product performing substantially the same functions;

design and development of a sizable (more than 20 percent of the source instructions comprising the existing product) interfacing software package which requires relatively little redesign of the existing product;

data processing system operations, data entry, and modification of values in the database.

The definition *includes* the following types of activity within the category of software maintenance:

redesign and redevelopment of small portions of an existing software product;

design and development of small interfacing software packages which require some redesign of the existing software product;

modification of the software product's code, documentation, or database structure.

Software maintenance can be classified into two main categories:

1. Software *update* which results in a changed functional specification for the software product.

2. Software *repair* which leaves the functional specification intact.

In turn, software *repair* can be classified into three main subcategories:

a. Corrective maintenance (of processing, performance, or implementation failures).

b. Adaptive maintenance (to changes in the processing or data environment).

c. Perfective maintenance (for enhancing performance or maintainability).

SOFTWARE MAINTENANCE EFFORT ESTIMATION*

The basic assumption underlying most maintenance models is that software maintenance costs are determined by substantially the same cost driver attributes that determine software development costs (see Chapter 13). The quantity used to determine the equivalent of product size for software maintenance is the *Annual Change Traffic* (ACT), that fraction of the software product's source in-

---

*Barry W. Boehm, *Software Engineering Economics*, © 1981. Reprinted by permission of Prentice-Hall, Inc., Englewood Cliffs, N.J.

structions which undergo change during a (typical) year, either through addition or modification.

If all of the cost driver attribute effort multipliers for maintenance are the same as those for development, the resulting annual maintenance effort estimate is:

$$(MM)_{AM} = (1.0)(ACT)(MM)_{DEVEL} \qquad [17\text{-}1]$$

MAINTENANCE PRODUCTIVITY RATIO

The maintenance productivity ratio $(DSI/MM)_{MOD}$ is the average number of instructions which can be modified per man-month of maintenance effort. It can be used to estimate the annual maintenance effort required for a product size $(DSI)_{DEVEL}$ by means of the annual change traffic parameter ACT:

$$(DSI)_{MOD/YR} = (ACT)(DSI)_{DEVEL}$$

$$(MM)_{AM} = \frac{(DSI)\ MOD/YR}{(DSI/MM)_{MOD}} \qquad [17\text{-}2]$$

Thus, a 32-KDSI product with an ACT of 10 percent and a maintenance productivity of $(DSI/MM)_{MOD} = 200$ would have $(DSI)_{MOD/YR} = (0.10)\ (32,000) = 3,200$ and an annual maintenance effort of $(MM)_{AM} = 3,200/200 = 16$ MM. The quantity $(DSI/MM)_{MOD}$ can also be used to support a task-unit approach to maintenance estimation in which each maintenance task is sized in terms of the number of instructions to be modified—$(DSI)_{MOD}$.

SOFTWARE MAINTENANCE PRODUCTION FUNCTION

Software maintenance is usually performed as a level-of-effort activity with the appropriate level of effort being determined from a cost-benefit, point-of-diminishing-returns judgement similar to the situation for software development.

A typical software maintenance cost-benefit production function is shown in Figure 17.1. The investment segment consists of those maintenance activities which must be performed if the program is not to deteriorate in value: emergency program fixes, accomodation of changes to the program's environment (hardware, operating system, master database, input data), and mandated enhancements (for example, new income tax reporting requirements).

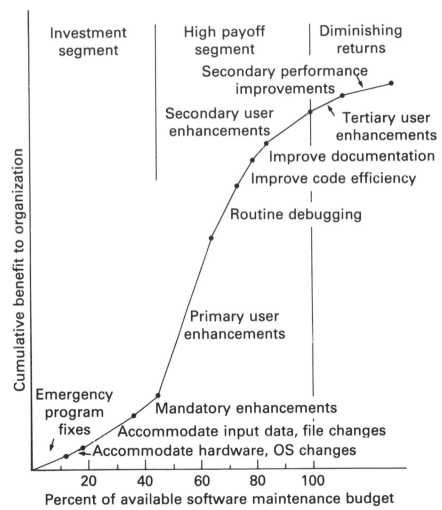

FIGURE 17.1. The software maintenance production function.

The high-payoff segment of the curve consists of primary-priority enhancements for users; primary improvements in program efficiency, reliability, and documentation; and a set of secondary user improvements which provide a lower but still positive excess of benefits over costs.

The diminishing-returns segment of the curve consists of the software maintenance organization's usual infinite backlog of "nice-to-have" features (limited-demand reports, pie chart displays, rewriting the poorly-structured but stable inventory module, etc.). All of these features would provide some benefit to the organization, but not as much in relation to their costs as the activities already underway or higher on the priority list.

DISTRIBUTION OF SOFTWARE MAINTENANCE EFFORT BY ACTIVITY

Although the benefits part of the software-maintenance production function in Figure 17.1 cannot be generally quantified, some aspects of the cost part can be quantified reasonably well.

Figure 17.2 shows how the software maintenance effort is typically distributed among the major categories of update and repair.

Corrective maintenance (emergency program fixes and routine debugging), generally the major portion of the hardware maintenance budget, tends to consume only a relatively small (21.7 Percent) portion of the software maintenance activity as defined here. Thus, achieving error-free software development does not eliminate the need for a significant budget level for software maintenance.

The major portion (41.8 percent) of the software maintenance effort is devoted to software updates (enhancements for users). Figure 17.3 shows how the software update effort is typically distributed in terms of the reports produced by the software system. It becomes clear from this distribution that flexible data structures and report generation capabilities play an important part in improving software maintenance efficiency.

The distribution of effort by activity in Figure 17.2 is the key to quantifying the cost (or percent of maintenance budget) portion of

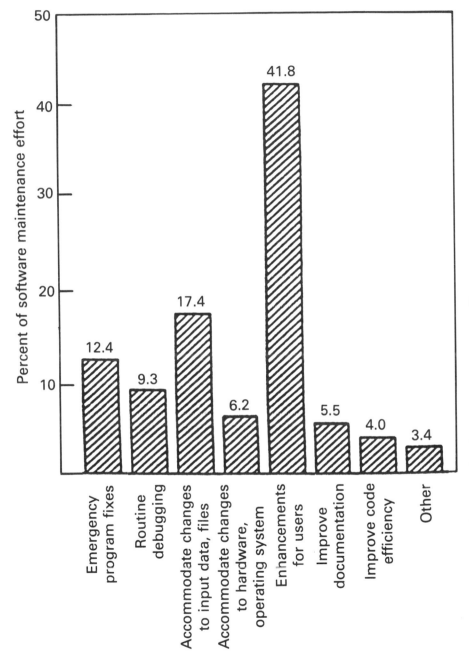

FIGURE 17.2. Distribution of software maintenance effort.

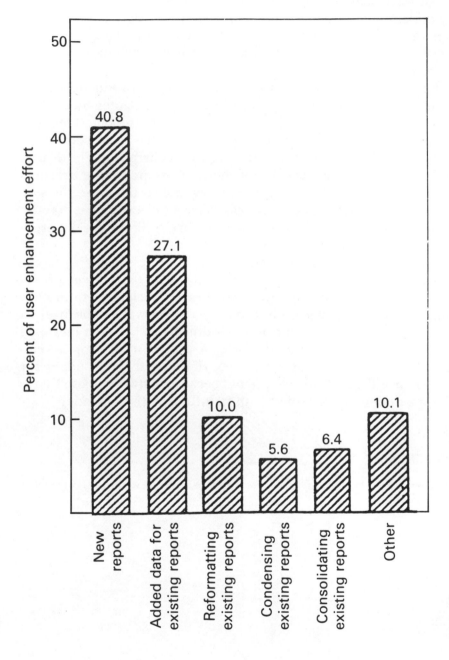

FIGURE 17.3. Distribution of user-enhancement effort

the software maintenance production function in Figure 17.1 in that the cumulative activity percentages in that figure are derived from the corresponding activity percentages in Figure 17.2 2.4 percent for emergency program fixes in the investment segment of Figure 17.1, etc.).

The most significant feature of the resulting production function in Figure 17.1 is the very high fraction of maintenance effort (40 to 50 percent) consumed by the investment segment. This represents a load of nondiscretionary work which has to be performed just to keep the system's value at roughly its current level. Clearly, this is an area in which the use of modern programming practices to reduce the need for emergency fixing and to minimize the side effects of environmental changes can have a powerful effect on the morale and effectiveness of the maintenance staff and on the organization's mission in general.

From a life cycle planning aspect, the main lesson for us in the maintenance production function is that *software maintenance is not optional*. For each dollar spent on software development, another dollar needs to be budgeted just to keep the software viable over its life cycle; after that, another optional dollar can be spent on desirable enhancement over the life cycle. A project to develop a long-life software product which allocates significantly less budget for maintenance than for development "because software doesn't have to be maintained" is a project with painful surprises ahead.

REFERENCE

Boehm, Barry W. *Software Engineering Economics.* Englewood Cliffs: Prentice-Hall, Inc., 1981.

Chapter
18
OTHER PRACTICAL ISSUES IN DATA PROCESSING PROJECT MANAGEMENT

Many software projects have gone awry for lack of calendar time. *Why is this disaster so common?*

First, our techniques of estimating are poorly developed. More seriously, they reflect an unvoiced assumption which is quite untrue, i.e., that all will go well.

Second, our estimating techniques fallaciously confuse effort with progress, hiding the assumption that men and months are interchangeable.

Third, because we are uncertain of our estimates, data processing/software managers often lack the courteous stubbornness required to make people wait for a good product.

Fourth, schedule progress is poorly monitored. Techniques proven and routine in other engineering disciplines are considered radical innovations in software engineering.

Fifth, when schedule slippage is recognized, the natural (and traditional) response is to add manpower. Like dousing a fire with gasoline, this makes matters much worse. More fire requires more gasoline and thus begins a regenerative cycle which ends in disaster.

Now, let us consider other aspects of the problem in more detail.

PERVASIVE OPTIMISM

The *first* false assumption that underlies the scheduling of systems programming is that all will go well, i.e. that each task will take only as long as it"ought" to take.

Computer programming involves a very tractable medium. The programmer builds from concepts and very flexible representations. Because the medium is traceable, we expect few difficulties in implementation; hence our pervasive optimism. Because our ideas are faulty, we have bugs; hence our optimism is unjustified.

In a single task, the assumption that all will go well has a probabilistic effect on the schedule. It might even go as planned, for there is a probability distribution for the delay that will be encountered, and "no delay" has a finite probability. A large data processing effort, however, consists of many tasks, some chained end-to-end. The probability that each will go well becomes small.

ILLUSTRATIVE EXAMPLE

Since a project network—together with the time and resources data—is a model of the actual project, it is easy to stimulate actual project progress. For the sake of demonstrating the principle, let us assume that a contractor has a network prepared that represents the project of constructing a building. He realizes that while almost all activities are stable and of predictable duration, there are uncertainties involved. One factor which can cause significant delays is the weather. The contractor identifies each activity that could be delayed by inclement weather and found the probability of such weather on any day. He checks his records for absenteeism among the various skills and records the relative frequency of occurrence for each skill classification.

To proceed with the simulation, it is necessary to assign ranges of random numbers to the various factors which can contribute to delays. The simulation of actual occurrences is then determined by the appearance of appropriate numbers in a random number table or as generated by the computer. The random number table in Appendix B is used for this example.

The results of the contractor's finding is summarized below:

PERSONNEL

TYPE	NO.	PROBABILITY OF ABSENCE	RANDOM NUMBERS RANGES
Mason	2	0.15	00-14
Carpenter	2	0.20	00-19
Plumber	2	0.20	00-19

WEATHER

	PROBABILITY	RANDOM NUMBERS RANGES
Inclement	0.28	00-27

Assuming that we are only looking at the first week of the project of constructing a building, the schedule shows that three activities should occur:

ACTIVITY NO.	DESCRIPTION	DURATION	CREW SIZE	SKILL
1	Lay basement wall	2	2	Masons
2	Frame	2	2	Carpenters
3	Plumbing in ground	3	2	Plumbers

This schedule is:

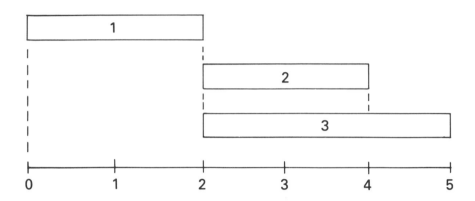

Note that activities 2 and 3 cannot start until 1 is complete. Assume that all possible levels of resources provide the same efficiency so that a man-day present is a man-day of progress:

Activity 1 has 2 × 2 = 4 mason days' work

Activity 2 has 2 × 2 = 4 carpenter days' work

Activity 3 has 2 × 3 = 6 plumber days' work

The simulation procedure is: If the situation above were part of the simulation, the steps to be followed would be:

Step 1: Check the weather for the first day (pick a two-digit random number from the random number table in Appendix B).

Result: The number picked is 37 which indicates good weather.

Step 2: If the weather is inclement, no work is done on that task. If the weather is good, check to see if the masons report for work. (Pick two-digit random numbers.) First mason: 76 present for work. Second mason: 24 present for work.

Step 3: Record the net progress for the first day's activity in a table similar to Table 18.1.

TABLE 18.1. Weekly critical activity summary—five weeks statement

CONTRACT_____ CONTRACT NO_____ PROJECT WEEK NUMBER_____ DATE_____

1	2	3	4	5	6	7	8	9
WEEK	ACTIVITY CODE	ACTIVITY DESCRIPTION	WEEKS BEFORE START DATE	CRITICAL WEEKS LOST	SKILL CODE	CRITICAL MAN-MACHINE WEEK LOST	REASON FOR BEING BEHIND SCHEDULE	ACTION TAKEN BY PROJECT MANAGER TO RECOVER LOST CRITICAL WEEKS

219

Step 4: Repeat steps 1, 2, and 3 for the second day.
Weather: 51-good weather

Mason: 05-first mason absent
82-second mason present

One mason-day of progress is recorded.

Step 5: Continue until the project is complete.

ESTIMATING AND SCHEDULING THE MAN-MONTH

The *second* fallacious thought mode is expressed in the very unit of effort used in estimating and scheduling: the man-month. Cost does indeed vary as the product of the number of men and months. Progress does not. Hence the man-month as a unit for measuring the size of a data processing job is a dangerous and deceptive myth. It implies that men and months are interchangeable.

Men and months are interchangeable commodities only when a task can be partitioned among many workers with no communication among them. This is true of reaping wheat or picking cotton; it is not even approximately true of data processing or systems programming.

When a task cannot be partitioned because of sequential constraints, the application of more effort has no effect on the schedule. The bearing of a child takes nine months no matter how many women are assigned. Many data processing tasks have this characteristic because of the sequential nature of debugging.

In tasks that can be partitioned but which require communication among the subtasks, the effort of communication must be added to the amount of work to be done. Therefore, the best that can be done is somewhat poorer than an even trade of men for months.

The added burden of communication is made up of two parts, training and intercommunication. Each worker must be trained in the technology, the goals of the effort, the overall strategy, and the plan of work. This training cannot be partitioned, so this part of the added effort varies linearly with the number of workers.

A large project can sustain a manpower buildup of 30 percent per year. More than that strains and even inhibits the evolution of the essential informal structure and its communication pathways. At the same time, a long project must anticipate a turnover of 20 percent per year, and the new people must be both technically trained and integrated into the formal structure.

Intercommunication is worse if each part of the task must be separately coordinated with each other part; the effort increases as $n (n - 1)/2$. Three workers require three times as much pairwise communication as two; four require six times as much as two. If, moreover, there is a conference among three, four, etc., workers to resolve things jointly, matters get worse. The added effort of communicating may fully counteract the division of the original task and thus lengthen the schedule.

Since software construction is inherently a systems effort—an exercise in complex interrelationships—communication effort is great and quickly dominates the decrease in individual task time brought about by partitioning. Adding more personnel then lengthens, not shortens, the schedule.

SYSTEM TEST

No parts of the schedule are so thoroughly affected by sequential constraints as component debugging and system tests. Furthermore, the time required depends on the number and subtlety of the errors encountered. Theoretically this number should be zero. Because of optimism, we usually expect the number of bugs to be smaller than it turns out to be. Therefore, testing is usually the most poorly scheduled part of programming.

Some data processing project managers have been successful in using the following rule of thumb for scheduling a software task:

1/3 planning

1/6 coding

1/4 component test and early system test

1/4 system test, all components in hand

This differs from conventional scheduling in several important ways:

1. The fraction devoted to planning is larger than normal. Even so, it is barely enough to produce a detailed and solid specification, and not enough to include research or exploration of totally new techniques.

2. The *half* of the schedule devoted to debugging of completed code is much larger than normal.

3. The part that is easy to estimate, i.e., coding, is given only one-sixth of the schedule.

In examining conventional scheduled projects, I have found that a few allowed one-half of the projected schedule for testing, but that most did indeed spend half of the actual schedule for that purpose. Many of these were on schedule until and except in system testing.

Failure to allow enough time for system tests, in particular, is peculiarly disastrous. Since the delay comes at the end of the schedule, no one is aware of schedule trouble until almost the delivery date. Bad news late and without warning is unsettling to the customer and to managers.

Furthermore, delay at this point has usually severe financial as well as psychological repercussions. The project is fully staffed and cost-per-day is maximum. More seriously, the software is to support other business effort (shipping of computers, operation of new facilities, etc.) and the secondary costs of delaying these are very high, for it is almost time for software shipment. Indeed, these secondary costs may outweigh all others. It is therefore very important to allow enough system test time in the original schedule.

SOME TYPICAL OPTIONS WHEN EXPECTED WORK IS NOT DONE

What does a data processing project manager do when an essential software project is behind schedule? Adding manpower may or may not help.

Let us consider an example. Suppose a data processing project is estimated at 12 man-months and assigned to three men for four months, and that there are the measurable mileposts A, B, C, and D which are scheduled to fall at the end of each month.

Now suppose the first milestone is not reached until two months have elapsed. *What are the alternatives facing the data processing project manager?*

1. Assume that the project must be done on time. Assume that only the first part of the task was misestimated. Then, nine man-months of effort remain, and two months, so 4½ persons will be needed. Add two persons to the three assigned.

2. Assume that the whole estimate was uniformly low. Then, 18 man-months, so nine persons will be needed. Add six persons to the three assigned.

3. Reschedule. Allow enough time in the new schedule to ensure that the work can be carefully and thoroughly done and that rescheduling will not have to be done again.

4. Trim the project task. In practice this tends to happen anyway, once the team observe schedule slippage. Where the secondary costs of delay are very high, this is the only feasible action. The data processing project manager's only alternatives are to trim it formally and carefully, to reschedule, or to watch the project task get silently trimmed by hasty design and incomplete testing.

In the first two cases, insisting that the unaltered task be completed in four months is disastrous. Consider the regenerative effects, for example, for the first alternative (Figure 18.1).

The two new men, however competent and however quickly recruited, will require training in the project task by one of the experienced men. If this takes a month, three man-months will have been devoted to work not in the original estimate. Furthermore, the task, originally partitioned three ways, must be repartitioned into five parts, hence some work already done will be lost and system testing must be lengthened. So, at the end of the third month, substantially more than seven man-months of effort remain, and five trained people and one month are available. As Figure 18.1 suggests, the product is just as late as if no one had been added.

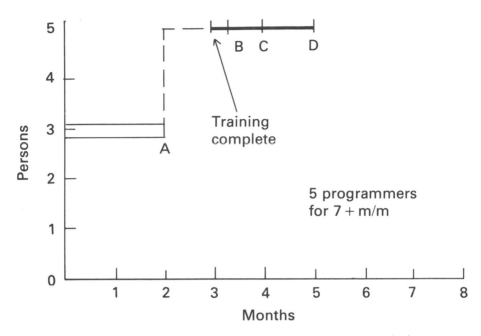

FIGURE 18.1. Adding manpower to a late project may not help.

To hope to get done in four months, considering only training time and not repartitioning and extra systems test, would require adding four persons, not two, at the end of the second month. To cover repartitioning and system test effects, one would have to add still more persons. Now, however, one has at least a seven-person team, not a three-person one; thus, such aspects as team organization and task division are different in kind, not merely in degree. Notice that by the end of the third month things look very black. The March 1 milestone has not been reached in spite of all the managerial effort. The temptation is very strong to repeat the cycle, adding yet more manpower.

The foregoing assumed that only the first milestone was misestimated. If on March 1 one makes the conservative assumption that the whole schedule was optimistic, one wants to add 6 persons just to the original task. Calculation of the training, repartitioning, and system testing effects is left as an exercise for the reader. Without any doubt, the regenerative disaster will yield a poorer product later than would rescheduling with the original three persons.

ADDING MANPOWER TO A LATE SOFTWARE PROJECT

The number of months of a project depends upon its sequential constraints. The maximum number of persons depends upon the number of independent subtasks. From these two quantities one can derive schedules using fewer persons and more months. (The only risk is product obsolescence). One cannot, however, get workable schedules using more persons and fewer months. Many software/data processing projects have gone awry for lack of calendar time than for all other causes combined.

SOME TRADE-OFFS FOR ESTIMATING PPOJECT TASK

How long will a system programming job take? How much effort will be required? How does one estimate?

I have earlier indicated ratios that seem to apply to planning time, coding, component test, and system test. First, one must say that one does not estimate the entire task by estimating the coding portion only and then applying the ratio. The coding is only one-sixth or so of the problem, and errors in its estimate or in the ratios could lead to ridiculous results.

Second, one must say that data for building isolated small programs are not applicable to programming systems products. For a program averaging about 3,200 words, for example, assume an average code-plus-debug time of about 178 hours for a single programmer, a figure which extrapolates to give an annual productivity of 35,800 statements per year. A program half that size took less than one-fourth as long, so an extrapolated productivity is almost 80,000 statements per year. Planning, documentation, testing, system integration, and training time must be added. The linear extrapolation of such figures is meaningless. (Extrapolation of times for the hundred- yard dash shows that a man can run a mile under three minutes!)

Figure 18.2 tells the sad story. It illustrates results reported from a study. This shows an exponent of 1.5; that is,

$$\text{Effort} = (\text{constant}) \times (\text{number of instructions})^{1.5}$$

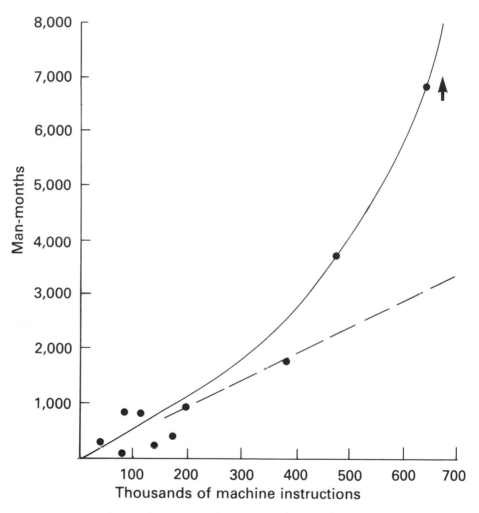

FIGURE 18.2. As project complexity increases, the number of man-months goes up exponentially.

A few studies on programming productivity have been made and several estimating techniques have been proposed. Here I shall give only a few items that seem especially illuminating. These data are shown in Table 18.2 and Figures 18.3 and 18.4.

Of these, Figure 18.3 is the most detailed and the most useful. The first two jobs are basically control programs; the second two are basically language translators. Productivity is stated in terms of debugged words per man-year. This includes programming, component test, and system test. It is not clear how much of the planning effort, or effort in machine support—writing and the like—is included.

The productivities likewise fall into two classifications: those for control progams are about 600 words per man-year; those for translators are about 2,200 words per man-year. Note that all four programs are of similar size—the variation is in the size of work groups, length of time, and number of modules. Which is cause and which is effect? Did the control programs require more people because they were more complicated? Or did they require more modules and more man-months because they were assigned more people? Did they take longer because of their greater complexity,

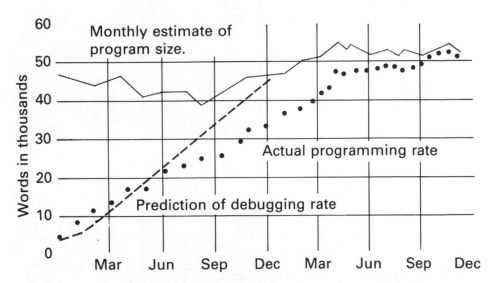

FIGURE 18.3. Prediction of programming effort on one project.

TABLE 18.2. Productivity differences between complex and less complex problems.

	PROG. UNITS	NUMBER OF PROGRAMMERS	YEARS	MAN-YEARS	PROGRAM WORDS	WORDS/ MAN-YR.
Operational	50	83	4	101	52,000	515
Maintenance	36	60	4	81	51,000	630
Compiler	13	9	2¼	17	38,000	2230
Translator (Data assembler)	15	13	2½	11	25,000	2270

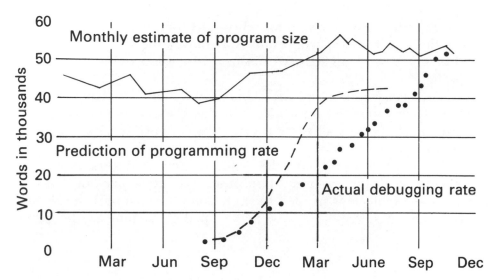

FIGURE 18.4. Predictions for debugging rates on a single project constrasted with actual figures.

or because more people were assigned? One can't be sure. The control programs were surely more complex. These uncertainties aside, the numbers describe the real productivities achieved by a large system using present-day programming techniques. As such they are a real contribution.

Figures 18.3 and 18.4 show some interesting data on programming and debugging rates as compared to predicted rates.

"THE OTHER ACTIVITY IS LATE"

A schedule slips a day; so what? Who gets excited about a one-day slip? We can make it up later. And the other activity ours fits into is late anyway.

As we have seen, one must get excited about a one-day slip. Such are the elements of catastrophe. However, not all one-day slips are equally disastrous.

How does one tell which slips matter? There is no substitute for a PERT chart (see Chapter 12) or a critical-path sohedule (see Chapter 11). Such a network shows who waits for what. It shows who is on the critical path, where any slip moves the end date. It also shows how much an activity can slip before it moves into the critical path.

The preparation of a PERT chart is the most valuable part of its use. Laying out the network, identifying the dependencies, and estimating the lags all force a great deal of very specific planning very early in a project.

As the project proceeds, the PERT chart provides the answer to the demoralizing excuse, "The other activity is late anyway." It shows how hustle is needed to keep one's own part off the critical path and it suggests ways to make up the lost time in the other part.

REFERENCES

Awani, Alfred O. *Project Management Techniques*. Princeton: Petrocelli Books, Inc., 1983.
Brooks, Jr. Frederick P. "The Mythical Man-Month". Reading: Addison-Wesley, 1975

Chapter
19
EVALUATION OF DATA PROCESSING SYSTEMS

The technology of computers has in the last several years been characterized by its phenomenal advances and improvements. As one generation of computers hits the market, new generations are being developed and tested. Examples of technological advances include the transition from integrated circuits to chips as well as new types of memory modules. These innovations have resulted in computers that are more compact, faster, more flexible, and less expensive.

The first generation of digital computers were relatively slow, had limited memory storage capacity, and were generally suited only for applications where total time for completing a computation was not restricted. For example, the processing of inventory records was not bound to any time constraint, so that performing such a function was superior to previous methods. However, for applications which required that a calculation be performed in real-time—real-time meaning that the calculation results be provided almost instantaneously (see Chapter 4)—the general-purpose digital computers were generally not fast enough. For instance, in simulating radar returns displayed to a trainee as the radar beam sweeps across a geographical area, terrain characteristics have to be displayed practically instantaneously—as they occur in operational situations. Therefore, the calculations have to be accomplished in such a short time that any time lag would not be discernible.

Traditionally used for the real-time calculations, analog computers performed well in simulators and similar applications. The inherent design incorporated elements that were precalculated, e.g., especially designed potentiometers, which generated continuous solutions to a particular input and therefore were natural real-time computers. One major shortcoming of the analog computer was its inflexibility to change. A new characteristic to be simulated required the designing and installing of new elements. The industry, involved with solving problems in real-time, had to live with the inherent disadvantages of the analog computer but waited with keen anticipation for the new generation of digital computers feasible for real-time applications. For many real-time applications, the latest digital computer design is fast and flexible enough to perform acceptably.

The fundamental parameters that must be considered by the data processing project manager prior to deciding whether the use of a digital computer is feasible for a particular application are memory capacity, word length, and speed.

THE GRAY RADAR PROJECT

Gray's top management would like to initiate a project to develop a Radar Landmass Simulator (RLS). A specification summary of the RLS identified the major requirements of the project for both the project manager and top management officials as follows:

The total land area to be simulated (elevation, reflectivity, and other characteristic features) is identified as 1,500 by 800 nautical miles.

Display must be able to resolve or distinguish objects as small as 250 feet on a side.

APPLICATION OF COMPUTER TO GRAY RADAR PROJECT

The first parameter to be considered for the radar landmass application is the amount of memory that the digital computer must possess. The total area can be divided into grids of 250-by-250 feet which total 6.9×10^8 grid areas. Based on the above, it might be deducted that the computer must have a memory capable of storing at least 6.9×10^8 words. This would be correct if no two grid areas were alike and therefore required a unique word to describe the terrain and other characteristics of each individual area. Since large numbers of grid areas have identical characteristics, the format of a single word could, for instance, describe a multitude of areas. In the case of a desert terrain, millions of areas would be identical and therefore only one memory location would be required to describe such a large number of areas. At any rate, the data processing project manager's analysis would establish that the memory capacity would be significantly less than 6.9×10^8 words and thus well within the computer's ability.

The second parameter that must be considered is the word length that the computer must possess. The more common general- purpose computers have word lengths of 16, 24 or 32 bits. One approach that the manager might take for establishing the word length is to analyze the word format to establish the most demanding word requirement.

His analysis of the problem might indicate that the greatest accuracy demand on the computer is that the simulated aircraft be pinpointed to within 100 yards or 300 feet at any instant. The 1,500-by-800 mile total area can be represented as a grid of lines at 16,000 100-yard intervals. The grid would consist of 30,000 lines and 16,000 lines in the X and Y coordinates, respectively. Therefore, the computer must be able to identify the more demanding parameter comprising each of the 30,000 lines in the X coordinate. A 15-bit word can count up to 32,767. Allowing 1 bit for a sign check, a 16-bit computer would be adequate for the radar landmass application. Figure 19.1 provides some of the word formats that the data processing project manager would sketch when considering the computer word size that might be required.

The data processing project manager would be required to make a similar analysis for other calculations to make certain that no other calculations may be required beyond the accuracy capability of the computers under consideration. Some of the types of computations for the RLS would include radar sweep, calculation for terrain contours, generation of shadow effects, etc. For purposes of this discussion, it can be established that the calculation to establish the X and Y axis aircraft position constitutes the most demanding requirement for computer computation.

The conclusion that he would reach is that a computer having a word length less than 16 bits would prove to be unacceptable and a larger word length of 24 bits would be oversized and not cost-effective. A 16-bit machine would be the best selection for the radar landmass application.

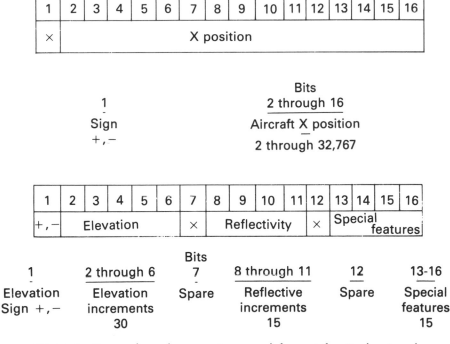

FIGURE 19.1. Examples of computer word format for Radar Landmass Simulation, x-axis aircraft position.

The third and, in most cases, the most critical parameter that must be considered for a computer application is timing. If the computer cannot perform its assigned functions within the required time frame it generally experiences a halt or ceases to function. Therefore, for applications which demand that data processing (e.g., a computation) be accomplished within a specific time frame, such as in the case of the landmass simulator, a timing analysis of the computer's ability to perform its functions is required.

Now let's assume that a review of the radar characteristics reveals that the fastest antenna rotation rate is a 360-degree revolution every four seconds and that its effective range at aircraft cruising altitude is 30 miles. Therefore, in any four-second period, the area that must be displayed is that contained in a circular area having a radius of 30 miles. The point of this analysis is that the computer, in the four-second time cycle, need only process data related to the 30-mile circle—or approximately 1.6 million 250-foot- square areas—instead of processing the 691,000,000 areas that would be necessary in the 1,500-by-800 mile total area. A digital computer with a two-microsecond computational speed would require 3.2 seconds to individually gain access to or retrieve each of the 1.6 million areas under consideration. In addition, the computer must perform other calculations, such as establishing the area being scanned by the rotating antenna, simulating the flight path of the aircraft, and simulating the sweep time.

Table 19.1 illustrates a summary of the computer requirements and the conclusion that would be drawn by the data processing project manager regarding the feasibility of using a digital computer for the Gray Radar project. The summary is based on a two-microsecond machine which the data processing project manager concluded was the fastest 16-bit computer available for the project.

As shown in the summary provided in Table 19.1, the total number of instructions that must be executed for each four-second cycle is 2,919,000. Based on a computer capable of executing an instruction in two microseconds (often referred to as computer iteration rate), the total time required to process all the instructions required by the RLS is 5,838 seconds. Since a fundamental requirement of the specification is to update all radar information every four seconds (based on maximum antenna speed, area to be

TABLE 19.1. Summary of timing functions for radar landmass simulation.

FUNCTION	MEMORY INSTRUCTIONS	INSTRUCTION FOR 4 SECOND CYCLE				TOTAL INSTRUCTIONS PER CYCLE
		4/CYCLE	3/CYCLE	2/CYCLE	1/CYCLE	
Area characteristics	1,600,000				1,600,000	1,600,000
Aircraft flight	15,000	15,000				60,000
Radar sweep	5,000		2,000		3,000	9,000
Terrain contours	500,000				500,000	500,000
Shadows	500,000				500,000	70,000
Other	100,000	25,000	25,000	25,000	25,000	250,000
						2,919,000

2.0×10^{-6} sec./instr. $\times$ 2.919×10^{6} instr./cycle $= 5.838$ sec./cycle

236

displayed, aircraft speed, etc.), the use of the two-microsecond computer is not fast enough (5,838 seconds required versus 4.000 seconds available). The data processing project manager would thus have to eliminate the technical approach using a digital computer for the radar landmass application.

The above demonstrates the type of analysis that the manager would make before deciding whether a general-purpose digital computer is feasible for a particular application. However, if other factors forced further consideration for applying a digital computer to perform the simulator functions, he could investigate options such as the following:

1. Use of special programming techniques.

2. Design and development of special data storage and retrieval modules.

3. Design and development of a special-purpose computer specifically for the RLS.

4. Utilization of a hybrid system (digital/analog computer system).

SOFTWARE ARCHITECTURE LIMITATIONS

It is normal for large, complex application systems to have a few problems once the systems are put into production. The new system goes through a certain amount of normal "settling" and the constantly changing user's environment causes changes to be made to the new system.

The data processing project manager needs to be able to distinguish when he is facing a surmountable problem or an unyielding constraint. To do this, he needs to be aware of some of the non-negotiable constraints of software. A constraint is non-negotiable and represents a problem or shortcoming of a system that necessitates redesign and rewrite of the system and/or moving the system to another environment. In short, when a data processing project manager is facing a true, constraint—hardware, software, or otherwise—by definition there is nothing that can be done to salvage the existing system in its existing form.

TYPICAL SOFTWARE CONSTRAINTS

The following are some of the more common software constraints:

arrival-rate limitations,

total transaction throughput,

processing limitations,

maintenance bind, and

database size limitations.

The above constraints will be examined in greater detail.

ARRIVAL RATE LIMITATIONS

In some cases the arrival rate of on-line activity (transactions) is so high that even in the face of a well-designed, well-written, well-tuned system with ample resources, response time is not adequate, nor will it be in the future. For example, suppose that a system can adequately handle a maximum arrival rate of 10 transactions per second. When the arrival rate rises above that, queue time will build. So, if total response time is 120 seconds for a given transaction, 118 of those seconds will typically have been spent in queues once the arrival rate goes beyond the amount the system can handle.

TOTAL TRANSACTION THROUGHPUT

This constraint is very similar to limitations of on-line arrival rates, with one large difference. Arrival-rate limitations apply to a short or finite amount of time, whereas transaction throughput applies all the time the system is up and functioning. As an example, suppose that a bank runs only 20,000 transactions a day and that software will support that amount of throughput if the transactions are reasonably spread out throughout the day. However, if all of those transactions are entered between 11:00 A.M. and 1:00 P.M., the arrival rate of the transactions will be such that response will not be adequate. On the other hand, if 200,000 transactions a day are to be run through a system that can handle a maximum of 100,000 (however they are distributed), the arrival-rate measurement is meaningless.

PROCESSING LIMITATIONS

Some types of processing simply cannot be done given the current hardware and software environment. For example, suppose a designer specifies a program that will scan an entire database on-line with a three- to five-second response time. With today's hardware and software this processing cannot be done if the database is of average size, and all the system timing that can be done will do nothing to alleviate the problem. The point is that if a certain kind of processing is required, it should be accomplished within the framework of what can be handled by the hardware and software, not at a cross-purpose to it. In the example above, it may be possible to redesign the datebase so that an entire scan is unnecessary.

MAINTENANCE BIND

Some software is in such a state that no changes to it can be made. This may be because

the system is old,

the system is very large and complex,

the system is not documented (either at all or adequately),

the system has been maintained to the point where nothing else can be changed without fear of disturbing something, or

a combination of these factors.

On occasion, systems reach a state of unmaintainability such that the very next change to the system, however small, will cause a rewrite.

DATABASE SIZE LIMITATIONS

Some applications and some database management systems have a limitation on the amount of data that can be handled. Usually, this limitation is pragmatic rather than technical. When the designer has specified more data to be handled than *can* be handled, something must give.

APPLICATION ARCHITECTURE LIMITATIONS

When application software is developed, the designer has in mind some framework around which the system will be built. When that framework is not fundamentally solid or when use of the system varies greatly from that anticipated by the developer, the system may have to be scrapped. For example, suppose that a designer wants to build an on-line system (see Chapter 4) without adhering to the standard work unit. Once the system is constructed, the designer throws hardware at the system and directs competent tuners to "give me performance," all to little or no long-term avail. The fact is that if the data processing project manager wants on-line performance, he must build it at the point of design, and the best way to do that is through the standard work unit. Performance cannot be retrofitted without restructuring the application.

In the case where a system is used beyond the boundaries anticipated by the designer, there is little to do except to restructure the system. For example, suppose an inventory system is built to keep track of office supplies. Once the system is functional, a data processing project manager sees how useful it is and decides to apply it to all the manufacturing inventory of the company, and then the system falls on its face because of transaction arrival rate, total amount of data handled, or for some other reason. If an inventory system for manufacturing goods is to be applied to a system designed to handle an order of magnitude or less of material, it is not surprising that a system rewrite is called for.

THE MEANING FOR DATA PROCESSING PROJECT MANAGEMENT

The major implications of the rapidly moving data processing field are that many of today's decision-making methods (for data processing) are rapidly becoming obsolete—and data processing management will have to change its methods accordingly.

1. *Equipment evaluation and selection.* This area is becoming so complex that mechanized evaluation appears to be the only realistic way of approaching the problem. The evaluation must include not only the hardware but also related software, such as operating system and program translators.

2. *Software selection.* The selection of software really constitutes a new decision area, especially for a large number of medium and small installations. This decision becomes critical as alternative software packages become available. The decision may become even more complex if hardware and software prices are separate, but in this case users may find it financially easier to obtain just the software they want.

3. *Reduced costs.* With computing the data storage costs being reduced rapidly, formerly uneconomic applications can be considered for conversion to the computer. One such application is the retention of large volumes of detailed transaction data for use by a management-reporting system. Also, new techniques can be considered, such as generalized file processing routines. If these routines are somewhat less efficient in their use of computer time and storage—and this point is not conceded by the developers of these routines—this is becoming a matter of less importance.

4. *New implementation methods.* Generalized file processing routines, decision tables, application packages, and time-shared systems promise much greater speed and reduced costs for converting many applications to the computer. Another benefit is that they will greatly ease the problems of making changes and improvements to applications already implemented by these methods.

5. *Computing utilities.* It is quite possible that computing utilities will offer much more powerful hardware-software combinations than the vast majority of independent installations can support. If data processing project management must choose between using a computing utility "now" which offers a powerful software system, or waiting several years before a more

limited system is available for their own computer, we suspect that many users will sign up with the computing utilities. They may well transfer more and more of their workload to these utilities as they integrate applications using the newer implementation methods.

REFERENCES

Canning, Richard G. and Sisson, Roger L. *The Management of Data Processing.* New York: John Wiley & Sons Inc., 1967.

Hajek, Victor G. *Management of Engineering Projects.* New York: McGraw- Hill, 1977.

Inmon, W. H. *Management Control of Data Processing: Preventing Management by Crisis.* Englewood Cliffs: Prentice-Hall, Inc., 1983.

20
IMPACT OF MICROCOMPUTERS ON BOTH PROJECTS AND PROJECT MANAGEMENT

With microcomputer technology advancing at a dizzying pace, computerized project management is no longer solely the reserve of the big-budget project manager.

As developers move to make mainframe style software available on personal computers, project management software has emerged as a sleeper that some say will join word processing and spreadsheets in the "must have" software library of every corporate executive.

Once the sole province of planners who masterminded complex and costly projects, project management techniques may soon guide small business in the same way that they have helped plan massive engineering endeavors. Techniques such as Program Evaluation and Review Technique (see Chapter 12) and Critical Path Method (see Chapter 11) help manage projects from their beginnings by breaking tasks into numerous segments and laying these in some kind of order. By making various computations, planners can determine factors such as the cost of the job, the time it will require and the number of people it will take to complete the task.

More importantly, the schemes will identify the crucial portions of the project. CPM determines which segments of a project will change the completion date if each is not completed on time. With this type of information, managers can tell how much slack time exists for each task and can schedule other tasks in such a way that the job gets done on time with the lowest cost.

The modern PERT chart did not emerge until the 1950s. Since then, PERT and variations on that technique have been used by planners mostly for very large construction and engineering projects, including the Alaska pipeline. Planners have performed much of the work manually, using a mainframe computer for the tedious calculations. Now that more computing power is creeping into desktop standalone computers, new products are bringing this planning capability to many people who are using it for more and smaller projects.

Within the last three years, planning programs that can assist planners with almost any task have become available for personal computers. One of these is The Primavera Project Planner from Primavera Systems Inc.

The Primavera Project Planner is a menu-driven project management program that offers sophisticated planning, monitoring, and tracking for managers well-vested in formal project management techniques. Primavera comes on four disks and is used on a PC XT or a PC with a hard disk drive. The program was originally developed for mainframe computers, so it's not surprising that it offers features seldom found in most personal computer project management software.

Primavera's ability to manage projects with up to 10,000 tasks is likely to satisfy the wants of any project manager using a PC. A single task can have 128 successor tasks (tasks whose start or finish depends on an active task) associated with it, in addition to six resources, variable and fixed costs, a code (which is useful when reports are generated), date constraints, and even a log of events.

USING TASKS

When a task is entered, the user is asked to provide a task number, a name, and an estimated duration. A task's duration can be specified by the user or calculated by the program based on needed or available resources using the resource leveling option. Additional information about a task is collected in seven screen forms that are displayed on demand. The forms are used to enter (and, to a limited extent, to display) information on successor tasks, resources, costs, task codes, time constraints, and project dates. A form for an electronic notepad records comments up to 400 characters long and appends them to the appropriate task.

The relationship between a task and its successors can take three forms: start-to-start, finish-to-finish, or finish-to-start. In the first relationship, a successor tasks starts a number of days after the preliminary task starts; in the second, a successor task cannot end until the preliminary task ends; in the third, the end of one task triggers the start of the next. The number of days a task must wait before it starts or end is also specified.

Task codes allow a project manager to produce very selective reports. For example, task codes can be linked to a supervisor responsible for overseeing the completion of certain tasks, to geographical locations, or to subprojects. At any point in the project, the project manager can print out a report detailing the supervisor's productivity in terms of tasks completed on schedule, resources expended, and associated costs. A task can have up to 20 codes.

RESOURCES AND COSTS

As noted earlier, tasks can be associated with all sorts of data. The same flexibility extends to the areas of resource and cost management. Six resources can be assigned to a task and 96 resource categories to a project—less than what mainframe packages offer but sufficient for managing many large projects. A resource's code, description, basic unit (such as manpower), and availability (normal units per day and maximum units per day before a certain date and after it for up to four dates) can all be recorded and linked to tasks and costs. Resource duration (the number of days a resource will be used) can be specified. With this information in hand, the Primavera Project Planner calculates the resources needed to complete a task (or a project) and compares actual data against budgeted quantities.

Costs are associated with tasks and resources and are assigned numeric and alphabetic codes. The alphabetic code designates cost categories, such as labor or equipment, while the numeric code defines subcategories, such as excavation or electrical under subcontract. A project can have up to six cost categories and a virtually unlimited number of subcategories.

Most importantly, Primavera offers resource leveling—a feature that averages out the availability of a task's vital resources and uses this information to determine its duration.

PROJECT CALENDAR

Primavera's project calendar embraces workweeks based on four to seven days. The user can specify a project's start and stop dates, and can take into account holidays and other nonworkdays. The project calendar can be printed in its entirety or by date range, in a detail or summary format.

PLANNING, MONITORING, AND TRACKING

Primavera schedules project tasks based on the Critical Path Method (CPM) using either the activity-on-arrow or activity-on-node methods. These approaches particularly illustrate Primavera's power to interrelate tasks, resources, and costs—the components that make up a project. These components can be changed with relative ease to generate alternative project models, even with models incorporating thousands of tasks.

Primavera excess at tracking and monitoring a project. The program will track resources and costs by task for the smallest allowable time period, and calculates variances. An unstarted task's duration, resource requirements, and start and stop dates can all be updated with actual results produced by completed tasks or tasks in progress; consumption of resources can likewise be monitored, with projected use compared against actual use. Primavera can create two project schedules—one based on the original project plan, the other on the plan and tracking data—and report the differences.

REPORTS

Primavera's reports give cost and resource summaries by task, disclose a supervisor's productivity, summarize the differences between estimated and actual project costs, and illustrate the complex task relationships that make up a project.

Reports fall into five categories:

1. network diagram
2. Gantt chart
3. resource reports
4. task list
5. cost reports.

NETWORK DIAGRAM

This chart portrays prerequisite and successor task relationships. A task's code, name, duration, remaining duration, percent completed, and earliest possible start and finish dates are shown. Reports can be selected based on total slack among various paths.

GANTT CHART

This task time line displays a project's critical path and indicates whether or not a project is on schedule. Task codes, earliest start and latest finish dates, durations and remaining durations are also displayed. Task information may be selected and summarized by task code and sorted by early start, late finish or slack time. The basic reporting unit is the day, week, or month.

RESOURCE REPORTS

Primavera produces five resource reports. The resource profile details an individual resource's use by day, week, or month. The cumulative resource profile is essentially a line graph that summarizes total resource use. The resource control report lists budgeted resources, resources expended to date and during the reported period, resources needed for completion, and variances. The resource usage report estimates the resources needed to complete a project on time and at the earliest and latest possible dates. The earned value report compares the value of work completed in resource units versus the actual resource units expended.

TASK LIST

Primavera's task list includes task codes, names, durations, percent completed, constraint dates, and prerequisite and successor task information. The report can include all tasks or those selected by resource, task code, early start date, late finish date, and slack time.

COST REPORTS

Cost reports closely mirror the form of resource reports. Cost profile, cumulative cost profile, cost control, cash flow, and earned value reports are available. Costs are reported by task, resource, or cost code.

A sample of The Primavera Project Planner reports/ screens directed toward a new product development schedule is presented in the following sections. Although the schedule is not specifically a data processing application, its logic activities are similar.

A Sample of the Primavera Project Planner Reports/Screens Directed Toward a New Product Development Schedule

PRIMAVERA UTILITIES

The following projects are contained in the directory:

HOME PNTG PNP4 PECO PHAR AERO PUBL BANK PNPO SYST

SELECT an existing project 1
LIST project names and titles 2
ADD a new project 3
DELETE a project. 4
DUPLICATE and rename project 5
MERGE several projects 6
CREATE a target schedule 7
BACKUP one or more projects 8
RESTORE one or more projects 9

EXIT PRIMAVERA X

Press selection

CONFIRM selection

Project name is PNP4

Project Title: Primavera New Product Devel.   PNP4
Company Name: Primavera Systems, Inc.

Report Center Heading: ***ACTUAL PROGRESS SCHEDULE*** (215) 667-8600

Project Start Date: 30JUL84   Project must Finish no later than:

Network Type (PDM or ADM):   PDM   5 Workdays Per Week

Schedule data date: 2NOV84

TARGET #   DATA DATE
-------------   ---------------
1   30JUL84
2
NOTE: If target does not show a data date,
it is not stored in your P3 directory.
MMMMMMMMMMMMMMMMMMMMMMMMMMMMMMMMMMMMMMMMMMMMMM
Commands: Advance   Edit   Help   Return

PROJECT DATA MENU   PNP4

Project data:
 Calendar 1
 Activity data 2

Dictionaries:
 Activity codes 3
 Resource codes 4
 Costs account codes 5

Calculations:
 Scheduling 6
 Leveling 7

Reports:
 Execution 8
 Specification 9

      Return to PRIMAVERA utility menu . . . . .R

      Exit PRIMAVERA X

Press selection

```
                        ACTIVITY DATA                      PNP4
                        --------------------

Activity number:        30                            TF:  63
          Title:   Final Design Review               PCT:   0

     ES: 21NOV84  EF:  6DEC84  Orig. duration  10   Actual start:
     LS: 28FEB85  LF: 13MAR85  Rem. duration   10   Actual finish:

Activity Codes:   PRODUCTMKG 4   4
MMMMMMMMMMMMMMMMMMMMMMMMMMMMMMMMMMMMMMMMMMMMMMMMMMM
FINANCIAL (COST)SUMMARY:
                     Resource 1         Resource 2         Resource 3
                     ------------------  ------------------  ----------------


Resource code          PRODUCMR          PRODMGRS          CORPEXEC
Cost acct code/type      2100E             2100E             7000A
Budgeted cost          1290.00           1185.00           1410.00
Actual cost to date       0.00              0.00              0.00
Percent expended            0                 0                 0
Percent complete            0                 0                 0
Earned value              0.00              0.00              0.00
Cost to complete       1290.00           1185.00           1410.00
Cost at completion     1290.00           1185.00           1410.00
Variance                  0.00              0.00              0.00
MMMMMMMMMMMMMMMMMMMMMMMMMMMMMMMMMMMMMMMMMMMMMMMMMM
Commands: Add Delete Edit Help More Next Return autoSort Transfer Window
Windows   : Act.codes Blank Constraints Dates Financial Log Resources
Successors
```

```
--------------------------------------------------------------------------------
                     PRIMAVERA PROJECT PLANNER
                 Activity Codes for Project PNP4              Page 1
--------------------------------------------------------------------------------
```

Code Name: RESP   Description: Respons. Group   Field Length = 10

Code Value	Code Title
MARKETING	Marketing Department
MARKETCOMM	Marketing Communications
PRODUCTMKG	New Product Marketing
CUSTOMSUPP	Customer Support
QC & QA	Quality Control and Assurance
PRODTRAING	New Product Training
DIRECTSALE	Direct Sales
RESEARCH	Research and Development
PROGDEVELT	New Product Program Development
SYSTEMTEST	New Product System Test
DOCUMENTN	Documentation and Editing
OPERATIONS	Operations Department
EXECOFFICE	Executive Officer Group
CONFIGURTN	Configuration Control
STRATEGIC	Long-range Strategic Planning Group
SCHEDULING	Project Scheduling and Control
NEWPRODMGR	New Product Department Manager
PROJECTMGR	New Product Project Leader/Manager
FIELDSALES	Field Sales Support

```
------------------------------------------------------------------------------------
                        PRIMAVERA PROJECT PLANNER              PNP4
1                       Summary of Cost Account Codes
------------------------------------------------------------------------------------
```

Cost Categories:

Code	Category Title	Code	Category Title
E	Engineer	M	Marketng
P	Productn	A	Administ
D	DataProc	F	Finance

Cost Account Titles:

Cost Account Number	Account Title
1000	Marketing
1100	Field Support
1200	Sales
2000	Research and Development
2100	New Product Development
2200	Product Documentation
3000	Data Processing
3100	Technical Support
3200	Design Engineering
4000	Operations
4100	Manufacturing Engineering
4200	Production
4300	Test and Erect
4400	Quality Assurance
4500	Quality Control
4600	Shipping and Receiving
5000	Personnel
5100	Labor Union
6000	Accounting
7000	Corporate

PRIMAVERA PROJECT PLANNER
Activity Codes for Project PNP 4   Page 2

Code Name: MILE   Description: Milestones   Field Length = 2

<u>Code Value</u>   <u>Code Title</u>

Code Value	Code Title
1	Project Planning Start
2	Product Requirements Spec.
3	Functional Design Plan
4	Final Design Review
5	Release to System Test
6	Release to Quality Assurance
7	Quality Assurance Complete
8	Release To Production
9	Release to Ship
10	Channel Roll-out Complete

Code Name: PHAS   Description: Project Phase   Field Length = 2

<u>Code Value</u>   <u>Code Title</u>

Code Value	Code Title
1	Project Phase I: Project Start-up
2	Project Phase II: Product Design and Specify
3	Project Phase III: Project Planning
4	Project Phase IV: Final Product Approvals
5	Project Phase V: Product Training
6	Project Phase VI: Marketing and Advertising/PR
7	Project Phase VII: Operations/Manufacturing

Resource Code Summary   PNP4

Code	Description
COORDINR	Product Coordinator
FIELDSUP	Field Support Staff
MARKSUPP	Marketing Support Staff
TECHSUPP	Marketing Technical Support Staff
MARKETQA	Marketing Quality Assurance
MARKETMR	Product Marketing Manager
PRODUCMR	Product Manager
TRAINSPL	Training Specialist
MARKETRN	Marketing: Training
MARKETCM	Marketing: Communications
SALESREP	Sales Representatives
CORPEXEC	Corporate Executive
OPERMGMT	Operations Management
OPERPERS	Operations Personnel
PRODMGRS	Product Development Directors & Managers
TESTCOOR	System Test Coordinator
WRITERS	Documentation Writers
EDITORS	Documentation Editors
SPECIAL	Documentation Specialist
SOFTENGR	Software Engineers
CONFIGCR	Configuration Control Coordinator

PNP4

Types of Reports

Schedule (tabular) reports 1
Barchart schedule 2
Network logic diagram 3
Resource reports 4
Costing reports 5

Return to Project Data Menu . . . . .R

Press selection

Primavera Systems, Inc.　　　PRIMAVERA PROJECT PLANNER　　　Primavera New Product Delev. PNP4

REPORT DATE 14SEP84 RUN NO. 56　　　***ACTUAL PROGRESS SCHEDULE***　　　(215) 667-8600　START DATE 30JUL84　FIN DATE

DATA DATE 2 NOV84　PAGE NO. 1

Schedule Report for Actual Progress vs. Target

ACTIVITY NUMBER	TAR DUR	CUR DUR	CUR PCT	CODE	ACTIVITY DESCRIPTION	CURRENT START	EARLY FINISH	TARGET START	EARLY FINISH	VAR.
2	10	0	100	STRATEGIC	Preliminary Strategic Marketing Planning	30JUL84A	10AUG84A	30JUL84	10AUG84	0
3	10	0	100	PRODUCTMKG	Preliminary New Product Planning	30JUL84A	10AUG84A	30JUL84	10AUG84	0
4	1	0	100	PROJECTMGR	Start Project Planning and Management	13AUG84A	13AUG84A	13AUG84	13AUG84	0
5	30	0	100	RESEARCH	Create/Prepare Product Specifications	14AUG84A	25SEP84A	14AUG84	25SEP84	0
6	3	0	100	PROJECTMGR	Approve/Edit Product Specifications	26SEP84A	28SEP84A	26SEP84	28SEP84	0
7	5	0	100	PROGDEVELT	Functional Design Specifications	10CT84A	50CT84A	10CT84	50CT84	0
8	3	0	100	NEWPRODMGR	Preliminary Documentation of Specifications	10CT84A	30CT84A	10CT84	30CT84	0
9	4	0	100	PRODUCTRNG	Preliminary Training Plan and Documentation	10CT84A	40CT84A	10CT84	40CT84	0
10	5	0	100	NEWPRODMGR	Detailed Project Planning	10CT84A	50CT84A	10CT84	50CT84	0
11	5	0	100	STRATEGIC	Preliminary Integrated Planning	10CT84A	50CT84A	10CT84	50CT84	0
12	3	0	100	NEWPRODMGR	Functional Design Plan Approved	80CT84A	100CT84A	80CT84	100CT84	0
13	3	0	100	QC & QA	Quality Assurance Standards Designed	110CT84A	150CT84A	110CT84	150CT84	0
22	5	0	100	PRODUCTMKG	Preliminary Packaging Design	110CT84A	260CT84A	110CT84	170CT84	-7
23	3	0	100	MARKETCOMM	Preliminary Marketing/Sales Forecast	110CT84A	150CT84A	110CT84	150CT84	0
20	3	0	100	FIELDSALES	Field Support Plan	110CT84A	150CT84A	110CT84	150CT84	0
21	5	0	100	PRODUCTRNG	Training Plan	110CT84A	170CT84A	110CT84	170CT84	0
27	3	0	100	MARKETCOMM	Advertising and Public Relations	110CT84A	150CT84A	110CT84	150CT84	0
28	3	0	100	MARKETCOMM	Collateral Plan	110CT84A	150CT84A	110CT84	150CT84	0
29	4	0	100	CUSTOMSUPP	Customer Support Plan	110CT84A	160CT84A	110CT84	160CT84	0
14	10	0	100	NEWPRODMGR	Project Design/Network Review	160CT84A	290CT84A	160CT84	290CT84	0
24	4	0	100	PRODUCTMKG	Preliminary Bill of Materials and Allocation	180CT84A	230CT84A	180CT84	230CT84	0
25	4	0	100	PRODUCTMKG	Costing and Economic Impact	240CT84A	260CT84A	240CT84	260CT84	0
36	65	59	10	PRODUCTMKG	Artistically Design Package	260CT84A	27FEB85	6DEC84	6MAR85	5
26	5	1	80	OPERATIONS	Preliminary Operations and Manufacturing	290CT84A	2NOV84	290CT84	2NOV84	0
15	15	13	13	OPERATIONS	Final Design	300CT84A	20NOV84	300CT84	19NOV84	-1
16	3	1	85	QC & QA	Final Test Specifications Approved	300CT84A	2NOV84	300CT84	1NOV84	-1
17	3	1	85	DOCUMENTN	Final Documentation Specifications	300CT84A	2NOV84	300CT84	1NOV84	-1
18	5	1	90	QC & QA	Final Quality Assurance Specification	300CT84A	2NOV84	300CT84	1NOV84	-1
19	5	1	70	PRODUCTMKG	Final User Interface Design	300CT84A	2NOV84	300CT84	5NOV84	1
30	10	10	0	PRODUCTMKG	Final Design Review	21NOV84	6DEC84	20NOV84	5DEC84	-1
41	56	56	0	MARKETCOMM	Advertising and Collateral	7DEC84	22FEB85	6DEC84	21FEB85	-1
32	40	40	0	PROGDEVELT	Create, Code and Implement Modules	7DEC84	31JAN85	6DEC84	30JAN85	-1
34	45	45	0	DOCUMENTN	Implement Documentation	7DEC84	7FEB85	6DEC84	6FEB85	-1
40	20	20	0	MARKETCOMM	Analyze Target Market and Liscensing	7DEC84	3JAN85	22FEB85	21MAR85	55

ACTIVITY NUMBER	ORIG DUR	REM DUR	PCT	CODE	ACTIVITY DESCRIPTION	EARLY START	EARLY FINISH	LATE START	LATE FINISH	TOTAL FLOAT
2	10	0	100	STRATEGIC	Preliminary Strategic Marketing Planning	30JUL84A	10AUG84A			
4*	1	0	100	SUCC	Start Project Planning and Management	13UAG84A	13UAG84A			
3	10	0	100	PRODUCTMKG	Preliminary New Product Planning	30JUL84A	10AUG84A			
4*	1	0	100	SUCC	Start Project Planning and Management	13UAG84A	13UAG84A			
4	1	0	100	PROJECTMGR	Start Project Planning and Management	13AUG84A	13AUG84A			
5*	30	0	100	SUCC	Create/Prepare Product Specifications	14AUG84A	25SEP84A			
6*	3	0	100	SUCC	Approve/Edit Product Specifications	26SEP84A	28SEP84A			
2*	10	0	100	PRED	Preliminary Strategic Marketing Planning	30JUL84A	10AUG84A			
3*	10	0	100	PRED	Preliminary New Product Planning	30JUL84A	10AUG84A			
5	30	0	100	RESEARCH	Create/Prepare Product Specifications	14AUG84A	25SEP84A			
6*	3	0	100	SUCC	Approve/Edit Product Specifications	26SEP84A	28SEP84A			
4*	1	0	100	PRED	Start Project Planning and Management	13AUG84A	13AUG84A			
6	3	0	100	PROJECTMGR	Approve/Edit Product Specifications	26SEP84A	28SEP84A			
7*	5	0	100	SUCC	Functional Design Specifications	1OCT84A	5OCT84A			
8*	3	0	100	SUCC	Preliminary Documentation of Specifications	1OCT84A	3OCT84A			
9*	4	0	100	SUCC	Preliminary Training Plan and Documentation	1OCT84A	4OCT84A			
10*	5	0	100	SUCC	Detailed Project Planning	1OCT84A	5OCT84A			
11*	5	0	100	SUCC	Preliminary Integrated Planning	1OCT84A	5OCT84A			
12*	3	0	100	SUCC	Functional Design Plan Approved	8OCT84A	10OCT84A			
5*	30	0	100	PRED	Create/Prepare Product Specifications	14AUG84A	25SEP84A			
4*	1	0	100	PRED	Start Project Planning and Management	13AUG84A	13AUG84A			
7	5	0	100	PROGDEVELT	Functional Design Specifications	1OCT84A	5OCT84A			
12*	3	0	100	SUCC	Functional Design Plan Approved	8OCT84A	10OCT84A			
6*	3	0	100	PRED	Approve/Edit Product Specifications	26SEP84A	28SEP84A			
8	3	0	100	NEWPRODMGR	Preliminary Documentation of Specifications	1OCT84A	3OCT84A			
12*	3	0	100	SUCC	Functional Design Plan Approved	8OCT84A	10OCT84A			
6*	3	0	100	PRED	Approve/Edit Product Specifications	26SEP84A	28SEP84A			
9	4	0	100	PRODUCTRNG	Preliminary Training Plan and Documentation	1OCT84A	4OCT84A			
12*	3	0	100	SUCC	Functional Design Plan Approved	8OCT84A	10OCT84A			
6*	3	0	100	PRED	Approve/Edit Product Specifications	26SEP84A	28SEP84A			

261

Schedule Report for Activity Code with Budget

DATA DATE 2NOV84   PAGE NO. 1

ACTIVITY NUMBER	ORIG DUR	REM DUR	PCT	CODE	ACTIVITY DESCRIPTION / BUDGET	EARNED	EARLY START	EARLY FINISH	LATE START	LATE FINISH	TOTAL FLOAT
3	10	0	100	PRODUCTMKG	Preliminary New Product Planning / 2160.00	2160.00	30JUL84A	10AUG84A			
23	3	0	100	PRODUCTMKG	Preliminary Marketing/Sales Forecast / 390.00	390.00	11OCT84A	15OCT84A			
24	4	0	100	PRODUCTMKG	Preliminary Bill of Materials and Allocation / 516.00	516.00	18OCT84A	23OCT84A			
25	3	0	100	PRODUCTMKG	Costing and Economic Impact / 1030.00	1030.00	24OCT84A	26OCT84A			
36	65	59	10	PRODUCTMKG	Artistically Design Package / 10237.50	1023.75	26OCT84A	27FEB85		27FEB85	0
19	5	1	70	PRODUCTMKG	Final User Interface Design / 645.00	451.50	30OCT84A	2NOV84		20NOV84	12
30	10	10	0	PRODUCTMKG	Final Design Review / 3885.00	.00	21NOV84	6DEC84	21NOV84	6DEC84	0
35	1	1	0	PRODUCTMKG	Review and Update Forecast / 129.00	.00	7DEC84	7DEC84	27FEB85	27FEB85	58
39	10	10	0	PRODUCTMKG	Develop Sales Precedures and Demonstrations / 3615.00	.00	7DEC84	20DEC84	5MAR85	18MAR85	62
31	5	5	0	PRODUCTMKT	Integrated Scheduling / 1290.00	.00	7DEC84	13DEC84	12MAR85	18MAR85	67
38	5	5	0	PRODUCTMKG	Develop Marketing Policies and Procedures / 1823.00	.00	7DEC84	13DEC84	12MAR85	18MAR85	67
57	5	5	0	PRODUCTMKG	Prepare Product Announcement and Industry Intro. / 1215.00	.00	8MAY85	14MAY85	9MAY85	15MAY85	1
62	2	2	0	PRODUCTMKG	Final Product and Specification Review / 690.00	.00	20MAY85	21MAY85	30MAY85	31MAY85	8
65	5	5	0	PRODUCTMKG	Release To Production / 1890.00	.00	3JUN85	7JUN85	3JUN85	7JUN85	0
71	5	5	0	PRODUCTMKG	Release To Shipping / 1245.00	.00	24JUN85	28JUN85	24JUN85	28JUN85	0
76	40	40	0	PRODUCTMKG	Channel Roll-out Monitor / 4560.00	.00	1JUL85	23AUG85	1JUL85	23AUG85	0
79	1	1	0	PRODUCTMKG	Channel Roll-out Complete / 498.00	.00	26AUG85	26AUG85	26AUG85	26AUG85	0

SUBTOTAL   PRODUCTMKG   35818.50   5571.25

REPORT TOTAL   35818.50   5571.25

262

REPORT DATE 7SEP84 RUN NO. 25   ***ACTUAL PROGRESS SCHEDULE***   (215) 667-8600   START DATE 30JUL84   FIN DATE

Detailed Schedule Report for Individual Activity   DATA DATE 2NOV84   PAGE NO. 1

ACTIVITY NUMBER	ORIG DUR	REM DUR	PCT	CODE	ACTIVITY DESCRIPTION	BUDGET	EARNED	EARLY START	EARLY FINISH	LATE START	LATE FINISH	TOTAL FLOAT
36	65	59	10		Artistically Design Package	10237.50	1023.75	26OCT84A	27FEB85		27FEB85	0
				1 2 3	Activity start due to advertising agency restriction; resource availability okayed by marketing management							
30*	10	10	0	PRED	Final Design Review			21NOV84	6DEC84	21NOV84	6DEC84	0
37*	13	13	0	SUCC	Preliminary Procurements			28FEB85	18MAR85	28FEB85	18MAR85	0
				UPDATE				IMPOSE DATE TYPE		DATE		

REPORT TOTAL

          =======   =======
          10237.50   1023.75

263

Time-Scaled Bar Chart showing Progress vs Target

WEEKLY-TIME PER. 1

PRIMAVERA
PROJECT PLANNER

TIMESCALE BARCHART

LEGEND

E - EARLY DATES
L - LATE DATES
+ - POSITIVE FLOAT
- - NEGATIVE FLOAT
/ - EARLY/LATE OVERLAP
A - ACTUAL DATES
* - DATA DATE
H - HOLIDAY
V - LEVELED DATES

Timescale: 08OCT84   17DEC84   25FEB85   06MAY85   15JUL85   23SEP85   02DEC8

| ....ACTIVITY DESCRIPTION......... | | | | | | | |
ACTIVITY NO	OD	RD	PCT	CODES	FLOATS	SCHEDULE	
Preliminary New Product Planning 3	10	0	100	PRODUCTMKG		PROGRESS	AA
						TARGET	/E
Preliminary Marketing/Sales Forecast 23	3	0	100	PRODUCTMKG		PROGRESS	
						TARGET	
Preliminary Bill of Materials and Allocation 24	4	0	100	PRODUCTMKG		PROGRESS	
						TARGET	
Costing and Economic Impact 25	3	0	100	PRODUCTMKG		PROGRESS	
						TARGET	
Artistically Design Package 36	65	59	10	PRODUCTMKG	0	PROGRESS	
						TARGET	
Final User Interface Design 19	5	1	70	PRODUCTMKG	12	PROGRESS	
						TARGET	
Final Design Review 30	10	10	0	PRODUCTMKG	0	PROGRESS	
						TARGET	
Review and Update Forecast 35	1	1	0	PRODUCTMKG	58	PROGRESS	
						TARGET	
Develop Sales Procedures and Demonstrations 39	10	10	0	PRODUCTMKG	62	PROGRESS	
						TARGET	
Integrated Scheduling 31	5	5	0	PRODUCTMKG	67	PROGRESS	
						TARGET	
Develop Marketing Policies and Procedures 38	5	5	0	PRODUCTMKG	67	PROGRESS	
						TARGET	
Prepare Product Announcement and Industry Intro. 57	5	5	0	PRODUCTMKG	1	PROGRESS	
						TARGET	
Final Product and Specification Review 62	2	2	0	PRODUCTMKG	8	PROGRESS	
						TARGET	
Release To Production 65	5	5	0	PRODUCTMKG	0	PROGRESS	
						TARGET	
Release To Shipping 71	5	5	0	PRODUCTMKG	0	PROGRESS	
						TARGET	

Network Logic Diagram for a Total Float   Data Date 2NOV84 PAGE NO.   1

```
XXXXXXXXXXXXXXXXXXXXXX
X                    X
X                    X
X                    X
X   NO PREDECESSORS  X------
X                    X
X                    X
X                    X
XXXXXXXXXXXXXXXXXXXXXX
```

```
              V
          XXXXXXXXXXXXXXXXXXXXXX    XXXXXXXXXXXXXXXXXXXXXX    XXXXXXXXXXXXXXXXXXXXXX    XXXXXXXXXXXXXXXXXXXXXX
          X ACT NO.        2 X      X ACT NO.        4  X     X ACT NO.        5 X      X ACT NO.        6 X
          X                  X      X                   X     X                  X      X                  X
TOTAL     X   Preliminary Stra X    X  Start Project Pl X     X  Create/Prepare P X     X  Approve/Edit Pro X
FLOAT     X   tegic Marketing X------X anning and Manag X------X roduct Specifica X-------X duct Specificati X---------
   0      X   Planning        X      X ement            X      X tions            X      X ons              X
          X                  X      X                   X     X                  X      X                  X
          XOD  10 RD   0 PCT100X     XOD  1 RD   0 PCT100X     XOD  3 RD  0 PCT100X      XOD  3RD   0 PCT 100X
          XXXXXXXXXXXXXXXXXXXXXX    XXXXXXXXXXXXXXXXXXXXXX    XXXXXXXXXXXXXXXXXXXXXX    XXXXXXXXXXXXXXXXXXXXXX
          ES 30JUL84A EF 10AUG84A    ES 13AUG84A EF 13AUG84A   ES 14AUG84A EF 25SEP84A   ES 26SEP84A EF 28SEP84A
```

```
              V
          XXXXXXXXXXXXXXXXXXXXXX    XXXXXXXXXXXXXXXXXXXXXX    XXXXXXXXXXXXXXXXXXXXXX    XXXXXXXXXXXXXXXXXXXXXX
          X ACT NO.        7 X      X ACT NO.       12  X     X ACT NO.       13 X      X ACT NO.       14 X
          X                  X      X                   X     X                  X      X                  X
TOTAL     X Functional Desig X      X Functional Desig X      X Quality Assuranc X      X Project Design/N X
FLOAT     X n Specifications X------X n Plan Approved  X------X e Standards Desi X-------X etwork Review    X---------
   0      X                  X      X                   X     X gned             X      X                  X
          X                  X      X                   X     X                  X      X                  X
          XOD  5 RD   0 PCT100X     XOD  3 RD   0 PCT100X     XOD  3 RD  0 PCT100X      XOD  10 RD   0 PCT100X
          XXXXXXXXXXXXXXXXXXXXXX    XXXXXXXXXXXXXXXXXXXXXX    XXXXXXXXXXXXXXXXXXXXXX    XXXXXXXXXXXXXXXXXXXXXX
          ES 10OCT84A EF  5OCT84A    ES  8OCT84A EF 10OCT84A   ES 11OCT84A EF 15OCT84A   ES 16OCT84A EF 29OCT84A
```

```
              V
          XXXXXXXXXXXXXXXXXXXXXX    XXXXXXXXXXXXXXXXXXXXXX    XXXXXXXXXXXXXXXXXXXXXX    XXXXXXXXXXXXXXXXXXXXXX
          X ACT NO.       15 X      X ACT NO.       30  X     X ACT NO.       36 X      X ACT NO.       37 X
          X                  X      X                   X     X                  X      X                  X
TOTAL     X Final Design     X      X Final Design Rev X      X Artistically Des X      X Preliminary Proc X
FLOAT     X                  X------X iew              X------X ign Package      X-------X urements         X---------
   0      X                  X      X                   X     X                  X      X                  X
          X                  X      X                   X     X                  X      X                  X
          XOD  15 RD  13 PCT 13X     XOD  10 RD  10 PCT  0X     XOD  65 RD  59 PCT 10X    XOD  13 RD  13 PCT  OX
          XXXXXXXXXXXXXXXXXXXXXX    XXXXXXXXXXXXXXXXXXXXXX    XXXXXXXXXXXXXXXXXXXXXX    XXXXXXXXXXXXXXXXXXXXXX
          ES 30OCT84A EF 20NOV84     ES 21NOV84  EF  6DEC84    ES 26OCT84A EF 27FEB85    ES 28FEB85  EF 16MAR85
```

Types of Resource Reports   PNP4

Profile of resource usage 1
Cumulative profile of resource usage 2
Control Report 3
Productivity 4
Earned value (units) Report 5
Tabular resource usage 6
        Return to Report Specification Menu .R

Press selection:

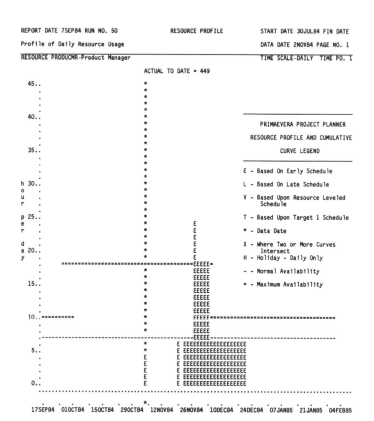

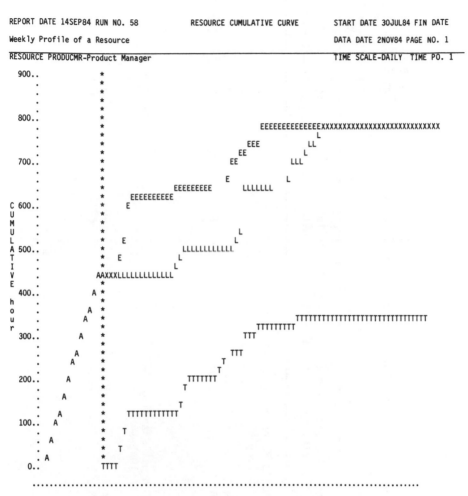

REPORT DATE 14SEP84 RUN NO. 58   RESOURCE CUMULATIVE CURVE   START DATE 30JUL84 FIN DATE

Weekly Profile of a Resource   DATA DATE 2NOV84 PAGE NO. 1

RESOURCE PRODUCMR-Product Manager   TIME SCALE-DAILY TIME PO. 1

Activity No.	Resource Ccde	Account Code	Account Category	Unit Meas	Budget	PCT CMP	Actual To Date	Actual This Period	Estimate To Complete	Forecast	Variance
2	Preliminary Strategic Marketing Planning										
	RD 0 AS 30JUL84 AF 10AUG84										
	PRODUCMR	2100M		Hour	60	100	60	0	0	60	0
	MARKETMR	1000M		Hour	60	100	60	0	0	60	0
3	Preliminary New Product Planning										
	RD 0 AS 30JUL84 AF 10AUG84										
	PRDUCMR	2100E		Hour	40	100	40	0	0	40	0
	MARKETMR	2100M		Hour	60	100	60	0	0	60	0

4   Start Project Planning and Management
     RD 0 AS 13AUG84 AF 13AUG84

     PRODUCMR   2100E   Hour   6   100   5   0   0   5   1

5   Create/Prepare Product Specifications
     RD 0 AS 14AUG84 AF 25SEP84

     PRODUCMR   3200   DataProc   Hour   180   100   175   0   0   175   5
     WRITERS   2200E   Hour   180   100   181   0   0   181   -1

6   Approve/Edit Product Specifications
     RD 0 AS 26SEP84 AF 28SEP84

     PRODUCMR   2100E   Hour   18   100   19   0   0   19   -1

Account Number	---Quantity--- Budget	To Date	Forecast	---Labor--- Budget	To Date	Forecast	---Labor Per Unit Quantity--- Budget	To Date	Forecast
1000 - Marketing									
LABOR UNIT PER MARKETCM (Hour)									
	1241	144	1277	402	44	404	.324	.306	.316
1100 - Field Support									
LABOR UNIT PER MARKETCM (Hour)									
	0	0	0	48	0	48	.000	.000	.000
1200 - Sales									
LABOR UNIT PER MARKETCM (Hour)									
	0	0	0	60	0	60	.000	.000	.000

270

2100 – New Product Development

LABOR UNIT PER PRODUCMR (Hour)

406	242	402
348	91	349
.857	.376	.868

2200 – Product Documentation

LABOR UNIT PER PRODUCMR (Hour)

18	15	33
156	34	190
8.667	2.267	5.758

1100 – Field Support

LABOR UNIT PER FIELDSUP (Hour)

18	20	20
48	0	48
2.667	.000	2.400

PRODUCMR – Product Manager

UNIT OF MEASURE – Hour

Activity No.	Resource Code	Account Code	Account Category	Unit Meas	Budget	PCT CMP	Actual To Date	Earned Value	Variance
2	PRODUCMR	2100M		Hour	60	100	60	60	0
3	PRODUCMR	2100E		Hour	40	100	40	40	0
4	PRODUCMR	2100E		Hour	6	100	5	6	1
5	PRODUCMR	3200D		Hour	180	100	175	180	5
6	PRODUCMR	2100E		Hour	18	100	19	18	-1
7	PRODUCMR	2100E		Hour	30	100	31	30	-1
8	PRODUCMR	2200E		Hour	18	100	15	18	3
11	PRODUCMR	2100A		Hour	30	100	28	30	2
12	PRODUCMR	2100A		Hour	18	100	18	18	0

19	PRODUCMR	2100E	Hour	30	85	26	26	0
23	PRODUCMR	1200M	Hour	18	100	17	18	1
25	PRODUCMR	2100A	Hour	18	100	15	18	3
30	PRODUCMR	2100E	Hour	60	0	0	0	0
31	PRODUCMR	1000M	Hour	30	0	0	0	0
35	PRODUCMR	1000P	Hour	6	0	0	0	0
37	PRODUCMR	4000P	Hour	13	0	0	0	0
38	PRODUCMR	2100M	Hour	30	0	0	0	0
39	PRODUCMR	1200M	Hour	60	0	0	0	0
52	PRODUCMR	4400P	Hour	30	0	0	0	0
57	PRODUCMR	1000M	Hour	30	0	0	0	0
61	PRODUCMR	4400P	Hour	0	0	0	0	0
62	PRODUCMR	4400E	Hour	12	0	0	0	0
65	PRODUCMR	2100E	Hour	30	0	0	0	0
71	PRODUCMR	2100P	Hour	30	0	0	0	0
79	PRODUCMR	2100E	Hour	6	0	0	0	0
TOTAL	PRODUCMR			803		449	461	12

Activity No.	Resource Code	Account Code XXXXXXXIXXXX	Account Category	Unit Meas	Budget	PCT CMP	Actual To Date	Earned Value	Variance
2	MARKETMR	1000M		Hour	60	100	60	60	0
9	MARKETMR	1000M		Hour	24	100	23	24	1
13	MARKETQA	1000M		Hour	18	100	21	18	-3
20	FIELDSUP	1100M		Hour	18	100	20	18	-2
21	MARKETRN	1000M		Hour	30	100	35	30	-5
22	MARKETCM	1000M		Hour	30	100	72	30	-42
23	PRODUCMR	1200M		Hour	18	100	17	18	1
27	MARKETCM	1000M		Hour	18	100	15	18	3
28	MARKETCM	1000M		Hour	18	100	15	18	3
29	TECHSUPP	1100M		Hour	24	100	20	24	4
31	PRODUCMR	1000M		Hour	30	0	0	0	0
35	PRODUCMR	1000M		Hour	6	0	0	0	0
36	MARKETCM	1000M		Hour	455	10	42	46	4
38	MARKETMR	1000M		Hour	30	0	0	0	0
38	TECHSUPP	1000M		Hour	30	0	0	0	0
39	PRODUCMR	1200M		Hour	60	0	0	0	0
39	MARKETCM	1000M		Hour	60	0	0	0	0
39	SOFTENGR	1000	DataProc	Hour	60	0	0	0	0
40	MARKETCM	1000M		Hour	180	0	0	0	0
41	MARKETCM	1000A		Hour	420	0	0	0	0
44	TECHSUPP	1100M		Hour	18	0	0	0	0
44	WRITERS	1100M		Hour	18	0	0	0	0
57	MARKETCM	1000M		Hour	30	0	0	0	0
57	PRODUCMR	1000M		Hour	30	0	0	0	0
63	SALESREP	1200M		Hour	60	0	0	0	0
64	MARKETCM	1000M		Hour	30	0	0	0	0
67	TECHSUPP	1100M		Hour	30	0	0	0	0
68	SALESREP	1200M		Hour	30	0	0	0	0
68	FIELDSUP	1200M		Hour	30	0	0	0	0
76	MARKETRN	1000M		Hour	240	0	0	0	0
77	FIELDSUP	1000E		Hour	60	0	0	0	0
	TOTAL	1000E		Hour	2165		340	304	-36

Tabular Usage Report of a Resource vs Target

PRODUCMR - Product Manager   UNIT OF MEASURE = Hour

Period Ending	Daily Avail- Normal	Maximum	Early Schedule Usage	Avg.Daily	Cumulative	Late Schedule Usage	Avg.Daily	Cumulative	Target 1 Schedule Usage	Avg.Daily	Cumulative
TO DATE											
08Nov84	7	7	4	.8	449	0	.0	449	12	2.4	454
15Nov84	7	7	0	.0	453	0	.0	449	0	.0	466
26Nov84	7	7	12	2.4	453	16	3.2	449	18	3.6	466
30Nov84	7	7	24	6.0	465	24	6.0	465	24	6.0	484
07Dec84	7	7	48	9.6	489	24	4.8	489	48	9.6	508
14Dec84	7	7	78	15.6	537	0	.0	513	36	7.2	556
21Dec84	7	7	24	4.8	615	0	.0	513	0	.0	592
28Dec84	7	7	0	.0	639	0	.0	513	0	.0	592
04Jan85	7	7	0	.0	639	0	.0	513	0	.0	592
11Jan85	7	7	0	.0	639	0	.0	513	0	.0	592
18Jan85	7	7	0	.0	639	0	.0	513	0	.0	592
25Jan85	7	7	0	.0	639	0	.0	513	0	.0	592
01Feb85	7	7	0	.0	639	0	.0	513	0	.0	592
08Feb85	7	7	0	.0	639	0	.0	513	0	.0	592
15Feb85	7	7	0	.0	639	0	.0	513	0	.0	592
22Feb85	7	7	0	.0	639	0	.0	513	0	.0	592
01Mar85	7	7	2	.4	641	8	1.6	521	0	.0	592
08Mar85	7	7	5	1.0	646	29	5.8	550	14	2.8	606
15Mar85	7	7	5	1.0	651	83	16.6	633	35	7.0	641
22Mar85	7	7	1	.2	652	19	3.8	652	23	4.6	664
29Mar85	7	7	0	.0	652	0	.0	652	1	.2	665
05Apr85	7	7	0	.0	652	0	.0	652	0	.0	665
12Apr85	7	7	0	.0	652	0	.0	652	0	.0	665
19Apr85	7	7	0	.0	652	0	.0	652	0	.0	665
26Apr85	7	7	0	.0	652	0	.0	652	0	.0	665
03May85	7	7	18	3.6	670	18	3.6	670	0	.0	665
10May85	7	7	30	6.0	700	24	4.8	694	18	3.6	683
17May85	7	7	12	2.4	712	18	3.6	712	30	6.0	713
24May85	7	7	12	2.4	724	0	.0	712	12	2.4	725
31May85	7	7	0	.0	724	12	2.4	724	12	2.4	737
07Jun85	7	7	30	6.0	754	30	6.0	754	0	.0	737
14Jun85	7	7	0	.0	754	0	.0	754	30	6.0	767
21Jun85	7	7	0	.0	754	0	.0	754	0	.0	767

Activity No.	Resource Code	Daily Usage	RES LAG	REM DUR	----Early Start---- DATE	TF	Norm	Max	--Delayed by Pred-- Date	TF	Norm	Max	---Delayed by Res-- Date	TF	Norm	Max	Leveled Start	Finish
2	Preliminary Strateg			10	30Jul84												30Jul84	10Aug84
	PRDUCMR	6		10	30Jul84	0	7	10									30Jul84	10Aug84
3	Preliminary New Pro			10	30Jul84	0							13Aug84	-10			13Aug84	24Aug84
	PRODUCMR	6		10	30Jul84	0	1	4					13Aug84	-10	7	10	13Aug84	24Aug84
4	Start Project Plann			1	13Aug84	0			27Aug84	-10							27Aug84	27Aug84
	PRODUCMR	6		1	13Aug84	0		4	27Aug84	-10	7	10					27Aug84	27Aug84
5	Create/Prepare Prod			30	14Aug84	0			28Aug84	-10							28Aug84	09Oct84
	PRODUCMR	6		30	14Aug84	0	1	4	28Aug84	-10	7	10					28Aug84	09Oct84
6	Approve/Edit Produc			3	26Sep84	0			10Oct84	-10							10Oct84	12Oct84
	PRODUCMR	6		3	26Sep84	0	1	4	10Oct84	-10	7	10					10Oct84	12Oct84

276

7 Functional Design PRODUCMR 6	S	5 5	01Oct84 10Oct84	0 0	1	4	15Oct84 -10 15Oct84 -10	7	10		15Oct84 15Oct84	19Oct84 19Oct84
11 Preliminary Integra PRODUCMR 6		5 5	01Oct84 01Oct84	0 0	1	4	15Oct84 -10 15Oct84 -10	1	4	22Oct84 -15 22Oct84 -15	7	10
8 Preliminary Documen PRODUCMR 6		3 3	01Oct84 01Oct84	2 2	1	4	15Oct84 -8 15Oct84 -8	1	4	29Oct84 -18 29Oct84 -18	7	10
12 Functional Design PRODUCMR 6	P	3 3	08Oct84 08Oct84	0 0	1	4	01Nov84 -18 01Nov84 -18	7	10		01Nov84 01Nov84	05Nov84 05Nov84
22 Preliminary Packagi MARKETCM 6		5 5	11Oct84 11Oct84	11 11	7	10	06Nov84 -7 06Nov84 -7	7	10		06Nov84 06Nov84	12Nov84 12Nov84
23 Preliminary Marketi PRODUCMR 6		3 3	11Oct84 11Oct84	17 17	1	4	06Nov84 -1 06Nov84 -1	7	10		06Nov84 06Nov84	08Nov84 08Nov84
25 Costing and Economi PRODUCMR 6		3 3	24Oct84 24Oct84	11 11	1	4	19Nov84 -7 19Nov84 -7	7	10		19Nov84 19Nov84	21Nov84 21Nov84

Types of Costing Reports   PNP4

Profile of resource cost................................1
Cumulative profile of resource cost 2,
Control Report 3
Cost, Price and Rates report 4
Earned value report.....................................5
Tabular cost report 6
        Return to Report Specification Menu....................R

Press selection:

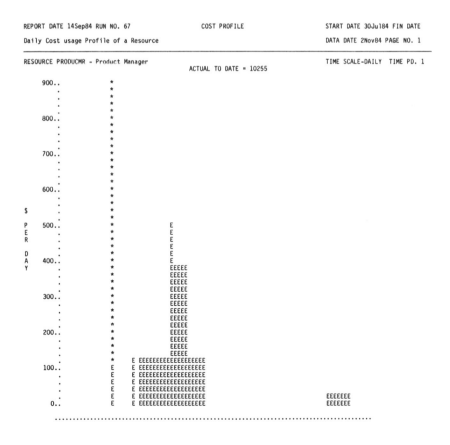

REPORT DATE 14Sep84 RUN NO. 67   COST PROFILE   START DATE 30Jul84 FIN DATE

Daily Cost usage Profile of a Resource   DATA DATE 2Nov84 PAGE NO. 1

RESOURCE PRODUCMR - Product Manager   TIME SCALE-DAILY TIME PD. 1
                                    ACTUAL TO DATE = 10255

```
        900..        *
          .          *
          .          *
          .          *
        800..        *
          .          *
          .          *
          .          *
        700..        *
          .          *
          .          *
          .          *
        600..        *
          .          *
    $     .          *
    P   500..        *        E
    E     .          *        E
    R     .          *        E
          .          *        E
    D     .          *        E
    A   400..        *        E
    Y     .          *        EEEEE
          .          *        EEEEE
          .          *        EEEEE
          .          *        EEEEE
        300..        *        EEEEE
          .          *        EEEEE
          .          *        EEEEE
          .          *        EEEEE
          .          *        EEEEE
        200..        *        EEEEE
          .          *        EEEEE
          .          *        EEEEE
          .          *        EEEEE
        100..        *      E EEEEEEEEEEEEEEEEEEE
          .          E      E EEEEEEEEEEEEEEEEEEE
          .          E      E EEEEEEEEEEEEEEEEEEE
          .          E      E EEEEEEEEEEEEEEEEEEE
          .          E      E EEEEEEEEEEEEEEEEEEE
          .          E      E EEEEEEEEEEEEEEEEEEE      EEEEEEE
          0..        E      E EEEEEEEEEEEEEEEEEEE      EEEEEEE
```

....

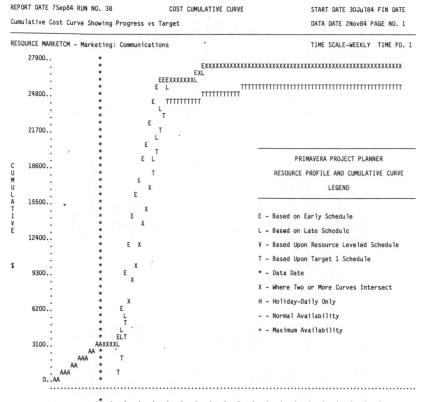

```
REPORT DATE 7Sep84 RUN NO. 38          COST CUMULATIVE CURVE          START DATE 30Jul84 FIN DATE

Cumulative Cost Curve Showing Progress vs Target                      DATA DATE 2Nov84 PAGE NO. 1
```

```
RESOURCE MARKETCM - Marketing: Communications                        TIME SCALE-WEEKLY  TIME PD. 1
```

```
      27900..          *
          .            *           EXXXXXXXXXXXXXXXXXXXXXXXXXXXXXXXXXXXXXXXXXXXXXXXXXXXXXXX
          .            *                 EXL
          .            *           EEEXXXXXXL
      24800..          *           E  L          TTTTTTTTTTTTTTTTTTTTTTTTTTTTTTTTTTTTTTTTTTTTTTTTTT
          .            *         E    TTTTTTTTTTTT
          .            *            E    TTTTTTTTTTT
          .            *              L
          .            *              T
      21700..          *            E    T
          .            *                 L
          .            *            E
          .            *                 T
          .            *            E  L
    C 18600..          *               T            PRIMAVERA PROJECT PLANNER
    U     .            *            E
    M     .            *                X           RESOURCE PROFILE AND CUMULATIVE CURVE
    U     .            *            E
    L     .            *                            LEGEND
    A 15500..          *              X
    T     .            *            E                E - Based on Early Schedule
    I     .            *              X
    V     .            *                              L - Based on Late Schedule
    E 12400..          *           E  X
          .            *                             V - Based Upon Resource Leveled Schedule
    $     .            *               X
       9300..          *           E                 T - Based Upon Target 1 Schedule
          .            *            X
          .            *                             * - Data Date
          .            *              X
       6200..          *           E                 X - Where Two or More Curves Intersect
          .            *           L
          .            *           T                 H - Holiday-Daily Only
          .            *           L
          .            *           ELT               - - Normal Availability
       3100..          AAXXXXL
          .          AA *                            = - Maximum Availability
          .       AAA   *    T
          .    AA        *
          .    AAA       *    T
        0..AA            *
          ............................................................
                     *
          08Oct84 17Dec84 25Feb85 06May85 15Jul85 23Sep85 02Dec85 10Feb86 01Apr86 30Jun86 08Sep86
```

Resource Cost Control Report with Summary   DATA DATE 2Nov84 PAGE NO. 1

PRODUCMR - Product Manager

UNIT OF MEASURE - Hour

Activity No.	Resource Code	Account Code	Account Category	Unit Meas	Budget	PCT CMP	Actual To Date	Actual This Period	Estimate To Complete	Forecast	Variance
2	PRODUCMR	2100M	Hour	1300.00	100	1300.00	.00	.00	1300.00	.00
3	PRODUCMR	2100E	Hour	860.00	100	860.00	.00	.00	860.00	.00
4	PRODUCMR	2100E	Hour	150.00	100	107.50	.00	.00	107.50	42.50
5	PRODUCMR	3200D	Hour	3900.00	100	3762.50	.00	.00	3762.50	137.50
6	PRODUCMR	2100E	Hour	400.00	100	475.00	.00	.00	475.00	-75.00
7	PRODUCMR	2100E	Hour	650.00	100	775.00	.00	.00	775.00	-125.00
8	PRODUCMR	2200E	Hour	390.00	100	375.00	.00	.00	375.00	15.00
11	PRODUCMR	2100A	Hour	645.00	100	700.00	.00	.00	700.00	-55.00
12	PRODUCMR	2100A	Hour	390.00	100	450.00	.00	.00	450.00	-60.00
19	PRODUCMR	2100E	Hour	645.00	85	650.00	.00	100.00	750.00	-105.00
23	PRODUCMR	1200M	Hour	390.00	100	425.00	.00	.00	425.00	-35.00

25	PRODUCMR	2100A	Hour	385.00	100	375.00	.00	.00	375.00	10.00
30	PRODUCMR	2100E	Hour	1290.00	0	.00	.00	1290.00	1290.00	.00
31	PRODUCMR	1000M	Hour	645.00	0	.00	.00	645.00	645.00	.00
35	PRODUCMR	1000P	Hour	129.00	0	.00	.00	129.00	129.00	.00
37	PRODUCMR	4000P	Hour	260.00	0	.00	.00	260.00	260.00	.00
38	PRODUCMR	2100M	Hour	645.00	0	.00	.00	645.00	645.00	.00
39	PRODUCMR	1200M	Hour	1290.00	0	.00	.00	1290.00	1290.00	.00
52	PRODUCMR	4400P	Hour	645.00	0	.00	.00	645.00	645.00	.00
57	PRODUCMR	1000M	Hour	645.00	0	.00	.00	645.00	645.00	.00
61	PRODUCMR	4400P	Hour	.00	0	.00	.00	.00	.00	.00
62	PRODUCMR	4400E	Hour	258.00	0	.00	.00	258.00	258.00	.00
65	PRODUCMR	2100E	Hour	645.00	0	.00	.00	645.00	645.00	.00
71	PRODUCMR	2100P	Hour	645.00	0	.00	.00	645.00	645.00	.00
79	PRODUCMR	2100E	Hour	129.00	0	.00	.00	129.00	129.00	.00
TOTAL PRODUCMR				17331.00		10255.00	.00	7326.00	17581.00	−250.00
REPORT COST TOTALS				17331.00		10255.00	.00	7326.00	17581.00	−250.00

Price - Rates Report per Resource

Account Number	....Quantity....			........Dollars........			...Dollars Per Unit Quantity...		
	Budget	To Date	Forecast	Budget	To Date	Forecast	Budget	To Date	Forecast

1000 - Marketing   COST PER MARKETCM (Hour)

| | 1241 | 144 | 1277 | 42149.50 | 5852.00 | 43136.50 | 33.964 | 40.639 | 33.780 |

1100 - Field Support   COST PER MARKETCM (Hour)

| | 0 | 0 | 0 | 1903.50 | 715.00 | 1868.50 | .000 | .000 | .000 |

1200 – Sales   COST PER MARKETCM (Hour)

| 0 | 0 | 3615.00 | 425.00 | 3650.00 | .000 | .000 | .000 |

1200 – Sales   COST PER SALESREP (Hour)

| 90 | 0 | 4080.00 | 425.00 | 4115.00 | 45.333 | .000 | 45.722 |

2100 – New Product Development   COST PER PRODUCMR (Hour)

| 406 | 242 | 21642.50 | 10078.50 | 21799.00 | 53.307 | 41.647 | 54.226 |

2200 – Product Documentation   COST PER PRODUCMR (Hour)

| 18 | 15 | 23815.00 | 5195.50 | 23770.50 | 1323.056 | 346.367 | 720.318 |

283

Earned Value Report by Resource

Activity No.	Resource Code	Account Code	Account Category	Unit Meas	Budget	PCT CMP	Actual To Date	Earned Value	Variance
	PRODUCMR - Product Manager						UNIT OF MEASURE - Hour		
2	PRODUCMR	2100M		Hour	1300.00	100	1300.00	1300.00	.00
3	PRODUCMR	2100E		Hour	860.00	100	860.00	860.00	.00
4	PRODUCMR	2100E		Hour	150.00	100	107.50	150.00	42.50
5	PRODUCMR	3200D		Hour	3900.00	100	3762.50	3900.00	137.58
6	PRODUCMR	2100E		Hour	400.00	100	475.00	400.00	-75.00
7	PRODUCMR	2100E		Hour	650.00	100	775.00	650.00	-125.00
8	PRODUCMR	2200E		Hour	390.00	100	375.00	390.00	15.00
11	PRODUCMR	2100A		Hour	645.00	100	700.00	645.00	-55.00
12	PRODUCMR	2100A		Hour	390.00	100	450.00	390.00	-60.00
19	PRODUCMR	2100E		Hour	645.00	85	650.00	548.25	-101.75
23	PRODUCMR	1200M		Hour	390.00	100	425.00	390.00	-35.00

25	PRODUCMR	2100A	Hour	385.00	100	375.00	385.00	10.00
30	PRODUCMR	2100E	Hour	1290.00	0	.00	.00	.00
31	PRODUCMR	1000M	Hour	645.00	0	.00	.00	.00
35	PRODUCMR	1000M	Hour	129.00	0	.00	.00	.00
37	PRODUCMR	4000P	Hour	260.00	0	.00	.00	.00
38	PRODUCMR	2100M	Hour	645.00	0	.00	.00	.00
39	PRODUCMR	1200M	Hour	1290.00	0	.00	.00	.00
52	PRODUCMR	4400P	Hour	645.00	0	.00	.00	.00
57	PRODUCMR	1000M	Hour	645.00	0	.00	.00	.00
61	PRODUCMR	4400P	Hour	.00	0	.00	.00	.00
62	PRODUCMR	4400E	Hour	258.00	0	.00	.00	.00
65	PRODUCMR	2100E	Hour	645.00	0	.00	.00	.00
71	PRODUCMR	2100P	Hour	645.00	0	.00	.00	.00
79	PRODUCMR	2100E	Hour	129.00	0	.00	.00	.00
TOTAL	PRODUCMR		Hour	17331.00		10255.00	10008.25	-246.75
REPORT COST TOTALS				17331.00		10255.00	10008.25	-246.75

REPORT DATE 7Sep84 RUN NO. 70   COST CONTROL ACCOUNT REPORT   START DATE 30Jul84 FIN DATE

Earned Value Report by Resource   DATA DATE 2Nov84 PAGE NO. 1

Activity No.	Resource Code XXXXXXX1XXXX	Account Code	Account Category	Unit Meas	Budget	PCT CMP	Actual To Date	Earned Value	Variance
2	MARKETMR	1000M		Hour	1300.00	100	1300.00	1300.00	.00
9	MARKETMR	1000M		Hour	520.00	100	437.00	520.00	83.00
13	MARKETQA	1000M		Hour	288.00	100	325.50	280.00	-45.50
20	FIELDSUP	1100M		Hour	325.00	100	360.00	325.00	-35.00
21	MARKETRN	1000M		Hour	570.00	100	665.00	570.00	-95.00
22	MARKETCM	1000M		Hour	570.00	100	1504.50	570.00	-934.50
23	PRODUCMR	1200M		Hour	390.00	100	425.00	390.00	-35.00
27	MARKETCM	1000M		Hour	340.00	100	337.50	340.00	2.50
28	MARKETCM	1000M		Hour	340.00	100	337.50	340.00	2.50
29	TECHSUPP	1100M		Hour	425.00	100	355.00	425.00	70.00
31	PRODUCMR	1000M		Hour	645.00	0	.00	.00	.00
35	PRODUCMR	1000M		Hour	192.00	0	.00	.00	.00
36	MARKETCM	1000M		Hour	10237.50	10	345.00	1023.75	678.75
38	MARKETMR	1000M		Hour	645.00	0	.00	.00	.00

38	TECHSUPP	1000M		Hour	533.00	0	.00	.00	.00
39	PRODUCMR	1200M		Hour	1290.00	0	.00	.00	.00
39	MARKETCM	1000M		Hour	1140.00	0	.00	.00	.00
39	SOFTENGR	1000D	DataProc	Hour	1185.00	0	.00	.00	.00
40	MARKETCM	1000M		Hour	3420.00	0	.00	.00	.00
41	MARKETCM	1000M		Hour	9450.00	0	.00	.00	.00
44	TECHSUPP	1100M		Hour	320.00	0	.00	.00	.00
44	WRITERS	1100M		Hour	301.00	0	.00	.00	.00
57	MARKETCM	1000M		Hour	570.00	0	.00	.00	.00
57	PRODUCMR	1000M		Hour	645.00	0	.00	.00	.00
63	SALESREP	1200M		Hour	930.00	0	.00	.00	.00
64	MARKETCM	1000M		Hour	570.00	0	.00	.00	.00
67	TECHSUPP	1100M		Hour	532.50	0	.00	.00	.00
68	SALESREP	1200M		Hour	465.00	0	.00	.00	.00
68	FIELDSUP	1200M		Hour	540.00	0	.00	.00	.00
76	MARKETRN	1000M		Hour	4560.00	0	.00	.00	.00
77	FIELDSUP	1000E		Hour	1080.00	0	.00	.00	.00
TOTAL	XXXXXXX1XXXX				44248.00		6392.00	6083.75	-308.25
	REPORT COST TOTALS				44248.00		6392.00	6083.75	-308.25

REPORT DATE 14Sep84 RUN NO. 62   RESOURCE USAGE REPORT - WEEKLY   START DATE 30Jul84 FIN DATE

Weekly Cost Usage Report vs. Target   DATA DATE 2Nov84 PAGE NO. 1

PRODUCMR - Product Manager   UNIT OF MEASURE = Hour

Period Ending	-Daily Avail- Normal	Maximum	------Early Schedule----- Usage	Avg.Daily	Cumulative	-----Late Schedule------ Usage	Avg.Daily	Cumulative	----Target 1 Schedule---- Usage	Avg.Daily	Cumulative
TO DATE					10255.00			10255.00			9847.00
08Nov84	0	0	100.00	20.0	10355.00	.00	.0	10255.00	258.00	51.6	10105.00
15Nov84	0	0	.00	.0	10355.00	.00	.0	10255.00	.00	.0	10105.00
26Nov84	0	0	258.00	51.6	10613.00	.00	.0	10255.00	387.00	77.4	10492.00
30Nov84	0	0	516.00	129.0	11129.00	.00	.0	10255.00	516.00	129.0	11008.00
07Dec84	0	0	1032.00	206.4	12161.00	.00	.0	10255.00	1032.00	206.4	12040.00
14Dec84	0	0	1677.00	335.4	13838.00	.00	.0	10255.00	774.00	154.8	12814.00
21Dec84	0	0	516.00	103.2	14354.00	.00	.0	10255.00	.00	.0	12814.00
28Dec84	0	0	.00	.0	14354.00	.00	.0	10255.00	.00	.0	12814.00
04Jan85	0	0	.00	.0	14354.00	.00	.0	10255.00	.00	.0	12814.00
11Jan85	0	0	.00	.0	14354.00	.00	.0	10255.00	.00	.0	12814.00
18Jan85	0	0	.00	.0	14354.00	.00	.0	10255.00	.00	.0	12814.00
25Jan85	0	0	.00	.0	14354.00	.00	.0	10255.00	.00	.0	12814.00
01Feb85	0	0	.00	.0	14354.00	.00	.0	10255.00	.00	.0	12814.00
08Feb85	0	0	.00	.0	14354.00	.00	.0	10255.00	.00	.0	12814.00

Date										
15Feb85	0	.00	.0	14354.00	.00	.0	10255.00	.00	.0	12814.00
22Feb85	0	.00	.0	14354.00	.00	.0	10255.00	.00	.0	12814.00
01Mar85	0	40.00	8.0	14394.00	358.00	71.6	10613.00	.00	.0	12814.00
08Mar85	0	100.00	20.0	14494.00	645.00	129.0	11258.00	298.00	59.6	13112.00
15Mar85	0	100.00	20.0	14594.00	387.00	77.4	11645.00	745.00	149.0	13857.00
22Mar85	0	20.00	4.0	14614.00	.00	.0	11645.00	487.00	97.4	14344.00
29Mar85	0	.00	.0	14614.00	.00	.0	11645.00	20.00	4.0	14364.00
05Apr85	0	.00	.0	14614.00	.00	.0	11645.00	.00	.0	14364.00
12Apr85	0	.00	.0	14614.00	.00	.0	11645.00	.00	.0	14364.00
19Apr85	0	.00	.0	14614.00	.00	.0	11645.00	.00	.0	14364.00
26Apr85	0	.00	.0	14614.00	.00	.0	11645.00	.00	.0	14364.00
03May85	0	387.00	77.4	15001.00	.00	.0	11645.00	.00	.0	14364.00
10May85	0	645.00	129.0	15646.00	.00	.0	11645.00	387.00	77.4	14751.00
17May85	0	258.00	51.6	15904.00	.00	.0	11645.00	645.00	129.0	15396.00
24May85	0	258.00	51.6	16162.00	.00	.0	11645.00	258.00	51.6	15654.00
31May85	0	.00	.0	16162.00	.00	.0	11645.00	258.00	51.6	15912.00
07Jun85	0	645.00	129.0	16807.00	189.00	37.8	11834.00	.00	.0	15912.00
14Jun85	0	.00	.0	16807.00	745.00	149.0	12579.00	645.00	129.0	16557.00
21Jun85	0	.00	.0	16807.00	2035.00	407.0	14614.00	.00	.0	16557.00
28Jun85	0	645.00	129.0	17452.00	.00	.0	14614.00	.00	.0	16557.00
05Jul85	0	.00	.0	17452.00	.00	.0	14614.00	645.00	129.00	17202.00

REFERENCES

Dauphinais, Bill and Darnell, Leonard. "Task Force". San Francisco: *PC World*, September 1984 (used with permission from Primavera Systems, Inc.).

Primavera Systems, Inc., "Primavera Project Planner". Bala Cynwyd, Pennsylvania.

Appendix
A
RANDOM VARIABLES*

Let us associate with each elementary event in S a real number x. This correspondence need not be unique, i.e., several elementary events may map into the same value x. This mapping of the elementary events onto the real line is called a random variable, denoted by X. We usually use capital letters to denote the random variable and small letters to denote particular values of the random variable. Note that no probabilities are implied in this mapping.

Example 1: Let X denote the sum of the dots on the faces up when rolling two dice. X can assume values 2,3, . . . 12. Only one elementary event of the experiment maps into the number 2; however, two map into 3, three into 4, etc. We now redefine the three axioms of probability in terms of random variables. Define

$$(F(x) = P(X \leq x)$$

as the *probability distribution function* of the random variable X. Then

AXIOM 1A

$F(x)$ is monotonic nondecreasing in x. If $a < b$, then $F(a) \leqslant F(b)$.

AXIOM 2A

$$F(\infty) = 1 \text{ and } F(-\infty) = 0$$

AXIOM 3A

$$P(a < X \leqslant b) = F(b) - F(a)$$

This follows immediately if we let event A = $[X \leqslant a]$, B = $[a < X \leqslant b]$, and event C = $A \cup B$ = $[X \leqslant b]$, and use axiom 3.

If the random variable X assumes only discrete values $x_1, x_2, \ldots$, then the probability distribution function is given by:

$$P\ (X \leqslant x_k) = F(x_k) = \sum_{i=1}^{k} p(\lambda_1), \quad k = 1, 2, \ldots$$

where $p(x_i)$ is the probability that $X = x_i$. The function $p(x_i)$ is called the probability (mass) function. Clearly $\Sigma_{i=1}^{x} p(x_i) = 1$. Try to find the probability function for the random variable "the sum of the dots on both dice."

If the random variable X is continuous, i.e., can assume any real value, then the probability distribution function is defined as:

$$P(X \leqslant a) = F(a) = \int_{-\infty}^{a} f(x)dx$$

where $f(x) = dF(x)/dx$ is called the *probability density function*.

The (approximate) probability of $f(x)dx$ is that the random variable assumes a value between x and $x + dx$, where dx is very small. Again, $\int_{-\infty}^{\infty} f(x)dx = 1$. Figure A.1 depicts some of these concepts.

Let X and Y be two random variables with a joint distribution function $P(X \leqslant a, Y \leqslant b) = F(a,b)$. For continuous random variables the joint distribution function is obtained by integrating the joint density functions $f(x,y)$ over both variables:

$$F(a,b) = \int_{-\infty}^{a} \int_{-\infty}^{b} f(x,y)\ dy\ dx$$

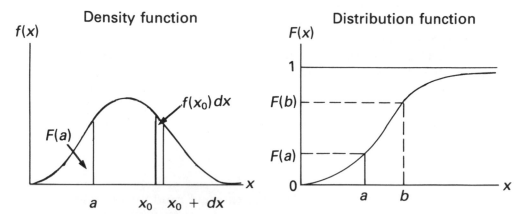

FIGURE A.1. Probability distribution and density functions for a continuous random variable.

If we are interested in the distribution of X or Y alone, regardless of what value the other random variable assumes, we find the so-called *marginal distribution* of X or Y. Its density function is defined as

$$g(x) = \int_{-\infty}^{+\infty} f(x,y)\, dy \quad \text{for } X,$$

or

$$h(y) = \int_{-\infty}^{+\infty} f(x,y)\, dx \quad \text{for } Y$$

Two random variables, X and Y, are said to be independent of one another if

$$f(x,y) = g(x)h(y)$$

If X and Y are mutually dependent, then the conditional density function of, say, X given $Y = y$ defined as

$$g(x\ y) = \frac{f(x,y)}{h(y)}$$

The reader is asked to define the corresponding expressions for discrete random variables.

It is often convenient to summarize the information contained in a probability distribution by a few summary measures. The two most important ones are the expected value and the variance of the random variable. The expected value, denoted by $E(X) = \mu$, is an indication of where the center of mass of the random variable is located. It is defined by

$$E(X) = \sum_{i=1}^{\infty} x_i\, p(x_i) \text{ for discrete random variables [A-2]}$$

and

$$E(X) = \int_{-\infty}^{\infty} xf(x)\ dx \text{ for continuous random variables [A-3]}$$

Thus, for a discrete random variable, $E(X)$ is seen to be the weighted sum of all values that the random variable can assume with the probabilities serving as weights.

The variance, denoted by VAR $(X) = \sigma^2$, is an indication of how dispersed the mass of the random variable is around its expected value μ . It is defined by

$$VAR(X) = \sum_{i=1}^{\infty} (x_i - \mu)^2 p(x_i) \text{ for discrete random variables [A-4]}$$

and

$$VAR(X) = \int_{-\infty}^{\infty} (x - \mu)^2 f(x)\ dx \text{ for continuous random variables [A-5]}$$

The square root of the variance is called the standard deviation, denoted by σ.

Example 2: Let X denote again the sum of the dots when rolling two dice. Then, you can verify that

$X = x_i$	2	3	4	5	6	7	8	9	10	11	12
$p(x_i)$	1/36	2/36	3/36	4/36	5/36	6/36	5/36	4/36	3/36	2/36	1/36

and

$$E(X) = 2(1/36) + 3(2/36) + 4(3/36) + 5(4/36) + 6(5/36) + 7(6/36) +$$
$$8(5/36) + 9(4/36) + 10(3/36) + 11(2/36) + 12(1/36) = 7$$
$$VAR(X) = (2-7)^2(1/36) + (3-7)^2(2/36) + (4-7)^2(3/36) + (5-7)^2(4/36)$$
$$+ (6-7)^2 (5/36) + (7-7)^2 (6/36) + (8-7)^2 (5/36)$$
$$+ (9-7)^2 (4/36) + (10-7)^2 (3/36) + (11-7)^2 (2/36)$$
$$+ (12-7)^2 (1/36) = 5\tfrac{5}{6}$$

and

$$\sigma = \sqrt{5\tfrac{5}{6}} = 2.415$$

Other measures of central location are the mode (value of X for the highest point in the probablility mass or density function) and the median (value of X that divides the entire mass or density function into two equal parts, i.e., the number M such that

$$P(X \leqslant M) = P(X \geqslant M) = \tfrac{1}{2}).$$

PROPERTIES OF $E(X)$

1. Let $Y = cX$, c constant, then

$$E(Y) = E(cX) = cE(X) \qquad\qquad\text{[A-6]}$$

2. Let $Y = X + c$, c constant, then,

$$E(Y) = E(X+c) = E(X) + c \qquad\qquad\text{[A-7]}$$

3. Let $Y = \Sigma_{j=1}^{k} X_j$, where each X_i is a random variable. Then

$$E(Y) = E(X_1 + X_2 + \cdots + X_k) = \sum_{j=1}^{k} E(X_j) \qquad \text{[A-8]}$$

PROPERTIES OF VAR (X)

1. Let $Y = cX$, c constant, then

$$\text{VAR}(Y) = \text{VAR}(cX) = c^2 \text{ VAR}(X) \qquad \text{[A-9]}$$

2. Let $Y = X + c$, c constant, then,

$$\text{VAR}(Y) = \text{VAR}(X + c) = \text{VAR}(X) \qquad \text{[A-10]}$$

3. Let $Y = \sum_{i=1}^{k} X_j$, where the X_j form a set of mutually independent random variables. Then

$$VAR(Y) = VAR(X_1 + X_2 + \cdots + X_k) = \sum_{j=1}^{k} VAR(X_j) \qquad \text{[A-11]}$$

Note that property 3 of VAR(X) requires the random variables to be mutually independent.

<u>Example 3.</u> Let X denote the random variable for monthly sales (in units sold) for a given product. Assume that X has the following probability function:

x_i	1	2	3	4
$p(x_i)$	0.4	0.3	0.2	0.1

Verify that $E(X) = 2$ and VAR $(X) = 1$.

Each unit sold brings in a revenue of \$4.00. Let Y denote the revenue in dollars generated by this product per month; $Y = 4X$

is also a random variable. If $c = 4$, then by [A-6] $E(Y) = 4E(X)$ $= 4(2) = 8$, and by [A-9] VAR $(Y) = 4^2 E(X) = 4^2 (2) = 32$.

Now consider sales over six months. Each month's sales follow the same probability distribution as above. Let X_i be the random variable for sales in month i and Y be sales over six months. $Y = \Sigma^6_{i=1} X_i$. Then, the expected sales over six months are

$$E(Y) = \sum_{i=1}^{6} E(X_i) = 2 + 2 + 2 + 2 + 2 + 2 = 12 \qquad \text{by [A-8]}$$

and the variance of sales over six months is

$$VAR(Y) = \sum_{i=1}^{6} VAR(X_i) = 1 + 1 + 1 + 1 + 1 + 1 = 6 \quad \text{by [A-11]}$$

assuming sales in consecutive months are independent.

Appendix
B
RANDOM NUMBER TABLE

54	57	63	63	58	95	98	07	09	73
85	82	87	42	43	75	47	24	63	47
20	19	14	34	10	02	39	49	98	21
55	78	40	99	55	82	66	37	07	97
80	09	53	36	63	62	13	85	71	21
77	05	34	86	14	33	56	30	67	80
19	02	53	33	77	27	66	54	62	03
73	79	77	04	17	19	03	80	15	61
96	54	60	67	86	26	21	73	79	69
40	90	53	32	34	06	66	40	97	81
46	92	96	52	00	61	75	31	07	96
49	05	23	22	14	34	78	38	36	55
77	18	58	80	01	10	98	95	05	39
48	62	19	03	77	17	49	77	27	73
74	10	16	14	50	26	37	04	08	24
58	78	52	77	20	48	63	35	43	01

95	23	19	97	81	38	15	74	24	55
75	43	05	23	16	91	79	65	31	79
76	82	87	43	02	47	28	96	37	09
71	23	37	92	10	87	31	95	11	23
25	92	17	43	99	33	47	34	08	40
94	58	83	14	24	50	29	28	80	23
26	31	82	62	30	47	20	30	70	75
63	63	52	90	55	72	57	41	11	44
39	50	26	41	29	18	67	99	32	18
77	29	28	00	74	18	73	87	50	28
97	79	73	95	05	49	87	30	78	47
08	21	70	96	29	29	13	95	19	89
11	20	19	14	44	17	49	91	68	13
00	80	13	05	41	19	85	68	14	18
63	50	36	65	03	77	01	20	36	46
77	21	65	31	06	79	73	83	06	80
14	24	70	86	18	54	66	34	90	47
35	35	12	52	97	75	37	93	44	16
97	69	43	95	96	54	38	23	16	96
46	86	11	21	60	47	11	27	48	41
22	87	52	80	24	52	90	52	72	45
56	16	97	65	16	10	03	86	14	45
72	57	68	09	59	03	69	61	92	22
87	40	79	88	63	55	99	50	16	95
08	32	38	20	35	34	97	67	87	29
36	48	42	67	72	48	58	70	99	30
63	40	84	30	63	48	69	60	39	45
74	05	45	55	90	28	12	76	85	66

INDEX